VISUALIZING BLACKNESS AND THE CREATION OF THE AFRICAN AMERICAN LITERARY TRADITION

Negative stereotypes of African Americans have long been disseminated through the visual arts. This original and incisive study examines how black writers use visual tropes as literary devices to challenge readers' conceptions of black identity. Lena Hill charts 200 years of African American literary history, from Phillis Wheatley to Ralph Ellison, and engages with a variety of canonical and lesser-known writers. Chapters interweave literary history, museum culture, and visual analysis of numerous illustrations with close readings of Booker T. Washington, Anne Spencer, Zora Neale Hurston, Melvin Tolson, and others. Together, these sections register the degree to which African American writers rely on vision – its modes, consequences, and insights – to demonstrate black intellectual and cultural sophistication. Hill's provocative study will interest scholars and students of African American literature and American literature more broadly.

LENA HILL is Assistant Professor of English and African American Studies at the University of Iowa. She is the coauthor of *Ralph Ellison's "Invisible Man": A Reference Guide* (2008). Her work has been published in journals such as *American Literature* and *African American Review*. She received her PhD from Yale University.

CAMBRIDGE STUDIES IN AMERICAN
LITERATURE AND CULTURE

Editor
Ross Posnock, *Columbia University*

Founding Editor
Albert Gelpi, *Stanford University*

Advisory Board
Alfred Bendixen, *Texas A&M University*
Sacvan Bercovitch, *Harvard University*
Ronald Bush, *St. John's College, University of Oxford*
Wai Chee Dimock, *Yale University*
Albert Gelpi, *Stanford University*
Gordon Hutner, *University of Illinois, Urbana-Champaign*
Walter Benn Michaels, *University of Illinois, Chicago*
Kenneth Warren, *University of Chicago*

Recent Books in This Series

167. LENA HILL
Visualizing Blackness and the Creation of the African American Literary
Tradition

168. ANDREW HEBARD
The Poetics of Sovereignty in American Literature, 1885–1910

169. CHRISTOPHER FREEBURG
Melville and the Idea of Blackness: Race and Imperialism in Nineteenth-
Century America

170. TIM ARMSTRONG
The Logic of Slavery: Debt, Technology, and Pain in American Literature

171. JUSTINE MURISON
The Politics of Anxiety in Nineteenth-Century American Literature

172. HSUAN L. HSU
Geography and the Production of Space in Nineteenth-Century American
Literature

173. DORRI BEAM
Style, Gender, and Fantasy in Nineteenth-Century American Women's
Writing

174. YOGITA GOYAL
Romance, Diaspora, and Black Atlantic Literature

175. MICHAEL CLUNE
American Literature and the Free Market, 1945–2000

VISUALIZING BLACKNESS AND THE CREATION OF THE AFRICAN AMERICAN LITERARY TRADITION

LENA HILL

University of Iowa

CAMBRIDGE
UNIVERSITY PRESS

CAMBRIDGE
UNIVERSITY PRESS

32 Avenue of the Americas, New York, NY 10013-2473, USA

Cambridge University Press is part of the University of Cambridge.

It furthers the University's mission by disseminating knowledge in the pursuit
of education, learning, and research at the highest international levels of excellence.

www.cambridge.org
Information on this title: www.cambridge.org/9781107041585

© Lena Hill 2014

This publication is in copyright. Subject to statutory exception
and to the provisions of relevant collective licensing agreements,
no reproduction of any part may take place without the written
permission of Cambridge University Press.

First published 2014

Printed in the United States of America

A catalog record for this publication is available from the British Library.

Library of Congress Cataloging in Publication Data
Hill, Lena M., author.
Visualizing Blackness and the creation of the African American literary
tradition / Lena Hill, University of Iowa.
pages   cm. – (Cambridge studies in American literature and culture; 167)
ISBN 978-1-107-04158-5 (hardback)
1. American literature – African American authors – History and criticism.   2. African
Americans in literature.   3. African Americans in art.   4. Blacks – Race identity.
5. African Americans – Intellectual life.   I. Title.   II. Series: Cambridge studies in
American literature and culture; 167. PS153.N5H55   2014
810.9896073–dc23   2013030422

ISBN 978-1-107-04158-5 Hardback

Cambridge University Press has no responsibility for the persistence or accuracy
of URLs for external or third-party Internet Web sites referred to in this publication
and does not guarantee that any content on such Web sites is, or will remain,
accurate or appropriate.

For Michael

Contents

Figures

x

Acknowledgments

This book ponders visual images inspired by texts, and I am fortunate to acknowledge the many people who have left indelible imprints on my work. My fascination with visual culture found invaluable guidance at Howard University from Hilda van Neck-Yoder, Allison Blakely, Jennifer Jordan, and Sandra Shannon. The Yale English department challenged and stimulated my thinking about words and pictures. For helping me shape early notions into definite forms, I thank Vera Kutzinski, Joseph Roach, Thomas Otten, Robert Stepto, Amy Hungerford, Wai Chee Dimok, Linda Peterson, Kelly Hager, and David Bromwich. Karin Roffman, Ayanna Cooper, and Vanessa Ryan sharpened my insights and encouraged my ideas.

The final contours of this project emerged at the University of Iowa. I am grateful to colleagues and friends in the English department, African American Studies program, and broader Iowa City community for contributing richly to my work. Kathleen Diffley, Claire Fox, and Naomi Greyser provided important feedback on individual chapters, and Harry Stecopoulos perceptively commented on the entire manuscript. I thank Teresa Mangum and the Obermann Center for granting me a Cmiel research semester. Group participants André Brock, Mary Campbell, Tim Havens, and especially Deborah Whaley helped me refine two chapters with their keen comments. I greatly appreciate Shanna Benjamin's penetrating and timely feedback on the introduction. For generously sharing research resources in addition to his luminous thinking about words and images, I am indebted to Garrett Stewart. I could not have finished this book without my research assistant, Chelsea Burke. You are simply the best. I thank my UI students for refreshing my thinking and regularly reminding me of why I love this work. I also benefited incalculably from Bridget Tsemo, Kathy Lavezzo, Chuck Swanson, Linda Bolton, Mary Lou Emery, Miriam Gilbert, Doris Witt, Sydné Mahone, Venise Berry, Lori Branch, Dee

Morris, Miriam Thaggert, Richard Turner, Fred Woodard, and Laura Rigal. Three chairs helped make this book a reality. Jon Wilcox provided able advice and readily smoothed my path, and Claire Sponsler went above and beyond to support this project. I will always be grateful for her intellectual acuity and kindness. Horace Porter read the entire manuscript and incisively commented on chapters multiple times. In addition to being a wonderful advocate, Horace represents the epitome of what one imagines in a mentor and wise friend. I thank him (and Carla) for contributing mightily to my scholarship as well as to our family's happiness in Iowa City. I am enormously appreciative of the feedback I gained at annual meetings of the American Literature Association, Modernist Studies Association, and Modern Language Association. I have gleaned much from Sara Blair, Herman Beavers, Adam Bradley, John Callahan, Pamela Caughie, Suzanne Churchill, Gene Jarrett, Adam McKible, and Patrice Rankine. Marc Connor and Larry Jackson have been special advocates to whom I am grateful. I have enjoyed sharing material from this book on different campuses. For these invitations and the ensuing conversations I thank Badia Ahad, Michael Chasar, Paula Krebs, Frann Michel, and Kenneth Warren. The anonymous readers for Cambridge offered immensely helpful suggestions, and Ray Ryan shepherded this book through the publication process with editorial expertise and welcome encouragement. I thank Ross Posnock for taking an interest in this project and supporting my work at every turn, and I appreciate Diana Witt's work on the index.

A number of institutions generously supported the research at the heart of this book. At Yale, where this project began, two Beinecke fellowships, a Mellon research grant, a Gignilliat fellowship, and a John Enders grant gave me my first opportunities to explore archives. As a Duke postdoctoral Fellow, I received summer funding from the Mellon Foundation. At the University of Iowa, I have been the grateful recipient of an Old Gold fellowship, an Arts and Humanities Initiative grant, and CLAS summer funding. These awards allowed me to spend time delving into numerous collections. At the Library of Congress, my best loved repository, I am indebted to the librarians and staff in the Manuscript and Prints and Photographs Reading Rooms who aided me with their catholic knowledge. In particular, I thank Alice Birney, Bruce Kirby, Patrick Kerwin, Jennifer Brathovde, and Joseph Jackson.

The collage of support that gave rise to this book most surely spills beyond academic walls. I am grateful to the Bethel A.M.E. Church family for spiritual sustenance, and I thank my girlfriends for the laughter and confidence that only one's girls can provide. I have been blessed to have angels in my midst to provide childcare. Irene Shell and Becky Long deserve special gratitude. I thank the Ronald McDonald House for giving me a calm space to finish this book in the midst of a storm. My family frames all that I do. I thank the Hills for their belief in me and especially Grandma Dell for embodying pure generosity. My sisters-in-law, brothers-in-law, nieces, and nephews prove the amazing way love multiplies as a family expands. My brother and sister are my best friends. Tony, thank you for dreaming big for me, sharing my political passions, and making me laugh. Kelly, I could not have completed this book without your listening ear and boundless support. Two days is too long to go without hearing your voice. To my parents, Carl and Gloria Moore, I thank you for your absolute faith in me and steady admonishment that I keep Christ first in my life. I admire you most in this world, and I treasure our daily conversations that keep me grounded and happy. I owe my little Hills, Caitlyn and Michael Carl, many apologies for too much time spent before the computer and deep gratitude for such good times away from it. You fill my heart in ways impossible to articulate. I dedicate this book to my husband, Michael. So much of it is rightfully yours. Thank you for investing your brilliance in my ideas and selflessly working through them with me until they emerge fully formed. In a world where chivalry has gone out of style, I count myself blessed to share life and love with you.

Materials by

Anne Spencer, including "The Sevignes," "Grapes Still Life," and letters to Grace and James Weldon Johnson, are reprinted here by permission of the Anne Spencer House & Garden Museum, Inc. Archives.

W.E.B. Du Bois, including lines from "The Burden of Black Women," are reprinted here with permission. I wish to thank the Crisis Publishing Co., Inc., the publisher of the magazine of the National Association for the Advancement of Colored People, for the use of the material first published in the November 1914 issue of *The Crisis*.

Gwendolyn Bennett, including "Quatrains" and "Advice" are reprinted courtesy of the Literary Representative for the Works of Gwendolyn B. Bennett, Schomburg Center for Research in Black Culture, New York Public Library, Astor, Lenox and Tilden Foundations.

Franz Boas, including his letter to Zora Neale Hurston, are reprinted here by permission of the American Philosophical Society.

Ralph Ellison, including references to his papers and unpublished letters, are reprinted here by permission of The Ralph and Fanny Ellison Charitable Trust.

An earlier version of Chapter 6 appeared in *American Literature*, published by Duke University Press, and I thank the press for permission to republish here.

Abbreviations

BSR	"Bathesda of Sinners Run," by Maud Irwin Owens
CE	*The Collected Essays of Ralph Ellison*, by Ralph Ellison
CW	*Complete Writings*, by Phillis Wheatley
FM	*Zora Neale Hurston: Folklore, Memoirs, and Other Writings*, by Zora Neale Hurston
HG	*Harlem Gallery*, by Melvin Tolson
IM	*Invisible Man*, by Ralph Ellison
NS	*Zora Neale Hurston: Novels & Stories*, by Zora Neale Hurston
PB	*Plum Bun: A Novel without a Moral*, by Jessie Fauset
Q	*Quicksand*, by Nella Larson
REP	*Ralph Ellison Papers*
RWP	*Richard Wright Papers*
SBF	*The Souls of Black Folk*, by W. E. B. Du Bois
TD	*Three Days Before the Shooting…*, by Ralph Ellison
US	*Up from Slavery*, by Booker T. Washington

Introduction: The Trope of the Picture Book

I visited her Mistress, and found by conversing with the African, that she was no Imposter; I asked her if she could write on any Subject; she said Yes ... I gave her your name, which she was acquainted with. She immediately wrote a rough Copy of the inclosed address & letter, which I promised to convey or deliver. I was astonish'd, and could hardly believe my own Eyes.

–Thomas Wooldridge, 1772[1]

What, then, was the experience of a man with a black skin, what *could* it be in this country? How could a Negro put pen to paper, how could he so much as think or breathe, without some impulsion to protest, be it harsh or mild, political or private, released or buried? ... What astonishes one most about *Invisible Man* is the apparent freedom it displays from the ideological and emotional penalties suffered by Negroes in this country.

–Irving Howe, 1963[2]

This study rethinks African American literary history by asserting that the manifold inscription of vision in literature is as important to the long arc of African American literary history as the well established presence of verbal arts. Specifically, this study explores black writers' reliance on the portrayal of African American vision – tropes designating the modes and consequences of sight as well as rendering the literal practices of looking – to validate black intelligence. Since Henry Louis Gates, Jr. traced the birth of African American literature to a legacy of signification that begins with the trope of the Talking Book, scholars have principally associated black literature with vernacular speech acts. Gates's *The Signifying Monkey: A Theory of African-American Literary Criticism* (1988) considers examples of the Talking Book trope in texts spanning from 1770 to 1815 and charts the ways African American writers signify on the trope to privilege the black voice in twentieth-century literature. By recovering and explicating this history, Gates demonstrates the centrality of reading, writing, and speaking to black literary production. African American writers dramatize verbal

I

literacy to substantiate black humanity, thereby challenging philosophical declarations conflating blackness with servility, immorality, and stupidity. This valuable history is indisputable, and I esteem it for the foundation it provides scholarship on the African American literary canon.

But the phenomenon of the Talking Book cannot be divorced from black writers' creation of what I term the trope of the Picture Book. For even as they verified African American intellect by displaying the power of black discourse, these writers found themselves forced to contend with a visually suffused society that defined blackness in derogatory terms. In addressing this reality, this study argues that African American writers devote as much energy to accentuating vision as proof of black mental power as to drawing on verbal tropes to revise the impoverished idea of blackness. Black writers use their texts to challenge readers who assess African American humanity through a visual lens. This study probes black writers' conversion of the multitudinous modes of vision traditionally employed to degrade African American subjectivity into meaningful methods of self-definition and national critique. To achieve this reclamation of black humanity, these writers connect vision to pedagogy. I describe their impulse to link myriad visual experiences to discrete opportunities for instruction as constituting the trope of the Picture Book. Although these textual moments do not include a literal book, this study argues that they underscore the central role vision plays in the African American literary tradition.

Beginning in the eighteenth century, black writers declare themselves seeing subjects, and the vision they exhibit proclaims them both gifted instructors and exceptional students. This assertion of what Nicholas Mirzoeff describes as "the right to look" reclaims the authority denied African Americans by the history of chattel slavery.[3] Across genres and time, they exhibit a wide range of visual knowledge that repeatedly connects African Americans to traditional sites of education and emerging institutions of cultural instruction. In fact, the initial questions that inspired this study lit upon the consistent nexus of visual acts and teaching paradigms. Why does Phillis Wheatley insist on modeling her religious vision to students at Cambridge University? Why do Booker T. Washington and W. E. B. Du Bois appeal to visual descriptions of ambition to validate their educational philosophies, ideas they portray in their writing as well as their carefully collected photographs? How do we explain Harlem Renaissance women writers' obsession with presenting black female speakers forced to adopt a pedagogical posture to instruct new observational practices of plastic art and black folk culture? What do we make of Melvin Tolson's abiding interest in the museum and Ralph Ellison's fascination with objects of art? Why do both men display a commitment to crafting characters who learn through analyzing visual art? In aiming to answer these questions, this study commences with the conclusion that black writers signify on visual practices in their literature to challenge the visual terms on which African Americans are excluded from full national belonging and artistic appreciation.

By codifying these practices as the trope of the Picture Book, I intentionally play on Western societies' reliance on pictures to define African Americans. Prior to large numbers of African slaves and black freeman inhabiting the United States, European explorers used visual description and images to establish narratives of black exoticism and savagery. Jennifer Morgan recounts the language white male planters and travelers employed from 1500 to 1770 to institute ideas of black monstrosity. She explains that "these meanings were inscribed well before the establishment of England's colonial American plantations."4 As publication opportunities flourished and illustrated travel narratives grew more popular, images of naked African women and men proliferated. During the eighteenth and nineteenth centuries, the expanding U.S. reading population eagerly looked to newspapers, magazines, and almanacs for images of blackness that confirmed the uncivilized, bestial status of African Americans.

In recognition of the power of these widespread images, black writers emphasize African American vision as a sly indictment of the special instruction needed by readers trained to interpret child-friendly pictures rather than words. If the term "picture book" primarily describes children's books that depend on illustrations to connote meaning, the trope of the Picture Book teasingly offers readers assistance with their interpretive work. Black writers highlight their character's visual engagement with the world, their ironic ability to make sense of the many images, art objects, and social exchanges organized around race that strive to define black character. In fact, African American adapters of the trope of the Picture Book acknowledge readers' desire to impose preconceived images of blackness onto literary speakers who appear solely via words even as they refuse this craving by portraying black Americans as seeing subjects as opposed to helpless objects. So although the figure of a book with pictures depicting black Americans does not constitute a major plot element in African American novels, stories, and poems, black characters forced to confront a society organized around visual definition and comprehension occupies a central position in black literature preceding the Black Arts Movement.

Contesting Willful Blindness

For nearly two hundred years, African American writers from Phillis Wheatley to Ralph Ellison faced the reality of readers interpreting their work through the veil of race. As the opening epigraph reveals, even though Thomas Wooldridge vouches for Wheatley's authenticity as a black woman capable of thinking and writing, he admits being "astonish'd" at the *sight* of her performing these tasks. One year later, when she published her slender volume of poems, the first book length publication by an African American, she not only needed a letter from her master to assure readers that a black woman had indeed written the verses, her volume also required a second letter "To the PUBLICK" signed by eighteen white men of Boston before her publisher felt comfortable presenting Wheatley's work as her own. Such authenticating documents became a mainstay of slave narratives and antebellum texts published by black writers, necessary testimony for white readers incapable of conceiving of literate and artistic African Americans.[5] What interests me most about this tradition of authentication is not that it was needed, but that it performed a particular type of work. It bridged the gap between how a white, male literate public understood the intellectual abilities of African Americans and the alternative, antithetical portrait Wheatley claimed for herself and her race through her poetry. In essence, the eighteen signatures carved out space for a black woman to teach readers to look beyond her skin color and confront her artistry.

In contrast to eighteenth-century white men who either marveled at the sight of black individuals performing impressive intellect, or required additional proof to validate such feats, the second epigraph shows Irving Howe questioning whether black literature reflects the realities of black life if it fails to focus on black suffering. Howe refuses to consider the possibility that Ellison, or any man defined by the appearance of "black skin" in the middle of the twentieth century, might craft fiction without being overwhelmed by the experience of racism. Howe's "astonish[ment]" at *Invisible Man* signals his skeptical view of Ellison's novel as a plausible barometer of modern black experience. Ellison, responding to Howe's willful blindness, claims that when a white liberal critic "looks at a Negro he sees not a human being but an abstract embodiment of living hell."[6] He proceeds to accuse Howe of substituting false pictures of African American life in a bid to protect conventional stereotypes. Ellison explains: "Prefabricated Negroes are sketched on sheets of paper and superimposed on the Negro community; then when someone thrusts his head through the page and yells, 'Watch out there, Jack, there're people living under here,' they are shocked and indignant.'[7] Even well-intentioned white readers, Ellison charges, cling to false images of blackness in the interest of perpetuating stereotypes they deem part and parcel of African American life.

The inability to consider black literature beyond their preconceived notions of blackness causes Wooldridge and Howe to misunderstand and misread the literary art of Wheatley and Ellison. This study contends that although these examples relate to specific literary figures, such interpretive misrecognition stems from a long history of criticism that considers how visual pictures are created in non-visual texts. Mirzoeff explains that to "visualize" acknowledges our tendency "to picture ... existence," to form pictures from mediums "that are not in themselves visual."[8] In recognition of their readers' insistent visualizing tendencies, black writers forthrightly assign their literary texts – works typically lacking pictorial illustration – the task of portraying African American critical looking, an activity their general audience cannot envisage. These writers understand that for most readers, their attempt to assign new meaning to blackness by focusing on black sight is superfluous. After all, black skin denotes what readers want it to connote. According to W. J. T. Mitchell: "The assumption is that 'blackness' is a transparently readable sign of racial identity, a perfectly sutured imagetext. Race is what can be *seen*"; by contrast, "[w]hiteness ... is invisible, unmarked ... but is equated with a normative subjectivity and humanity from which 'race' is a visible deviation."[9] Black writers resist such reasoning from their earliest publications. Accordingly, *Visualizing Blackness* argues that rather than ignoring the challenge of most readers' interpretive postures, black writers tackle misapprehension directly by using their texts to "visualize" blackness: to dramatize the act and power of black vision in place of traditional images of racial degradation. Thus, this study ponders how the black literary tradition has been shaped by a commitment to defining black humanity by attending to visual practices even when blackness is not itself pictorially rendered within the pages of a work.

This study casts a critical eye across 200 years of African American literary production to recount black writers' most prevalent responses to readers' penchant for misreading blackness. In focusing on modes of vision in Phillis Wheatley, Frederick Douglass, Harriet Jacobs, Booker T. Washington, W. E. B. Du Bois, Anne Spencer, Angelina Grimké, Gwendolyn Bennett, Nella Larsen, Maude Irwin Owens, Jessie Fauset, Zora Neale Hurston, Melvin Tolson, and Ralph Ellison, *Visualizing Blackness* interrogates U.S. literary history from slavery through segregation, tracing the thread of visual knowing and learning as it unravels across time. As illuminated in the opening epigraph, Wheatley not only holds the distinction of being the first African American writer to publish a book, but she also bore the chore of being incessantly discussed as a visual testament to black intellectual capacity. Her dependence on her verse to respond to this objectification makes her a necessary starting point for this study. And although Tolson and Ellison craft their final works after the era of segregation proper, their literary projects reflect an enduring commitment to examining a pre-1960s U.S. landscape. Accordingly, their texts provide a fitting conclusion for my survey. Studying this long interval – the pre-abolition era through the pre-Black Arts years – and the specific modes and methods of vision embraced by writers, underscores *how* and *why* this historical period produces writers dedicated to connecting visuality to pedagogy in African American literature.

Mitchell defines visuality as "practices of seeing the world and especially of seeing other people," and Martin Jay explains it as "the distinct historical manifestations of visual experience in all its possible modes."[10] Both definitions underscore the social nature of vision. From the late eighteenth until the middle of the twentieth century, black writers' investment in visuality shows them decrying the error of a national vision dedicated to promulgating naïve or false conceptions of racial identity so as to validate white authority. Black writers concede what Michele Wallace declares an undeniable truth: "How one is seen (as black) and, therefore, what one sees (in a white world) is always already crucial to one's existence as an Afro-American. ... However, not being seen by those who don't want to see you ... often leads ... to the interpretation that you are unable to see."[11] Consequently, African American writers craft texts around figures who perform their ability to see in ways that instruct readers by dramatizing both pedagogical prowess and a special aptitude as students.

For black writers who come of age before the Black Arts Movement, the work of demonstrating the ability to teach and learn from sight assumes a markedly different cast from writers shaped by the cultural reality of the late 1960s and beyond. As Lawrence Jackson reveals in his magisterial *The Indignant Generation: A Narrative History of African American Writers and Critics, 1934–1960* (2010), the cultural sensibility defining writers immediately preceding the Black Arts Movement reflects the singular experience of segregation. Kenneth Warren goes so far as to distinguish black literature of the segregation era as constituting the only works that might legitimately be described as African American literature.[12] Both Jackson and Warren emphasize black writers' investment in defensive identity formation during the years preceding the civil rights movement to draw stark differences between African Americans publishing before 1960 and those who hit the literary scene later.

My study, however, considers two key pre-integration historical moments that highlight black writers' concentrated fight against readers' willful blindness: the slavery years through the early Harlem Renaissance and the later years of the New Negro Movement through what might be described as the pre-Black Arts Movement. Slavery and segregation, two periods of U.S. history during which African Americans were legally denied equal rights, uniquely impact black ideas regarding visuality. This division tracks black writers' evolution from approaching visuality as a means to define African Americans' superior moral vision to examining the ways black vision comes to denote a modern crisis of cultural identity. The literature of both eras, although by no means uniform, affirms the persistent link writers forge between their representation of black vision and pedagogy. To establish this connection, writers invariably focus on traditional pieces of art and conventional observational practices. Conversely, many African American artists who begin publishing during and beyond the Black Arts years demonstrate a willingness to engage abstract art objects and present more experimental portrayals of looking. Their continued reliance on vision and visual art, though moving in new directions, represents a continuum with earlier African American literature. Works from Ishmael Reed's *Mumbo Jumbo* (1972) to John Edgar Wideman's *Sent for You Yesterday* (1983) to Edward P. Jones's *The Known World* (2003) reveal black writers focusing on vision and visual objects in extremely unconventional ways. Reed's art-nappers, Wideman's abstract painters, and Jones's revisionist tapestry access new territory that builds on the foundational period I analyze even as their work reflects the reality of a post-1960s literary sensibility. This creative philosophy marks a changing of the guard that represents fertile ground for additional scholarship. This study lays the groundwork for such research as I elucidate the appeal and use of vision in shaping the inception of the African American literary canon and explain the significance of its role in moving the tradition forward.

Faith in Vision over Objects

In contrast to scholarship contending that black writers focus on the black voice to distract readers from concentrating on black appearance, I spotlight the central positioning of the trope of the Picture Book, the literary move to foreground sight. Thus, this study parts ways with the long focus on verbal culture as well as with the rich and expanding field of sound studies. My synoptic analysis distills the significance of black writers' investment in establishing African American command over visually acquired knowledge and linking such mastery to an argument for black humanity. By defining black character in terms of African Americans' ability to discern moral, national, and cultural truths – all portrayed in terms overwrought with the language of vision – these writers encourage readers to confront how aesthetic notions of racial difference impact interpretations of black identity. Labeling their literature as invested in "aesthetics" draws attention to their participation in debates linking humanity to appearance and identifying sight as a sense connoting freedom, moral authority, and artistic capacity. Mary Lou Emery, trenchantly tracing a parallel phenomenon in the work of twentieth-century Caribbean writers and artists, returns to David Hume's essay "On National Characters" to argue that his "judgment of black people as inferior" is "crucial to an empiricist philosophy in which sight is privileged as a sensory basis for knowledge of reality."[13] She proceeds to contend that Caribbean artists acknowledge this reality and therefore engage vision forthrightly as the means by which the modern subject possessing knowledge of the world is established. African American writers similarly respond to philosophers who unabashedly declare black skin visually, or "aesthetically," displeasing by revealing the depravity of such superficial claims.[14] As black writers question the consequences of such an immoral gauge of humanity, they convert a philosophical discussion into an ethical one and creatively explore the costs of these perspectives through their literature.

This decision to educate readers on the dangers of allowing aesthetics to frame discussions of morality and citizenship shapes black writing from its beginning. Ivy Wilson profitably ponders African Americans' consideration of aesthetics in nineteenth-century art that manipulates visuality to represent national belonging. Departing from a strictly Kantian sense of aesthetics concerned with formalist evaluations and preoccupied with pleasure, Wilson examines black writers' investment in connecting art to formal politics. To this end, he focuses on moments of "mimesis and representation" in texts seeking to size up the shadowy political position of African Americans.[15] Wilson's excellent work refines black writers' appeal to visuality as they challenge their liminal political position, and his research offers a provocative exploration of the ways aesthetic concerns intersect with discussions of civic inclusion. Thus, Wilson provides a useful point of departure as I trace the link between vision and representations of black intellect in literature to argue that African American writers have long depended on visuality to trouble traditional discussions of black humanity and national character.

My focus on the multiple ways black writers emphasize vision as a pedagogical tool works against a notion of black sight as monolithic.[16] But even in its variation, the portrayal of vision in black literature of the period I study largely reflects an Enlightenment faith in sight as opposed to subscribing to the anti-ocularism popularized by French theorists of the twentieth century.[17] In the many texts that emphasize the act of looking, black writers celebrate the ways visual perception informs African American character. Even as they acknowledge the dangerous underside of the ocularcentrism of Western culture – that is, the privileging of vision over other senses central to black cultural existence, such as sound – African American writers retain a belief in the ability to enlighten themselves, and their potentially wayward readers, by developing, executing, and preserving the capacity to interpret the world visually. Thus, I do not appeal to Freudian and Lacanian philosophy to argue that a tyrannically visual society built on racially blinkered cues has damaged black psychology. Instead, I contend that black writers remain committed to a kind of Cartesian perspectivalism, a belief in their natural ability to deploy vision to articulate their most profound revelations. In other words, black writers retain a "visually privileged order of knowledge."[18] *Visualizing Blackness* takes as its central project the discovery of how pre-Black Arts African American writers consistently seek to exhibit the achievement of such visually acquired wisdom.

By focusing on the ways writers portray black Americans interpreting what they see, as opposed to concentrating on deciphering visual objects described in their texts, this study shifts my analysis away from the approaches taken by scholarly works with a similar emphasis on visualization. For instance, David Brody's *Visualizing American Empire* (2010) concentrates on photographs, arts magazines, maps, parades, and world fairs to establish how American visualizing practices between 1898 and 1913 contributed to U.S. colonial expansion in the Philippines. Similarly, Melissa Dabakis's *Visualizing Labor in American Sculpture* (1999) explores the ways sculptural expression from 1880 to 1935 captures the complicated nature of U.S. labor formation. For both Brody and Dabakis, the work of "visualizing" depends almost exclusively on material objects, specific tangible artifacts, and visual mediums that tease out complicated notions of national identity.

My project, however, primarily analyzes how writers craft and signify on scenes that dramatize African American analyses of what they see without a consistent emphasis on the objects of such vision. Although African American writers exhibit a high awareness of the ways material culture defines race and racial understanding at particular historical moments, and sometimes draw directly from this backdrop, there is less focus on art objects per se, and more emphasis on the visual exchanges that generate, challenge, or alter accepted meanings of race. This is particularly true in the early literature I examine. Texts produced after the Harlem Renaissance devote more energy to art objects, but these exchanges prioritize the originality of black visual evaluation over particular objects. Whether they craft scenes depicting religious experience, creative production, educational philosophy, or the acquisition of intellectual knowledge, black writers underscore African Americans' dependence on sight to form independent, authoritative interpretations of U.S. society.

And even as this study refrains from entering physiological discussions of vision or pursuing the history of modern optics, it offers an extended consideration of the traditions of visual production that dominate black literature. The trope of the Picture Book, in drawing together various modes of visual knowing, unveils the enduring commitment that characterizes black writers' turn to vision. Wheatley challenges Cambridge students to execute spiritual and physical vision, imploring, "[s]ee [Jesus] with hands outstretch upon the cross," so they might share the undefiled Christian vision of an "*Ethiop*"; Douglass entreats readers to share the moral indignation he feels upon "witness[ing]" the "horrible exhibition" of his Aunt's beating; Washington discloses that the "first sight of the large ... school building" of Hampton gave him "new life" as he impresses the importance of black education on his audience; Anne Spencer directs readers to view *The Good Darky* statue with consternation, insisting, "[g]o, see it, read it, with whatever heart you have left"; Hurston conveys Janie's museum visitor disposition by stressing her inclination for seeking designated sites of observation such as the "front gate" which she leans over to "gaze up and down the road." The sheer magnitude of scenes in which African Americans foreground sight to formulate autonomous explanations of the U.S. – construals that they suggest their audience would do well to adopt – highlights the crucial role black vision plays in defining black identity and insisting on its centrality to understanding American character.

As a result of moving my emphasis away from an abiding concern with material objects to consider African American visualizing practices more broadly, I often uncover the generative nature of black vision. Sustained examinations of literary scenes denoting black vision substantiate the complexity of African American identity. In fact, what bell hooks describes as "black looks"[19] – the practice of African Americans looking at material representations of blackness or of being looked on in material objects such as photographs – I translate into "black visualizations," literary images of African Americans viewing the world or of being generally misread. In the texts of this study, the interpretive work performed by African American literary speakers attests to their cultural independence and authority. Consequently, *Visualizing Blackness* traces the glory of black humanity primarily through the historical evolution of black writing that focuses on visual practices as opposed to the revolutionary capacity of the photograph or other visual technologies.

By principally concerning itself with narrative tropes of vision, this book examines moments of visual discernment in literature to reassess the development of the African American literary tradition according to questions of sight rather than issues of voice. And although I am not preoccupied with pictorially illustrated literature, my work often intersects with and builds on scholarship guided by this interest. After all, the study of illustrated texts and analyses of black writers' interest in visual art and technology is certainly one way to approach questions related to the importance of visuality to literary texts. For instance, Michael Chaney and Ivy Wilson valuably examine the impact of nineteenth-century visual art, iconography, and visual apparatuses on the writing and political identity of black slaves; Anne Carroll and Martha Nadel investigate interart texts of the Harlem Renaissance to uncover the formative ways image and text shaped modern black identity; and Sara Blair, Jacqueline Goldsby, and Miriam Thaggert implement a range of approaches to probe the rich ways photography introduces new modes of seeing that influence black literature from Reconstruction through the 1970s. However, I approach the writers in this study by emphasizing the importance they place on acquiring knowledge through sight as opposed to stressing their work with visual media. Although writers' engagement with visual art and technology invariably enters this study – indeed, photographs occupy a central position in Chapter 2 – such concerns take a back seat to my persistent examination of writers' focus on vision. *Visualizing Blackness* reveals visuality as indispensable to the history, development, and theoretical contours of the African American literary tradition.

Sights of Instruction

By shifting the discussion of black literature from a verbal to a visual emphasis, a different set of issues emerges in stark relief. I examine the texts in this study with the aid of two frames that distinguish forms of the Picture Book trope and concentrate on distinct historical periods. Part I, "Sights of Instruction," traces the establishment and evolution of the trope of the Picture Book from Phillis Wheatley's poetry through 1920s publications by Harlem Renaissance women. My analysis of these texts aims to clarify how moments of visual instruction offer new modes for defining African American character. For the most part, these writers enjoy an unmitigated belief in the integrity of their vision, a rectitude they trace to the moral authority garnered by their social position in the nation. Women of the Harlem Renaissance reveal the first consistent signs of doubt regarding the moral authority of African American vision – an indication of their early affinity with a modernist perspective – but even they retain an inherent awareness of the error of those who prescribe deprecating visions of blackness. In contrast to the trope of the Talking Book which is usually founded on a moment of confusion and cultural deficiency that presents black writers seeking entrance into the Western world of letters, the Picture Book commences as a trope demarcating superior knowledge and self-sufficiency.

In recognition of the seminal position held by Wheatley's *Poems on Various Subjects, Religious and Moral* (1773), and her deliberate approach to visualizing blackness, I identify her work as inaugurating the trope of the Picture Book. Contrasting her poetry to publications by her black contemporaries clarifies both the role of her work in the formation of the African American literary canon and the basic elements of the Picture Book trope. For instance, James Gronniosaw's *A Narrative of the Most remarkable Particulars in the Life of James Albert Ukawsaw Gronniosaw, an African Prince, As Related by Himself* (1770) and Olaudah Equiano's *The Interesting Narrative of the Life of Olaudah Equiano, or Gustavus Vassa, the African* (1789) provide instructive examples of the trope of the Talking Book. Comparing the place of vision in their narrative accounts of their captivity, enslavement, and conversion to Christianity provides telling differences with Wheatley's portrayal of vision in her book of verse. Gronniosaw commences the trope of the Talking Book through his careful description of his desire to read:

> I was never so surprised in my whole life as when I saw the book talk to my master; for I thought it did, as I observed him to look upon it, and move

his lips. – I wished it would do so to me. ... I open'd it and put my ear down close upon it, in great hope that it wou'd say something to me; but was very sorry and greatly disappointed when I found it would not speak, this thought immediately presented itself to me, that every body and every thing despis'd me because I was black.[20]

For Gronniosaw, his failure to communicate with the book provides additional proof of the blight of physical blackness. This scene of instruction formed around the stubbornly silent book teaches him to despise his appearance and distrust his sight.

Equiano adopts Gronniosaw's point of view when he conveys his passionate desire to learn to read:

I was astonished at the wisdom of the white people in all things I saw. ... I had often seen my master and Dick employed in reading; and I had a great curiosity to talk to the books, as I thought they did; and so to learn how all things had a beginning: for that purpose I have often taken up a book, and have talked to it, and then put my ears to it, when alone, in hopes it would answer me; and I have been very much concerned when I found it remained silent.[21]

Later, he admits that he "looked upon" white people "as men superior to" blacks "and therefore ... had the stronger desire to resemble them."[22] These moments vividly illustrate the components of the Talking Book trope. In each instance, the black speaker observes a white individual reading, wishes to make the book talk to him, and interprets verbal illiteracy as a marker of racial inferiority. The black man's failure to read initially appears as a failure to interpret what he sees. Both Gronniosaw and Equiano are inspired to read by their high regard for white appearance and wisdom, and they view verbal literacy as an important form of imitation. Their inability to comprehend the written word results in feelings of cultural inadequacy.

The seminal feature I identify as establishing the trope of the Picture Book – an unabashed confidence in the authority of black vision – emerges clearly in Wheatley's poems and tenders a sharp distinction with writers' invested in the trope of the Talking Book. Although scholars have long condemned Wheatley for abdicating her duty to write forcefully against slavery, more recent critics consider the subtle ways her poetry seeks to intervene in discussions of African American equality.[23] My readings examine the way Wheatley's attention to race and vision facilitates her revisions of common conceptions of black inferiority. She repeatedly credits her creative genius, moral righteousness, and religious constancy to her enlightened view of blackness, race relations, and Christ. As I demonstrate in Chapter 1, she alternately assumes the posture of instructor and model art student, using both roles to highlight black creative superiority and moral authority. These attributes, achieved through her visionary prowess, illuminate the goals of the trope of the Picture Book.

Many writers signify on her verse directly and adopt a similar posture of uncertainty and humility even as they shrewdly teach their readers to subscribe to their vision of U.S. society. The authors of the slave narratives profess confusion and doubt about the sights around them, echoing Wheatley's speaker in a poem such as "To Maecenus," but they clearly instruct their readers to endorse their point of view. Additionally, as these writers develop the trope of the Picture Book, they acknowledge the changing visual technologies influencing their historical context. For instance, the ex-slave narrators subtly connect the truth of their vision to the technology of the daguerreotype and extol their honest portrayals of interactions between white and black Americans as necessary contributions to the national welfare. As they structure scenes around visual instruction in their texts, they encourage their audience to embrace and trust their vision just as they are learning to trust and value emergent technologies that record the world around them. Thus, slave narrators simultaneously extol the authority of their sight even when it diverges sharply from the expectations of their audience. By presenting black subjects who see and interpret the world around them in more convincing terms than their white counterparts, these writers declare their instructional authority.

Lessons from the Museum

Part II, "Lessons from the Museum," focuses on variations of one site of instruction. It contemplates the ways that museum culture pervades black literature of the twentieth century. In contrast to their predecessors who emphasize a largely uncomplicated belief in their visual authority, the late and post-Harlem Renaissance writers of this section detail their protagonist's struggle to regain an unadulterated perspective of U.S. society. The difficulty of their endeavor enacts the modern struggle to repair a fractured identity and underscores the need for sophisticated tools of visual observation. To this end, writers craft scenes of instruction that endorse, replicate, or exploit the principles of museum conduct. In fact, if the trope of the Picture Book is initially defined by the possession of special powers of insight rooted in black moral authority, as we move beyond the era defined as the "The Museum Age" – the period from 1880 to 1920 – visual tropes become heavily inflected by concepts disseminated by the museum.

Tony Bennett explains that the public museum was founded for the purpose of instructing citizens. By providing them with knowledge on how to see themselves and their place in the world, the museum embraced its role as an instructional site. Scholars have long interrogated how institutions dedicated to the display of cultural objects and visual art codify ethnic groups and instruct individuals to read racial difference, and black writers through the middle of the twentieth century demonstrate a growing interest in recreating museum culture in their texts. This insertion of museums into literature participates in what Karin Roffman describes as modern American women writers' complicated reflection on the way that demonstrating expertise in such institutions "became the means by which authority could be established" in their creative and professional lives.[24] In his examination of literature that engages the museum, Les Harrison explains that "the museum's practice is one of representing its objects to convey a given message; its practice is representational. The museum and the literary text then become analogous as sites where the existing power structures and power relations in society are confirmed or contested."[25]

Writers such as Zora Neale Hurston, Melvin Tolson, and Ralph Ellison turn to the "analogous" space of the museum to stress the importance of not only learning by sight but from deliberately organized scenes. Through either staging visual experiences structured by institutional rules for acquiring knowledge, or inserting fictional museums into their work, these writers portray moments of visual discovery – and the spaces that foster such opportunities – as critical to identity formation. Because their works emerge after "The Museum Age," writers of the mid-twentieth century reap the benefit of writing for a reading public more familiar with the museum experience than their predecessors. Consequently, they confidently draw on the representative world of the museum to infuse their literary worlds with new powers of instruction.

As an institution, the museum does not recommend itself as a homogeneous site with uniform goals. Instead, African American writers appeal to particular types and notions of the museum. Their works illustrate the acquisition of knowledge through interpretations of display; portray the impact of experiences occurring in museum spaces; and depict encounters that represent the surge of museum culture beyond the museum proper. The writers I study introduce singular ideas of the museum, together with the individual histories attending each type, into their literary explorations of black experience. Their texts rely most conspicuously on the natural history museum and art museum. As I discuss in Chapter 4, the natural history museum served as the first home for anthropologists – as well as other scientists – and shaped early discussions of race and culture. Carla Yanni explains that these institutions, where "objects were collected not only for political meaning but also for their visual power," transform "museum vision into a 'way of seeing'" such that "once an object rests in a museum, there is no way to view it other than as an object of visual worth."[26] Her description of "museum vision" helps make sense of black writers' reliance on a type of museum burdened with a history of objectifying ethnic minorities in troubling ways. Yanni reminds us that in the nineteenth century natural history museum context, "[l]ay consumers of science were also encouraged to learn by looking: vision was a credible way of understanding the world, especially in science museums."[27]

Notwithstanding the significant role museums of natural history played in affecting ideas about race, the art museum garners the lion's share of scholarly attention in literary study.[28] Scholars identify the 1793 opening of the Louvre Museum in Paris as the birth of the modern public art museum, but in the U.S., that distinction belongs to Charles Willson Peale's Philadelphia Museum. Black writers' investment in the art museum, an institution driven by educational goals, makes plain their drive to realign the national discussion of race from accentuating racialized objects to studying black interpretation. The turn from a focus on African American writers' construction of visually discerning figures in the literary texts of Part I, to a concentration on black writers' dependence on museums to instruct readers' vision in Part II, facilitates my analysis of the consistent yet evolving appeal to visuality in pre-Black Arts literature. By approaching their work through these frames, *Visualizing Blackness* highlights black writers' refutations of U.S. society's misguided reliance on established pictorial notions of black humanity. The focus on the museum in Part II adds a new direction for contemplating African American literature invested in visuality. My study draws from scholars' fine work to expand and rethink the field of African American visual-verbal scholarship and to assert that writers' investment in visuality informs the very shape of the black literary canon. Within a sweeping historical scope, I probe multiple literary genres including fiction, nonfiction, and poetry. In surveying the most persistent examples of their dependence on the trope of the Picture Book, *Visualizing Blackness* contends that African American writers become sophisticated practitioners of vision out of necessity.

Individual chapters develop the important ways writers exploit visuality. Chapters 1 and 2 consider the popular and high art visual portrayals of blackness that provide a backdrop for writers' revisionary texts.

Chapter 1, "Witnessing Moral Authority in Pre-Abolition Literature," examines how early African American writers showcase their visual assessment of the nation that teaches readers to revise popular conceptions of black character and recognize the visual perception of black citizens. It contrasts Scipio Moorhead's frontispiece of Wheatley with contemporary paintings and suggests that his visual portrayal anticipates Wheatley's celebration of sight in terms of her imagination and religious devotion, two attributes that confirm her independent moral character. Analyses of her poems confirm her consistent appeal to vision to portray her creative and spiritual authority. Turning to the nineteenth-century authors of slave narratives, the chapter probes Douglass's and Jacobs's relentlessly honest observations of slavery in first person narratives that parallel the work of the daguerreotype and replicate nineteenth century genre paintings that figure African Americans on the margins of U.S. citizenship. They offer their moral wholeness as an antidote to a nation fractured by a refusal to face race relations forthrightly.

The works examined in Chapter 2, "Picturing Education and Labor in Washington and Du Bois," emphasize Booker T. Washington's and W. E. B. Du Bois's literary and photographic representations of the education of black workers. By considering their most canonical texts, *Up from Slavery* (1901) and *The Souls of Black Folk* (1903), alongside the photographic collections they supported, I ponder the complexity of their formation of the racialized seeing subject. As educators, they carefully revise the trope of the Picture Book to depict the inspired vision of the black masses determined to succeed. Du Bois unveils the danger of denying the American Dream to young rural souls whereas Washington extols the power embodied by visions of educational institutions. Although their portrayals diverge sharply from each other as well as from images promulgated by mainstream media and literature, both men trumpet spirited cases for entrusting black Americans with contributing to the country's progress. Washington in particular uncovers an unexpectedly progressive strategy for portraying African American education.

Chapter 3, "Gazing upon Plastic Art in the Harlem Renaissance," refines the discussion of labor to focus specifically on the black female artist. Moving forward to the 1920s, this chapter studies how New Negro women's poetry and fiction appeal to visual art to revise stereotypical images of black humanity. Turning to ekphrasis, the chapter argues that black women seek to "still" their work to contemplate the complexity of their modern outlook. Narrowly defined by Leo Spitzer as "the poetic description of a pictorial or sculptural work of art" and more broadly described by James Heffernan as "the verbal representation of visual representation," ekphrasis recalls the long history behind verbal texts' investment in visual art.[29] As they insert a pause in the action of their texts, they extol the potential for black female artists to impact U.S. race relations. I study the poetry of Anne Spencer, Angelina Grimké, and Gwendolyn Bennett as well as fiction by Nella Larsen, Maude Irwin Owens, and Jessie Fauset to highlight the ways women focus on visual art across genres. Together, their texts present African American female creativity as invested in radically redefining political and aesthetic ideas across the entire black community. Renaissance women writers also demonstrate an avid interest in the painted portrait. Francoise Meltzer's analysis of the portrait suggests that because it is "'other' to the verbal economy of the text," the portrait "functions as a good barometer for literature's views of itself, on representation, and on the power of writing."[30] For women of the Harlem Renaissance, depending on ekphrasis and visual portraits facilitates their visualization of black womanhood as well as their enhancement of the trope of the Picture Book.

Chapter 4, "Zora Neale Hurston: Seeing by the Rules of the Natural History Museum," commences Part II. I begin this chapter by reviewing Hurston's training as an anthropologist and considering the formative role the natural history museum initially played in publishing anthropological research. Using her studies with Franz Boas as a backdrop, this chapter argues that Hurston connects her written texts to the museum by championing the acquisition of knowledge through careful observation. It also suggests that she portrays her protagonists as ethnographers whose growing insight of their communities displays the importance of cultural authority achieved through sophisticated vision. After examining her early short stories to establish Hurston's penchant for enlisting fiction to challenge scientific pronouncements of black intellectual inferiority, I analyze *Jonah's Gourd Vine* (1934), *Their Eyes Were Watching God* (1937), and *Moses, Man of the Mountain* (1939). These novels lay bare her method for visualizing African American intelligence in ways that simultaneously recall and refute the earlier scientific fascination with measuring skulls and brains to gauge intellectual aptitude. The chapter argues that the protagonists of her mature novels assume the roles of participant-observers who adopt the tools of anthropology to learn more about their culture and themselves. As protagonists demonstrate their visual dexterity, readers are invited to assess the knowledge they collect, thereby fulfilling the expectations established by exhibits in natural history museums.

In Chapter 5, "Melvin Tolson: Gaining Modernist Perspective in the Art Gallery," I shift my attention from the natural history museum to examine Tolson's investment in the art museum. Concentrating on the volumes of verse that form the bookends of his career, *A Gallery of Harlem Portraits* (c. 1935) and *Harlem Gallery* (1965), I suggest that the art museum comes to represent a space for publication, a means for contemplating how avant-garde black art might reach an expanded audience. After reviewing early U.S. museum history, including the distinct development of African American public museums as well as historically black college and university museums, I argue that Tolson portrays the art museum as a site where the black critic and black artist close ranks to champion modernist art by African Americans. Signifying on the trope of the Picture Book, Tolson foregrounds the curator's visual authority that enables his sophisticated understanding of how modern black art proves culturally relevant to diverse black audiences. Tolson draws on his career as a college professor to insist on the power of both "high" and "low" African American art to unveil the complexity of black identity.

I conclude *Visualizing Blackness* with Chapter 6, "Ralph Ellison: Understanding Black Identity beyond Museum Walls." This chapter contends that Ellison appeals to museum culture to expose how as an institution, the museum develops rules that pervade social interactions throughout society. Building on André Malraux's concept of a "museum without walls," I argue that in both *Invisible Man* (1952) and his unfinished second novel which he worked on until 1993, Ellison constructs scenes according to exhibition rules or around art objects to demonstrate the need for sophisticated reading in everyday affairs, particularly those highly charged relationships between people of different races. Close readings of both *Invisible Man* and *Three Days Before the Shooting...* allow me to trace Ellison's careful attention to theories of visual display and interpretation as he asserts the need to recognize and respect the sophisticated perspective born of black cultural experience. His success serves as a final testament to the formative role of visual aesthetics in shaping the tradition of African American literature.

As these chapters suggest, *Visualizing Blackness* is not a prolonged contemplation of whether or how painting is or is not like poetry, or how visual art objects are or are not like books. By investigating the many ways black writers stage moments of visual instruction to shape definitions of black identity, this study eschews overly neat packaging. Instead, each chapter takes up an important historical moment in African American letters and aims to recover the rich diversity of black writers' appeal to visual aesthetics. Put simply, *Visualizing Blackness* examines the most formative ways African American writers appeal to visuality in shaping their literary works. By following the evolution of the trope of the Picture Book, I provide a critical apparatus for analyzing a fundamental issue in the African American literary canon. This apparatus, considered within the expansive frame *Visualizing Blackness* offers, represents a starting point for other scholars to build on rather than a definitive end.

PART ONE

Sights of Instruction

CHAPTER I

Witnessing Moral Authority in Pre-Abolition Literature

And entering in [a river], we see a number of blacke soules, Whose likelinesse seem'd men to be, but all as blacke as coles.

Their Captaine comes to me as naked as my naile, Not having witte or honestie to cover once his taile.
                                                    – Robert Baker, 1562, 1589[1]

Has Mr. Jefferson declared to the world, that we are inferior to the whites, both in the endowments of our bodies and of minds? ... But is Mr. Jefferson's assertions true? viz. "that it is unfortunate for us that our Creator has been pleased to make us *black*?"
                                                    – David Walker, 1829[2]

African Americans entered the U.S. imagination defined by an outer appearance that white Westerners interpreted as proof of an inner immorality. The sixteenth-century British explorer's poem recording his initial view of black Africans captures this early Western reflex to connect black skin with a black soul and nudity with stupidity as well as moral corruptness. Almost 300 years later, the African American activist David Walker tackled the staying power of such ideas. His incredulous response to Thomas Jefferson's claim that African Americans' physical appearance indicated their deficient intellectual capacity addresses two prongs undergirding the logic for U.S. slavery: black slaves' physical unattractiveness, together with their mental deficiencies, fitted them for slavery and little else. In examining Jefferson's prejudiced views, however, Walker questions whether one of the nation's founding fathers thought himself above God. Just as the sixteenth-century explorer implies that black nakedness confirms immorality, Jefferson maintains that black Americans' aesthetically unpleasant appearance denies them access to a mature moral nature. Walker, forthrightly appraising this logic, repudiates Jefferson's visual authority, which he traces back to a morally flawed foundation.

23

His fiery *Appeal* (1829) captures the confluence of eighteenth- and nineteenth-century African American writers' arguments against slavery. Notwithstanding their distinct historical contexts, these writers emphasize their visual interpretation of the world to substantiate their legitimacy as both artists and potential citizens. They willingly assume the pedagogical role necessary to correct misguided vision. Walker's focus on the absurdity of white America's obsession with blackness locates white immorality in religious terms, but his transgressor exemplar, Thomas Jefferson, demonstrates the ways this religious immorality bleeds into national politics. Black American writers note this double adulteration from their earliest publications and accordingly develop literary methods that distinguish their high artistic and political standards. Their publications, in both verse and narrative forms, reflect an unwavering commitment to challenging the visualizing practices of their audience by presenting black Americans as possessing powers of vision often connected to the artistic practices of their era. This strategy leads to their creation of the trope of the Picture Book, narrative moments that link vision to instruction.

As the epigraphs make clear, black writers' decisions to connect black vision to moral character stemmed from the majority's relentless designation of blackness as a sign of wickedness. Africans had been introduced to Europeans chiefly in visual terms, and for large numbers of white Westerners who would never interact with blacks, skin color signified much about their character. From the late eighteenth to the mid-nineteenth century, blackness equaled slavery in most Americans' minds. Reviewing a broad range of publications from the period, Milton Cantor notes the difficulty of disputing the "popular notion that slavery was 'connected with the Black Colour and Liberty with the White.'"[3] The nearly 100-year period explored in this chapter, from 1773 to 1861 – or from the publication of Phillis Wheatley's *Poems on Various Subjects, Religious, and Moral* to Harriet Jacobs's *Incidents in the Life of a Slave Girl* – includes the colonies' move from dependence on Great Britain to independence following the Revolutionary War, and then from a unified republic to a divided land approaching the Civil War. Additionally, this era saw the force of the Enlightenment and its celebration of neoclassical ideas give way to the age of Romanticism, but not before African American writers deeply imbibed the passionate advocacy for improving one's mental capacity, one's knowledge of the world. And during this period, many philosophers argued that knowledge was most directly procured through a development of the most noble of the senses: sight.

African American writers actively participated in this celebration of vision as they subscribed to the philosophical pronouncements connecting sight to the attainment of knowledge. During the late eighteenth century, philosophers and artists alike continued to connect intelligence and imagination to a visual engagement with the world. Visual perception proved the moral independence of the thinking subject. Even as black writers embraced Cartesian perspectivalism, which suggested that all people possessed a universal point of view endowed by God, they revealed the increasing truth that racial preconceptions often corrupted white vision. In fact, the questions they raise by contrasting their vision with that of their white counterparts prove all the more striking when considered against the general Enlightenment attitude toward sight.

This span of years also witnessed a sea change in how white Americans viewed blacks. The visual and written records portray the interdependent nature of the representative arts in establishing, effecting, and evolving race relations. Consequently, as African Americans laid the groundwork for a literary tradition, they remained acutely aware of the rampant visual depictions of black skin surrounding them and the impact these images wielded on assessments of their humanity. This chapter explores these writers' methods for visualizing black sight to celebrate their morality in spite of national narratives defining them as servants lacking an independent moral compass. By focusing on Wheatley's poetry before considering Frederick Douglass's and Harriet Jacobs's slave narratives, I explain how their work establishes the trope of the Picture Book and provides a sturdy base for this study. Together, these pre-abolition writers challenge white conceptions of African American character as they invite readers to behold black speakers deftly negotiating the increasingly visually laden society around them.

Wheatley's New Image for the Mind's Eye

In establishing the trope of the Picture Book, Wheatley emphasizes two modes of vision that challenge her readers' conceptions of African Americans. Wheatley presents black imagination and religious devotion in terms of sight. By picturing herself as a kind of religious seer while foregrounding her physical blackness, she contests the popular assumption of black Americans' spiritual, intellectual, and artistic blindness. At the same time, she exploits the popular conversion narrative that Phillip Richards argues allowed black Americans to become "an exemplary figure for the white audience."[4] Wheatley's attention to vision also underscores her familiarity with the reading practices of colonial Americans who remained enthralled with British neoclassicism.[5] Although colonial readers in cities such as Boston enjoyed access to homegrown writing in newspapers, magazines, almanacs, and pamphlets, American bookstores of the 1760s and 1770s primarily stocked British texts. As a result, colonial taste in poetry from 1765 to 1790 remained devoted to the aesthetics epitomized by Alexander Pope. Like his neoclassical peers, Pope's ekphrastic verse assumed readers could readily visualize well-known pieces of plastic art. Additionally, his celebrated philosophical poems, *Essay on Criticism* (1711) and *An Essay on Man* (1734), refined Enlightenment ideas relating reason, nature, and morality. In linking his philosophical and ethical ideas, Pope attempted to define a practical morality and provided an unabashed explanation of the poet's role in assisting readers to understand man's relationship to God.

Wheatley's familiarity with Pope is well established, and her verse shows her following his example in assuming an instructional posture as she urges readers to contemplate their spirituality. But instead of directing her audience to see classical art objects in their mind's eye, she teaches her audience to visualize a morally upstanding, discerning African American speaker. Most scholarship that considers Wheatley's embrace of neoclassicism attends to accusations proclaiming her an untalented imitator, but Eric Slauter helpfully explains the historical significance of such charges.[6] After noting the transitional nature of the late eighteenth century, as colonial Americans shifted from identifying with neoclassicism to romantic ideals, Slauter observes that the burgeoning clash of principles resulted in a "discourse about cultural 'slavery' and the dangers of mental dependency."[7] For the colonial leaders anxious to prove the American right to self-government, the failure to display original ideas – in art or politics – became tantamount to a failure to deserve national independence.

The slippery extension of such arguments to address African Americans was not lost on Wheatley. Few critics, however, have noted Wheatley's direct challenge of this logic through her portrayal of the creative and inspired vision of black Americans in her poetry. Whereas major English poets of the era, such as Pope, Dryden, and Gray, embraced *ut pictura poesis* and strove to bring a picture before their reader's eye – often an image drawn from classical paintings or sculptures – in an effort to proclaim the truth of nature and all human experience, Wheatley demonstrates a commitment to infusing her poetry with pictures of African American visualizing practices, images at odds with traditional notions of black inhumanity. Using herself as a prime example, she offers readers an opportunity to assess her moral and aesthetic insights, described in terms of visual acuity, and she rejects philosophical theories relegating black Americans to the position of slaves.

Even as she occasionally turns to classical subjects in ekphrastic poems such as "NIOBE in Distress for her Children slain by APOLLO, from Ovid's Metamorphoses, Book VI. and from a view of the Painting of Mr. Richard Wilson," Wheatley more frequently seeks to visualize the black artist as an instructor with intellectual and moral authority. She was certainly familiar with the contours of the sister arts discussion, and as John Shields points out, she likely read Horace's *Art of Poetry* and found encouragement for "exploring the connection between poetry and painting."[8] Yet the sophistication of Wheatley's own understanding of the relationship between visual and verbal art did not obscure her awareness of her audience. Her repeated references to her black skin reflect her awareness that, for the vast majority of her readers, her verse directs their eyes back to her dark body. Winthrop Jordan bluntly explains, "Phillis Wheatley ... became antislavery's most prized exhibit, her name virtually a household term for the Negro's mental equality."[9] Wheatley's work seeks to refine this exhibit, and her revision of expected visualizations of black character begins with Scipio Moorhead's frontispiece published in the first edition of her *Poems on Various Subjects, Religious and Moral* (see Figure 1.1).

As one of the few surviving visual depictions of Wheatley, Moorhead's engraving has long provided scholars a rich object of analysis. Frontispiece portraits were rare additions to eighteenth-century books – especially for a living author – and even more noteworthy for women. Wheatley enjoyed the distinction of being "the first colonial American woman of any race to have her portrait printed alongside her writings."[10] David Grimstead describes the portrait as "an icon of the dignified, respectable, literary, and especially thoughtful black" that offers a "quiet refutation ... of the tacit prejudice" that proclaimed African Americans "incapable of being fully intelligent and respectable humans."[11] Betsy Erkkilä declares that the portrait dually represents Wheatley's "[r]evolutionary" position by depicting "a black woman reading, thinking, and writing" even as it "enchains her" with the inscription "Phillis Wheatley, Negro Servant to John Wheatley, of Boston."[12] Walter Nott proclaims the picture a "palpable presence" that "constitutes the graphic representation of Wheatley's public presence and the power it produces," a veritable "emblem of the book as a whole."[13] And Astrid Franke, taking issue with these racially motivated readings, calls for greater attention to the "cultural context in which the engraving" existed, an approach that leads to her provocative comparison of Wheatley's

PHILLIS WHEATLEY NEGRO SERVANT to Mr JOHN WHEATLEY, of BOSTON.

Publifhed according to Act of Parliament, Septr. 1, 1773 by Arch^{d.} Bell,
Bookfeller N°. 8 near the Saracens Head Aldgate.

Figure 1.1 Anonymous, *Phillis Wheatley, poet* (1773). Engraving after Scipio Moorhead. National Portrait Gallery, Smithsonian Institution, Washington, DC. Photo credit: National Portrait Gallery, Smithsonian Institution / Art Resource, NY.

portrait to the contemporary portrait of the Countess of Huntingdon, Wheatley's patron. Franke concludes that both portraits partake in the "iconography of melancholy" and reflect "a mournful reflexivity proceeding from the insights of the religious convert and the poetic genius."[14]

These scholarly contemplations of Wheatley's famous frontispiece confirm the crucial role it played for eighteenth-century readers and continues to play for current critics of her work. Scholars such as Mary Balkun cogently argue that Wheatley persistently strove to direct readers' attention away from her physical body so as to emphasize her mind and explain the frontispiece as simply a result of the Countess of Huntingdon's desires, but my reading concurs with Robert Kendrick's assessment of both the portrait and her poetic exhibition of her body.[15] Insisting that the frontispiece raises new questions, Kendrick maintains that Wheatley "does not simply want abstract recognition, equality as a matter of discourse, but equality as a matter of physical, lived contact with her audience. She must be *seen* equally." What is more, he contends that this "emphasis on the body, and her body, continues throughout her poetry."[16]

Building on his compelling line of reasoning, together with Franke's contention that the eighteenth-century cultural context holds valuable clues for analyzing Wheatley's portrait as well as her verse, we might read Moorhead's engraving as actively contributing to an analysis of themes central to the poems it precedes. Studied beside the most common portrayals of blackness of the period, her portrait radically revises visualizations of African American intellectualism, artistry, and morality. Unlike later periods, the rather narrow field of U.S. visual culture during the late eighteenth through the mid-nineteenth century empowered trends shaping ideas about African Americans.[17] High art consigned black subjects almost exclusively to the roles of servant and entertainer. Given the subjects Wheatley's poetry addresses, she was likely aware of the unimaginative nature of such representations. A brief overview of such works establishes the stereotypes that her verse and frontispiece seek to dismantle.[18]

Justus Engelhardt Kühn's *Portrait of Henry Darnall III* began the effort to define black character in relation to white authority with his portrayal of the young Henry in full aristocratic dress complemented by his nameless black servant commensurately attired (see Figure 1.2). The black boy's adoring attitude, contrasted with Henry's youthful confidence, augurs the relationship between black and white men. The neoclassical background, the dividing balustrade, and the slave boy's silver collar and retention of the game bird young Henry has felled firmly establish the position of the black slave: he serves as an accoutrement of gentlemanly status. As such, he stands outside the boundaries of official citizenship, closely aligned with the animals over which white colonists reigned. *Alexander Spotswood Payne and his Brother, John Robert Dandridge Payne with their Nurse* (c. 1790) by an unknown artist and Ralph Earl's *Gentleman with Negro Attendant* (see Figure 1.3) replicate Kühn's representation of black servitude by placing the black subjects in positions that mimic the posture of Henry's servant. Of course, the earlier completion of famous paintings such as John Trumbull's

[1912.1.3] Henry Darnall III. Oil on canvas by Justus Englehardt Kühn, c. 1710. Museum Department. Copy of original owned by the Maryland Historical Society. No reproduction or use without permission.

Figure 1.2 Justus Englehardt Kühn, *Henry Darnall III* (c. 1710). Courtesy of the Maryland Historical Society, Museum Department, Baltimore, MD, (192.1.3).

George Washington (see Figure 1.4) and *The Death of General Warren at the Battle of Bunker Hill* (1786) signaled the entrenched nature of black servitude. Together, this collection of eighteenth-century portrayals of black identity purposefully defines black Americans as servants whose moral rectitude rests on their fidelity to their masters. The paintings train white

Figure 1.3 Ralph Earl, *Gentleman with Negro Attendant* (c. 1785–1788). Courtesy of the New Britain Museum of American Art, New Britain, CT. Harriet Russell Stanley Fund, 1948.06.

and black viewers alike to infer that African Americans depend on white power for moral integrity.

Whereas the Dutch and other Europeans boast long histories of representing blacks in a variety of roles, most frequently as a member of the Magi, American artists produced far fewer notable exceptions of blacks filling the servant station.[19] John Singleton Copley's *Watson and the Shark* (1778) stands as the best known example of an eighteenth-century piece breaking with the tradition of relegating African Americans to definitive servant roles, and even Copley's painting stops short of casting the

Figure 1.4 John Trumbull, *George Washington* (1780). Bequest of Charles Allen Munn, 1924 (24.109.88). The Metropolitan Museum of Art, New York, NY. Digital Image © The Metropolitan Museum of Art / Art Resource, NY.

black man as heroic.[20] Of course, the largest number of colonists viewed blacks in less remarkable forms of print media. Barbara Lacey superbly examines "imprints – books, pamphlets, broadsides, magazines, and selected newspapers – published between 1640 and 1800" to probe how visual images in the most accessible published material influenced early American racial attitudes.[21] The vast majority of visual depictions of blacks emerged in relation to slave advertisements, and these broadsides emphasized the African roots of the future bondsmen and women. The illustrations encourage what Lacey describes as the white potential purchaser's "power of the observer over the observed; they gazed at an exotic people who became objects to be studied at a distance."[22]

Advertisements for runaways extended the narrative initiated by auction notices and further defined blacks as servants without a fully developed moral sensibility. These images imply that without the civilizing attempts of slave masters, blacks would devolve to their barbaric ways and pose a threat to all. Even the vast array of abolitionist images piled onto depictions of blacks' natural subservience to whites. In 1787, the mass-produced seal of the Committee for Affecting the Abolition of the Slave Trade, a Quaker group, featured a muscular black male figure wearing only white drapery around his midsection and chains connecting his ankles to his wrists raised in a gesture of supplication. The image strengthens the narrative of black dependence on whites. The same might be concluded from the most widely distributed image by antislavery activists: the 1789 diagram of *The Brooks*, a slave vessel diagram published in magazines and pamphlets. The image both emphasized the horrific conditions on board a slave ship and, albeit unintentionally, corroborated the idea that blacks lack individuality. Thus, abolitionist images ironically substantiated proslavery illustrations that call attention to blacks' slave status rather than their moral rectitude and individual agency.[23]

Wheatley's portrait diverges from high art portrayals of blackness that precede and succeed hers while it also acknowledges the defamatory work achieved by popular illustrations. Placed in the company of Kühn's *Portrait of Henry Darnall III* (see Figure 1.1), Trumbull's *George Washington* (see Figure 1.4), and Earl's *Gentleman with Negro Attendant* (see Figure 1.3), Moorhead's picture of Wheatley disrupts visual definitions of black servitude and the accepted correlation of morality with visual proof of a black slave's devotion to a white master. In each of the eighteenth-century portraits that include black servants, their looks of adoration signal their moral nature: Henry Darnell's boy in waiting, the Negro attendant, and Washington's manservant perform their righteousness through faithful upward gazes fastened on white authority. Conversely, Wheatley's upturned eyes find no white master to contemplate. Where her painted peers focus on white power, she ruminates on artistic accomplishment.

Thus, in place of the dividing balustrade that confirms the exclusion of Darnell's servant from participating in neoclassical culture, Wheatley sits before a desk with accoutrements that corroborate her contributions to American poetry. Instead of the Eastern looking costume that establishes Washington's servant as "other," Wheatley wears conservative attire that attests to her identification with colonial America. Even as she remains circumscribed by words that decree her physical servant status, her gaze asserts her independent, imaginative thoughts.

Moorhead's portrait also foregrounds Wheatley's gender, an additional hurdle for some readers to overcome, and asserts the reality of a black woman participating in the production of neoclassical art. When she published her collection in 1773, the reading public was highly gendered, making her knowledge of Greek literature and facility with Latin all the more noteworthy.[24] Women only began finding encouragement to increase their classical learning when new social opportunities involving both men and women, such as salons and tea tables, necessitated classical knowledge for glittering conversation. But even in preparation for these settings, women were instructed to maintain a narrow reading list of classical texts.[25] Wheatley's reading well exceeded this list, and her writing also focuses on unexpected classical themes that give rise to a consideration of artistic skill and moral righteousness. In fact, the portrait that figures Wheatley as a black American female writer challenges her audience's expectations of both a woman and an African. Although many women possessed the ability to read, far fewer women of any race could write. Carretta notes that "only about half the white American female population of the eighteenth century may have been sufficiently literate to sign a name to a will."[26] Wheatley's portrait, then, clears the way for the literary posture she assumes in her verse. Her words enact a devotion to artistic excellence that substantiates her upstanding moral nature and plays on the exceptional visionary position of the poet speaker even as she foregrounds her racial blackness.

The Poetic Work of Visualizing Black Character

Wheatley's poet speakers exhibit the role of vision in nurturing artistic imagination and developing Christian devotion. "To Maecenas," the poem that commences her volume, begins the work of establishing her visual authority by somewhat surprisingly designating her a student. Shields notes that Wheatley discreetly reflects back on the frontispiece in the opening poem as she carefully assumes an unobjectionable artistic posture: "[S]he declares 'here I sit, and mourn a grov'ling mind" but "the inclusion of [the] portrait makes a rebellious statement: Wheatley sits non-humbly and aggressively before a writing desk, on which one sees paper with writing on it ... obviously promising still more writing to come."[27] The visual image conflates the roles of student and thinker. Although the poem ostensibly opens with Wheatley soliciting Maecenas's attention and approval, the second stanza promptly reveals its principal objective of teaching readers to adopt the appropriate posture toward a talented black artist. She describes her powers of aesthetic appreciation in terms of exceptional sight and links her penetrating vision to the authenticity of her creative ability. The poet speaker directs her words toward a tried-and-true patron of the arts, acknowledging the necessity of seeking worthy listeners, readers who "feel the same" and boast an "equal genius" as the greatest poets of Western literature.[28] And even more importantly, she vividly portrays her own untrained taste in terms of vision:

> While *Homer* paints lo! circumfus'd in air,
>
>   ...
>
> Great Sire of verse, before my mortal eyes,
> The lightening blaze across the vaulted skies,
> And, as the thunder shakes the heav'nly plains,
> A deep-felt horror thrills through all my veins.
> When gentler strains demand thy graceful song,
> The length'ning line moves languishing along.
> When great *Patroclus* courts *Achilles'* aid,
> The grateful tribute of my tears is paid (*CW*, 9)

Rather than present herself as an imperceptive novice needing guidance, Wheatley displays her instinctive aesthetic appreciation and genuine response to great art, proof of her intellectual precociousness. What initially appears to be an admission that she depends on "mortal eyes" as opposed to Homer's god-like artistic status is really Wheatley's clever assertion of her own inspired aesthetic judgment. Homer's poetic pictures appear only to those possessing the interpretive skills to see meaning and imagine the images his verse describes; verbal literacy is not enough. Wheatley's "thrills through her veins" alternating with her grateful "tears" bespeak the natural passion she feels when experiencing great art through her "mortal eyes." She requires no teacher to instruct her on Homer's achievement for she boasts an innate ability to recognize great art. In fact, the admiration she feels highlights what Jennifer Billingsley describes as Wheatley's paradoxical position of being both an "agent of wonder in the

Age of Reason" and a champion of aesthetic awe in terms that anticipate Kant's appeal to imagination to escape the bounds of reason.[29]

Thus, Wheatley links the wonder her readers felt with regard to her race to her wondrous creative ability. She foregrounds her blackness and reminds her audience of black artists who preceded her: "The happier *Terence** all the choir inspir'd ... / But say, ye *Muses*, why this partial grace, / To one alone of *Afric*'s sable race" (*CW*, 10). Yet even as she laments the small cadre of black poets who have achieved notoriety for their verse, she is inspired with new confidence. Despite the Muses' stinginess, she vows to push ahead and even embraces a playful persona in relation to Maecenas: "I'll snatch a laurel from thin honour'd head" (*CW*, 10).[30] The agency she exhibits proclaims her faith in her own talents, and the assertive nature of her procurement of Maecenas's support, a veiled reference to the Countess of Huntingdon's patronage, attests to her belief in the accomplishment of her "lays." Wheatley concludes the opening poem of her collection with a bold declaration of her artistic worthiness that forthrightly contests those writers who deny African American creative ability and clears the way for the instructional position she assumes throughout the collection: she smoothly transitions from student to teacher.

"To Maecenus" lays the foundation for the trope of the Picture Book with its deliberate portrayal of Wheatley as a visionary student who responds passionately to Western literature in visual terms, but it is in the third poem of her collection that Wheatley crafts a racialized poetic identity that instructs the implied white reader as she connects blackness to artistic fervor and moral stature. In "To the University of CAMBRIDGE, in NEW-ENGLAND," she tightly ties poetic and religious vision, hints that black Americans retain the purest relationship with Christ, and implies that the potency of her spiritual vision accounts for her Christian constancy. She explains that "an intrinsic ardor prompts" her to write even as she contemplates the marvel of having not been long departed from the largely unchristian Africa (*CW*, 11). As in "To Maecenas," what first seems to be a focus on her unworthiness – here defined by her brief exposure to Christianity – becomes an opportunity to broadcast her extraordinary powers of vision, art, and morality. She directs the Cambridge students to "[s]ee [Jesus] with hands out-stretch upon the cross," implicitly acknowledging the possibility that some of these "sons of science" may not be blessed with such visionary powers (*CW*, 12). Her verse, like Homer's great work, possesses the power to inspire readers to recall iconic images crucial to Christian faith. Reminding the students that "An *Ethiop*" offers such advice, Wheatley links her devoutness to her racial identification and contrasts her constancy with the white students' more likely tendency to stray from a path of religious fidelity.[31] She also conflates her black body with the iconic crucified body of Christ, directing the students' eyes to this faith-inspired visionary knowledge first shared by "messengers from heav'n" (*CW*, 12). Her imploring remonstrance that students visualize the crucified son of God presents Christ as the sole pictorial presentation, other than Wheatley's repeated references to herself as a "native" of "Egyptian gloom" and an "*Ethiop*" (*CW*, 11, 12). As the bearer of the good news, the black body to which Wheatley alludes gets both subsumed and amplified by Christ's perfect body and the countless paintings that visualize his sacrifice. Thus, Wheatley seems devoted to encouraging her listeners to imagine an iconic visual image – Christ on the cross – as they simultaneously ponder the blackness of the poet urging such contemplation.

Her emphasis on her power to keep her eyes on Christ, and to use her poetic creations to encourage others to follow her lead, places Wheatley in a vastly different position than black writers recounting their attempts to conquer the Talking Book. The moment of visual instruction that I identify as a key component of the Picture Book portrays the African American speaker as enlightened. Conversely, the silence of the Talking Book highlights black slaves' failed attainment of Western culture. Wheatley claims a power to see in contrast to her audience's possible blindness to Christ's example. What is more, as in "To Maecenas," Wheatley declares her ability as unlearned in contrast to the Cambridge students whom she hints might lose sight of their *intellectually* – as opposed to *spiritually* – acquired beliefs. And finally, she foregrounds her black body only to redefine its visual meaning. Her blackness augurs a pure and steadfast commitment to Christ as well as a willingness to perform the work of proselytizing. As other scholars have noted, Wheatley boldly assumes ministerial robes and offers a jeremiad of sorts.

Even her most maligned poem, "On being brought from AFRICA to AMERICA," piles on to the portrayal of her visual authority and pedagogical prowess. After acknowledging the spiritual salvation made possible through her arrival in America, she directs her attention to morally compromised Christians: "Some view our sable race with scornful eye, / 'Their colour is a diabolic die.' / Remember, *Christians*, *Negros*, black as *Cain*, / May be refin'd, and join th' angelic train" (*CW*, 13). In the broader context of her collection and its concerted effort to demonstrate her inspired vision, her description of the "scornful eye" of those who connect black skin to exclusion from the Christian family critiques their theological ignorance. Even an African knows this. White Christians' failure to interpret visual blackness as anything other than an opportunity to evangelize leaves her forced to play the role of missionary in the U.S. She must again adopt the role of instructor and teach mistaken Christians to focus on spreading the gospel as opposed to indulging sinful preconceptions. Her previously "benighted soul," as well as "*Negros*, black as Cain," represents the interior blackness that Christians should work to enlighten as opposed to focusing on "sable" skin which is only of note to wayward believers distracted from the work Christ desires from his followers (*CW*, 13).

"To S. M. a young *African* Painter, on seeing his Works" offers a final, striking example of Wheatley's consistent portrayal of black artistry and morality in terms of enlightened vision. The poem is noteworthy as both an example of Wheatley's desire to compare the work of visual and verbal artists, as well as an instructive illustration of her willingness to draw direct contrasts between the role vision plays for black artists compared to white poets and painters. Like a number of poems in her collection, "To S. M." reflects the influence of the contemporary white poet, Mather Byles. Not only was he one of the best known poets in eighteenth-century America, Byles was also Wheatley's neighbor and one of the eighteen white men whose signature authenticated her work. In her portrayal of the relationship between black visual and verbal artists, Wheatley revises Byles's similar project in his poem "To Pictorio, on the Sight of his Pictures" published in his collection, *Poems on Several Occasions* (1744). Byles uses his poetry to celebrate friendship between painters and poets, but he extols the impact American freedom imparts to visual and verbal artists alike. Comparing "To Pictorio" to "To S. M." effectively proves Wheatley's investment in portraying black artists' possession of a weightier moral vision.

Wheatley and Byles appear inspired by similar goals, but their distinctly different views of the artistic landscape of eighteenth-century America leads them to pen very different verses. Byles's poem probably first appeared as a broadside, but its initial publication was in the *London Daily Courant* in 1730 under the title "To Mr. Smibert on the Sight of his Pictures."[32] Henry Foote suggests that the unsigned poem commemorates Smibert's exhibition "not later than early March, 1730," an event marking "the first exhibition of art ever held in Boston."[33] Most critics who discuss Byles's poem refer to the revised version titled "To Pictorio, on the Sight of his Pictures," which he published in his 1744 collection. Nevertheless, his initial dedication of the poem to John Smibert, one of the first painters of portraits in colonial America, heightens the similarities between his poem and Wheatley's.

Byles undoubtedly sought to celebrate an early American painter in an effort to promote the fledgling American artistic tradition. Wheatley's poem on Moorhead provides a parallel attempt to advance an African American artistic tradition built on black artists' inspired vision. She explores the artistic camaraderie African American painters and poets enjoy and the moral rectitude they advocate. Wheatley introduces her verse as resulting from the visual inspiration of Moorhead's painting, but she concentrates on the nature of the black artist and displays her continued willingness to use her inspired vision to support Christian fidelity. In responding to the work of a fellow artist of color, she fortifies the trope of the Picture Book by trumpeting the visionary qualities that render black artists inspired instructors.

She commences by voicing her feelings on seeing Moorhead's work, but she goes further to model the appropriate response to art like Moorhead's:

> To show the lab'ring bosom's deep intent,
> And thought in living characters to paint,
> When first thy pencil did those beauties give,
> And breathing figures learnt from thee to live,
> How did those prospects give my soul delight,
> A new creation rushing on my sight? (*CW*, 59)

Wheatley admires Moorhead's ability to represent the deepest thoughts of the working painter whose skill infuses pictured characters with lifelike mental capacities. But rather than belabor Moorhead's visual achievements, Wheatley quickly shifts to the impact of his work on her, an ideal viewer almost collapsed with Moorhead's painted figures. She claims that his pencil not only produces beauty, but additionally she notes that, "breathing figures learnt from thee to live." Whether the "breathing figures" are the lifelike characters on his canvas or the living viewers of his pictures, the poet speaker receives extreme pleasure from his accomplishment, a "new creation" materializing before her eyes. She celebrates Moorhead's instructional success in terms that echo her praise of Homer in "To Maecenus."

Byles also expresses delight over Smibert's work: "Landskips how gay! arise in ev'ry Light, / And fresh Creations rush upon the Sight."[34] Yet, Byles's pen only arrives to these words in the seventh stanza after cataloging the many paintings he viewed at Smibert's exhibition. In stark contrast to Wheatley's opening lines that focus on the impact of Moorhead's painting, Byles's opening stanzas focus on the complete absence of high art in America, which he repeatedly describes as "barb'rous" and bereft of the "softer Arts" so that "No heav'nly Pencil the free Stroke could give, / Nor the warm Canvas felt its Colors live."[35] Byles concludes his first three stanzas of the original poem by noting that only after the first 100 years of the colonies' existence can they celebrate "[a] *Smibert* painted and a ....wrote. // Thy Fame, O *Smibert*, shall the Muse rehearse, / And sing her Sister-Art in softer Verse."[36] When he published the poem in his collection, however, Byles changes the lines to read, "Pictorio painted, and Maecenas wrote. // Thy Fame, Pictorio, shall the Muse rehearse, / And sing her Sister-Art in softer Verse." [37] He clearly refers to himself as the writer. Byles seeks to affirm the idea that colonial artists are successfully taming the wilds of America to produce original and impressive work. Wheatley pursues a different objective.

Her first lines serve as a prologue to her celebration of Moorhead's potential to inspire Christian revelation through the cultivation of spiritual sight. She follows her wonder with an injunction and hope for the accomplishments born from artistic community: "On deathless glories fix thine ardent views: / Still may the painter's and the poet's fire / To aid thy pencil, and thy verse conspire!" (*CW*, 60). Wheatley contemplates the rewards of pure artists' products by drawing on what Ivy Wilson describes as the "visual basis for ekphrasis that is enhanced by things only the mind can see."[38] By enjoining Moorhead to remain focused on heavenly rewards, she realizes the power of great art to transcend mere earthly admiration. She also implies that their passage from a mortal to immortal state will allow them to achieve their potential as artists enjoying the right to address "nobler themes" in "purer language" (*CW*, 60). She suggests that their subjects and languages will no longer suffer under limitations based on skin color.

Her focus diverges sharply from Byles's concluding sentiments. He devotes the final twenty lines of his poem to advocating friendship between poets and painters as he simultaneously applauds the superb work of new colonial artists like himself and Smibert:

> Yet, Smibert, on the kindred muse attend,
> And let the Painter prove the Poet's Friend.
> In the same Studies nature we pursue,
> I the Description touch, the Picture you;
>
> . . .
>
> Now, with bold Hand, we strike the strong Design,
> Mature in Thought now soften ev'ry line.
> Now, unrestrain'd, in freer Airs surprize,
> And sudden at our Word new Worlds arise;[39]

For Byles, the most striking similarity between his work and Smibert's is their ability to prove the sophistication of the American artist. Notwithstanding the views of contemporary critics, he describes their work as "Mature" and likely to improve in the "freer Airs" of America. Of course, the "free" atmosphere that America represents to Byles and Smibert, Wheatley and Moorhead must seek in heaven.

Rather than bemoan this state of affairs, Wheatley celebrates the loftier goals that inspire black artists. In contrast to Byles's focus on cultivating national pride, she extols her ability to view accomplished art with sufficient understanding to direct her eyes to spiritual subjects. Her poet speaker transforms the view of Moorhead's painting into an opportunity to remind artists that great paintings should lead their eyes back to heavenly sights: "But when these shades of time are chas'd away, / And darkness ends in everlasting day, / On what seraphic pinions shall we move, / And view the landscapes in the realms above?" (*CW*, 60). In other words, black artists such as Wheatley and Moorhead seek to produce art that stimulates their audiences to visualize heaven as opposed merely to arousing national pride. Wheatley links her artistry to Moorhead's in an effort to proclaim the moral righteousness of black artists even as she anticipates a moment when they will enjoy greater artistic freedom and agency. And ever so subtly, she challenges her audience to recognize the concessions black artists are forced to make as a result of the compromised aesthetic sensibilities of their audience. If their audience can learn to visualize blackness as successfully as black artists visualize heaven, creative individuals such as Wheatley and Moorhead will finally escape being circumscribed by their readers' notions about race.

The Slave Narrator's View of the National Body

By contending that the trope of the Picture Book is comprised by moments in Wheatley's verse connecting vision to creative and moral instructional authority, I stress black writers' presentations of themselves as necessary teachers. If Wheatley's attention to visual instruction pours the foundation for this trope of vision, Frederick Douglass and Harriet Jacobs lay the bricks that strengthen it. In their most widely read texts, *The Narrative of the Life of Frederick Douglass, An American Slave, Written by Himself* (1845) and *Incidents in the Life of a Slave Girl* (1861) respectively, Douglass and Jacobs self-consciously represent their view of the nation as an argument for the abolition of slavery. They, too, presume the nobility of sight and blame Americans who abdicate moral vision for many ills facing the nation. The canonical positions their texts claim make slave narrative authors crucial to assessing the centrality of vision in the creation of the African American literary tradition.

The vision they celebrate, however, is often physical as opposed to Wheatley's attention to serving as a spiritual and artistic seer. These authors connect their sight to a moral authority that arises from their willingness to assess difficult scenes honestly. Douglass links his escape from slavery – both emotionally and physically – to his ability to read and write. Nevertheless, crucial scenes in both his text and Jacobs's narrative stress the exceptional nature of black American visual observation as necessary to freeing white Americans from the morally reprehensible institution. Whereas Wheatley emphasizes her spiritual insight and blackness to challenge the notion that African Americans lacked the artistic ability to portray an inviolable moral authority, the authors of nineteenth-century slave narratives demonstrate how their truthful spectatorship portrays the need for a morally grounded national identity. They draw attention to their black bodies to contrast their persistent moral wholeness with a national body fractured by violent disagreement and moral compromise. In an environment of national division, ex-slaves offer stories staging the path toward the creation of a political philosophy capable of reuniting a splintering union.

Douglass's and Jacobs's narratives offer pictures of the brutal environment black slaves endured, a reality endorsed by the founding documents of the country. In particular, the Three-fifths Compromise provided a rich backdrop against which African Americans accentuated the country's moral hypocrisy. Found in Article 1 of the Constitution, the compromise determined levels of representation and taxation by adding the total number of "free Persons," excluding "Indians," to "three-fifths of all other Persons." With these words, the Constitution defined African American slaves as fragmented citizens. Slave narrative authors exploit this act of lawful bodily dissection by linking their morally holistic vision to their brutalized bodies in provocative and condemnatory ways. The fragmented black bodies that result from the violence of slavery implicitly indict the authors of the Constitution for defining African Americans in inhumane terms. Moreover, as Northern and Southern political sentiments diverged over the issue of slavery, the narratives of ex-slaves drew attention to the increasingly fragmented U.S. body politic they critique. The authors of slave narratives highlight their unique ability to showcase national truthfulness. In fact, Douglass, who initially adopted the position that the Constitution advocated slavery, pointed to the Three-fifths Compromise to argue that the founding document "instructed" slaveholders "to add as many to his stock as possible" to attain greater "wealth" and "more political power." [40] He and Jacobs bid to replace such instruction with the ink of their powerful pens.

Their narratives highlight their visual recording of slave experiences and implicitly engage the broader U.S. visual landscape. By the end of the Revolutionary War, the antebellum era witnessed significant developments in the portrayal of blacks in high art. As writers and readers cultivated a stronger sense of national character, artists defined and refined their portrayals of African Americans. In Ivy Wilson's examination of nineteenth-century American genre painting, he notes that the most well-known artists of the era employ a "compositional logic ... to illustrate forms of democratic belonging in the United States." Artists from Sidney Mount to Winslow Homer routinely pictured black Americans on the margins, denying African Americans access to "private spaces" so as to keep them "precluded from the inner sanctum of social belonging." [41] I want to suggest that Douglass and Jacobs use their narratives to replicate and challenge these painted restrictions. They occupy hidden or separate positions like their African American painted counterparts, but the scenes they witness contrast vividly with the gay subjects often depicted in American genre paintings. In other words, they seek peripheral, concealed, shadowy sites – such as closets and attic sheds – to mimic high art portrayals that exclude them from the heart of U.S. citizenship; however, their descriptions of white-American behavior bespeak their central roles in delineating national identity. They unveil true images of American character that many citizens ignore, deny, or intentionally suppress.

As they narrate their experiences as slaves, Douglass and Jacobs also revise the minstrel-like appearance often assigned to their painted equivalents. Paintings by John Lewis Krimmel and his best known descendent, Sidney Mount, never moved beyond portraying black Americans as an important, yet limited, element in American society. [42] Even as respected U.S. artists produced more emotionally complex portrayals of African Americans, these positive, high art portrayals were dwarfed by the teeming visualizations of African Americans in printed media and literature of the early to mid-nineteenth century. Like their eighteenth-century counterparts, white citizens of the nineteenth century interacted with images of black Americans predominantly via advertisements for runaway slaves, newspapers, magazines, broadsides, pamphlets, sheet music, novels, and children's books. [43] As the U.S. publishing industry grew more robust, the number of printed materials multiplied, leading scholars to designate the first thirty years of the nineteenth century as the "Classified Ad Period." Drawing on the earliest printers' specimen book in 1809, Marcus Wood concludes that the type ornaments reflect a basic idea: "pictures come first, the words can be fitted in afterwards."[44]

In addition to the growth of the U.S. advertising culture, the birth of minstrel shows and interest in black music spawned an industry defined by an obsession with demeaning images of blackness. Comic operas showcasing debased depictions of African Americans toured the U.S. as early as 1793, but not until Thomas Dartmouth Rice introduced the song *Jim Crow* in 1828 did such shows become an integral part of U.S. performance.[45] Rice's comic imitation of an elderly black man indulging in exuberant singing and outlandish dancing propelled the song into a hit. With one of the earliest sheet music songs to enjoy a wide distribution in the U.S., Rice set the stage for a new genre of exploitative performance supported by particularly humiliating visual advertising. Although the minstrel Sambo released blacks from the servant role, the demeaning new stereotype moved African Americans even further away from being viewed as morally responsible citizens, a fact not missed by the authors of slave narratives.

In her landmark study of the antebellum slave narrative, Francis Smith Foster identifies the period between 1831 and 1865 as the "golden age of the slave narrative."[46] This interval parallels the rise of the daguerreotype which enjoyed its greatest popularity from 1839 to the mid-1850s. This confluence of a heightened interest in first person accounts of slavery and new access to photographic portraits aided black writers seeking to highlight their power to convey an accurate vision of the national body. Writers such as Douglass and Jacobs quickly grasped the significance of a technology perfectly aligned with their narrative endeavors. Daguerreotypes were created by an intricate process that began with a sheet of copper that was thinly plated with silver. After this plate was suspended in iodine, exposed to light, developed in mercury, and finally fixed permanently in a solution of salt before being refined with gold chloride, a highly detailed image was produced.[47] For the ex-slave authors, the one-of-a-kind portraits provided an apt comparison to the bodily reality of slavery. The weighty, material images were comprised of the same silver and gold metals implicated in the inhuman trading of black bodies, whereas the technological process that produced the images invested them with a connotation of truth. Indeed, the word daguerreotype incited discussions of these images' ability to operate as moral x-rays.[48] Antebellum Americans viewed the images as offering "direct and intimate experience with unique objects."[49] In a similar vein, the authors of slave narratives presented their texts as giving readers access to their original, unique bodies.

The new photographic technology empowered black Americans to produce their own images to combat the negative portrayals of blackness so pervasive in U.S. society. In his 1861 speech "Pictures and Progress," Douglass proclaimed the democratizing nature of the daguerreotype:

> Men of all conditions may see themselves as others see them. What was once the exclusive luxury of the rich and great is now within reach of all. The humbled servant girl whose income is but a few shillings per week may now possess a more perfect likeness of herself than noble ladies and court royalty, with all its precious treasures could purchase fifty years ago.[50]

What is more, the daguerreotype process, wherein the original is directly linked to the image produced, connected the early photographic process to what Alan Trachtenberg describes as the "written expression of ideas" and with a truth rooted in unshakable moral authority.[51] Deborah Willis's excellent history on African American photographers recounts that these men "sought to integrate elements of romanticism and classicism into their work, echoing the work of painters in the eighteenth century."[52] African American professionals such as James Presley Ball and Augustus Washington strove to recuperate a respectable image of blackness from the derogatory images promulgated in paintings and popular advertisements. Ball and Washington also pursued political aims with their photographs liberating African Americans from a visual history that yoked them to servitude.[53]

With the invention of the daguerreotype, ex-slave authors discovered a visual analogue for portraying the truth of their words and the morality of their work. Comparing one of the earliest known daguerreotypes of Douglass to the engraved frontispieces of the British and American first editions of his 1845 *Narrative* provides a case in point. The daguerreotype – thought to date from the mid-1840s around the same time as the *Narrative* – presents Douglass looking more youthful than the frontispiece image, but it articulates a more forceful, vital nature than its engraved counterparts (see Figure 1.5). Although Douglass appears slight in physical build, his face boasts an uncompromising seriousness. The resolute line of his lips and unflinching stare bespeak potency not present in the engraved pictures. Whereas the portrait for the American first edition captures a similar element of Douglass's vigorous character with its portrayal of his closed fists and determined expression, the British picture transforms him into a polished gentleman bearing little resemblance to the man who emerges in the pages that follow (see Figure 1.6).

Figure 1.5 Frederick Douglass (c. 1840). Courtesy of Greg French, Early Photography.

A number of scholars have discussed these images and noted Douglass's angry response to the British portrait.[54] The ex-slave denounces the stamp of artistic intervention that renders the frontispiece a false advertisement of his character, and he particularly deplores the softening of his facial demeanor so that he appears with "a much more kindly and amiable expression than is generally thought to characterize the face of a fugitive slave." For Douglass, such untruthful doctoring did not represent a singular misstep but a cultural practice:

> It seems to us next to impossible for white men to take likenesses of black men, without most grossly exaggerating their distinctive features. And the reason is obvious. Artists, like all other white persons, have adopted a theory respecting the distinctive features of Negro physiognomy.

Figure 1.6 Frederick Douglass (1845). Image courtesy of Documenting the American South, The University of North Carolina at Chapel Hill Libraries.

John Stauffer concludes that "Douglass's criticism of white artists helps to explain why he was so taken with photography" and came to extol it as a technology of truth that distinguished humanity's investment in accurate representations of both the material and spiritual worlds.[55] Focusing on Douglass's passionate celebration of man's imaginary powers, Stauffer quotes the ex-slave's celebration of the new picture-making ability: "Poets, prophets, and reformers are all picture-makers – and this ability is the secret of their power and of their achievements. They see what ought to be by the reflection of what is, and endeavor to remove the contradiction."[56]

Douglass's Honest Pictures of Slavery

Like Wheatley, the posture Douglass displays in his photographic portrait anticipates the role he assumes in his written texts. He unquestionably approaches his narrative as an opportunity to educate readers about how African Americans view the nation. Douglass looks unflinchingly on the state of the fracturing union. From his position of observation, he provides honest visions and offers a pathway to national unity. With pens in hand, ex-slaves such as Douglass and Jacobs translate their former servant status into a voluntary service of righting the country's moral compass. Their narratives not only contest rampant pictures of degraded blackness promulgated in high and low art, they also accuse the U.S. of falsifying the national record. The physiognomic distortions portraying black inhumanity painted by Krimmel, performed by Rice, and illustrated on everything from sheet music to children's books receive a forceful challenge from these authors' visualizing practices. With their texts, they reclaim a central position in the endeavor of picturing American identity.

My brief analysis of Douglass's and Jacobs's works acknowledges the range of excellent criticism exploring their multifaceted investment in vision. The remainder of this chapter builds on this criticism through succinct readings of Douglass's *Narrative* and Jacobs's *Incidents*. Together, they not only signify the major thematic strains of the slave narrative, they also attest to a consistent interest in visuality pervading the genre. To chart the evolution of the trope of the Picture Book, I want to consider one of the most critically analyzed moments in Douglass's canonical text. In the iconic scene where young Frederick witnesses the brutal beating of his Aunt Hester, Douglass formulates a key strategy that inflects his subsequent exploitation of visual media: he portrays the black slave's role as a witness to white brutality as a necessary purveyor of truth. In the first chapter of his *Narrative*, Douglass details his master's sadistic actions, Captain Anthony's "pleasure in whipping a slave":

> I have often been awakened at the dawn of day by the most heart-rending shrieks of an own aunt of mine, whom he used to tie up to a joist, and whip upon her naked back till she was literally covered with blood. No words, no tears, no prayers, from his gory victim, seemed to move his iron heart from its bloody purpose. ... I remember the first time I ever witnessed this horrible exhibition. I was quite a child, but I well remember it. I never shall forget it whilst I remember any thing. It was the first of a long series of such outrages, of which I was doomed to be a witness and a participant. It struck me with awful force. It was the blood-stained gate, the entrance to the hell of slavery, through which I was about to pass. It was a most terrible spectacle. I wish I could commit to paper the feelings with which I beheld it.[57]

After providing further details of the scene, he recalls his master's words: "Now, you d – d b – h, I'll learn you how to disobey my orders!" The sight of Captain Anthony's violence leads Douglass to admit, "I was so terrified and horror-stricken at the sight, that I hid myself in a closet, and dared not venture out till long after the bloody transaction was over. ... It was all new to me. I had never seen any thing like it before."[58]

Douglass's report of Aunt Hester's brutal beating reminds us of the pedagogical role slave masters assigned the performance of their brutality. It serves as the foundation of formative studies ranging from Saidiya Hartman's declaration of it as "the primal scene" that "establishes the centrality of violence to the making of the slave" to Frank Moten's bold identification of Hester's shrieks as contributing to a "musical encounter" representative of the "phonic materiality" produced by resisting black objects.[59] But most fundamentally, the scene foregrounds the moral authority of the black slave's untutored vision.[60] Building on Wheatley's example of African Americans' spiritually discerning vision, Douglass portrays his vision as underpinning an instinctive recognition of slavery as a hell-like institution that transmogrifies men like Captain Anthony. As a "witness" of the "most terrible spectacle," he realizes the importance of visual instruction.[61] His master's promise to "learn" Aunt Hester to follow his orders inspires Douglass to view the incident as educational; but, rather than see Captain Anthony's lesson as indicative of a superior morality, he interprets it as emblematic of American slavery's wickedness.[62] He comprehends his master's lash and abhorrent sexual desire as constituting "the blood-stained gate" of the U.S. slave institution. This lesson baldly contradicts the lesson of the Talking Book which served to remind slaves of their unchristian status and denied access to the Bible.

Many scholars shrewdly note that as the black child slave, Douglass, hiding in the closet witnessing and arguably voyeuristically participating in the bloody transaction, stands in for the naïve white reader.[63] Additionally, Douglass emphasizes the feminization he suffers.[64] He is unmanned by his failure to act, opting instead to hide like his reader and assume a parallel position of moral abdication. Nevertheless, his portrayal retains the position of visual authority so crucial to the creation of the Picture Book trope. By describing the sight, and offering his view of the plantation that serves as a microcosm of southern U.S. society, he represents the sole purveyor of moral authority. Consequently, he inverts the power dynamic established by the political reality of U.S. law: the black slave claims an unparalleled position of authority, a position attained through uncompromised vision. His vision offers instruction on matters of national conscience. If the Talking Book signals the moral necessity of African Americans gaining the ability to read the Bible and enjoy spiritual salvation, the Picture Book conveys the black slave's singular authority to educate the nation on matters of moral integrity. Aunt Hester's beating assigns shame to the white master and the black slave child standing in for the white reading audience. Douglass must mature to the point where his actions parallel his beliefs; like his readers, he must not only read and reject the horrible spectacle but accept the responsibility of preventing future such episodes.

The famous passage highlights the fragmentation black bodies suffer under the brutality of American slavery. Douglass's ekphrastic display of Aunt Hester adds a new element to the figure of the Picture Book: black authors' exhibition of extraordinary vision while visually objectifying the black body as a truthful portrait of the state of the nation. The details associated with his aunt's body – "her naked back ... covered in blood" and "the blood-clotted cowskin" – become increasingly disconnected from her person and attached to his master.[65] Aunt Hester's naked back becomes the material object that represents Captain Anthony's savagery. As a trustworthy observer of and recorder for the country, Douglass's presentation anticipates the power of photographs like the 1863 image of the slave, Gordon, whose scarred back became famous when *Harper's Weekly* published three photographs of his brutally disfigured form in 1863. Acknowledging the force of the image at the time of its publication, *The New York Independent* proclaimed: "This Card Photograph should be multiplied by the 100,000 and scattered over the states. It tells the story in a way that even Mrs. Stowe cannot approach, because it tells the story to the eye."[66] Douglass enlists his words to produce comparable visual evidence documenting the savagery of white slave masters. For Douglass, retelling the story in detail allows his work to reconnect the pieces of Aunt Hester's body only to have them crumble into blood more dramatically. His "horror-striken" state "at the sight" of this transaction hopefully mirrors that of the reader.[67]

In this way, he aligns his vision with the reader's, preparing for a shared national identity founded on the rejection of the fragmented black body, a potent symbol of national division. In Douglass's culminating physical confrontation in his *Narrative*, the Baltimore shipyard fight, he exposes white anxiety over the black slave's status as a visual recorder of truth. The white ship carpenters attempt to educate Douglass in the ways of the country, and he describes their abuse as his "school for eight months." The shipbuilders verbally terrorize him with oaths promising to "blast [his] eyes" and "knock [his] brains out."[68] When white apprentices attack him, viciously kicking his left eye, Douglass recalls: "My eyeball seemed to have burst. When they saw my eye closed, and badly swollen, they left me."[69] Their threats and physical attack confirm their violent desire to blind and intellectually subdue African Americans in a bid to deny the true path forward for the nation. Douglass's achievement of reaching the North and reporting the sights of general prosperity as well as the particular success of black citizens of New Bedford provides a final testament of the escaped slave providing a symbol of American triumph. As he gazes on the sights of freedom, he notes that free blacks "better understood the moral, religious, and political character of the nation, – than nine tenths of the slaveholders."[70]

His move marks a distinction of the early trope of the Picture Book: rather than adopt the attitude and way of life performed by white Americans, black writers use their texts to demonstrate the superiority of African American vision. Dismissing the white tendency to view the black body as aesthetically unpleasing and therefore ripe for enslavement, Douglass makes no attempt to portray himself in the threads of respectable fashion and comportment. Instead, he implicitly questions the morality of those who would deny his humanity based on their vision of his physical appearance. By connecting his spirit and person while highlighting the sophisticated quality of his sight, he rejects the morally flawed white body of American citizens who condone slavery.

Jacobs's Revision of Black Womanhood

Harriet Jacobs's *Incidents* extends Douglass's focus on emphasizing slave vision as a means of instructing readers on black American character. But Jacobs trains her sights specifically on black women. A good deal of criticism explores Jacobs's appeals to visual culture by contemplating the rich symbolism of the loophole retreat.[71] I want to build on these arguments to emphasize the national implications of her development of the trope of the Picture Book. By presenting her self-imposed captivity as an experience equating the black female body with the marks of the white invalid woman, Jacobs reinserts what might initially be deemed her morally compromised body into the heart of acceptable national icons: the frail mother. Her erasure of the gulf separating these purportedly paradoxical images allows her to clear new space for defining black female character. To this end, Jacobs declares accepted standards of feminine virtue outmoded in relation to slave women and argues for adopting more complicated definitions that acknowledge the country's fractured foundation. As she strives to portray psychological fragmentation as more dangerous than the kinds of physical torment and exploitation emphasized in Douglass's *Narrative*, she commences the pedagogical work necessary to make sense of her radical picture of black feminine morality.

Ironically, Jacobs achieves her revised definition of appropriate black womanhood by pitting her vision against her grandmother's view of the country. Although Brent repeatedly proclaims her respect and love for her grandmother, she also presents her grandmother as a woman who has fully embraced the dictates of respectable white womanhood. Aunt Marthy enjoys wide esteem throughout the community, profits from a measure of independence and agency, and represents a source of physical sustenance for Linda and the broader community in the form of her tasty crackers. Nevertheless, Linda implies that her grandmother fails to provide the critical help she needs. Like the well-meaning white mistresses who neglect to free Aunt Marthy and die leaving Linda and her family to the mercy of less caring hands, her grandmother fails to protect her granddaughter from the polluting conduct of Dr. Sands.

Aunt Marthy's decision to wrap herself in a cloak of virtue effectively robs Linda of a potential confidant. In fact, when her grandmother discovers Linda's pregnancy, her response mirrors that of the narrow-minded white women Jacobs seeks to soften with her narrative: "'O Linda! Has it come to this? I had rather see you dead than to see you as you now are. You are a disgrace to your dead mother.' She tore from my fingers my mother's wedding ring and her silver thimble."[72] By espousing the tenets of proper womanhood defined by white society, Aunt Marthy blinds herself to the truth of Linda's predicament and elects to punish her granddaughter as if she were headed toward a simple domestic life symbolized by her mother's ring and thimble. As Linda writes of her travails and hopes to elicit sympathy from her readers, Aunt Marthy, who even looks somewhat white, becomes a strange stand-in for her broader audience. Challenging her grandmother's philosophy, Jacobs argues that "the slave woman ought not to be judged by the same standard as others."[73] Jacobs implies that such standards stand on an immoral foundation.

Thus, she comes to represent a new generation of black womanhood, a new worldview. Before ascending to the loophole retreat, Brent struggles to gain a point of view capable of altering her self-image and circumstances. When her master calls her into his "study" to confront her desire to wed a free black carpenter, Brent stares at him before he is aware of her presence: "I stood a moment gazing at the hateful man who claimed a right to rule me, body and soul. I did not want him to know how my heart was bleeding. He looked fixedly at me."[74] Her words establish the war of looks Jacobs wages against Dr. Flint and the slave-holding nation more generally. Although she struggles to escape the power of his fixing looks – as if he would like to transform her into a daguerreotype for his pocket – she strives just as mightily against his attempt to own her "soul." Unlike Douglass's Aunt Hester who sheds bodily blood under the violence of her lascivious master, Jacobs fights to hide her figuratively "bleeding" heart from Dr. Flint's grasp. Her description of her emotional state becomes the most representative part of her person. Notwithstanding Dr. Flint's attempts to "fix" her, she refuses his entrance into her most private worlds.

Later, when she sees her "master watching" her and her lover "from his window," she understands the necessity of protecting her feelings as well as her physical body.[75] Unlike Aunt Marthy, who insists on participating in the slave auction to vivify Dr. Sands's immorality, Brent seeks to recalibrate the very terms of visual power. From her perch in the attic confinement, reminiscent of Douglass's closet, she secures a broader view of the town, a microcosm of U.S. society. As she manages to "read and sew," she also relishes watching her children.[76] Having contrived a new form of the domestic space that advocates for the cult of domesticity celebrate, she self-consciously redefines the core purpose of black womanhood and the terms on which slave women should be judged. Her most important role as a mother is not providing domestic comfort; instead, she excels by refusing the terms of black maternity slave society defined.

By contriving a means to observe white citizens from her unseen perch, she works to destabilize the terms on which U.S. slave society was organized. She rejects white visualizations of black slave women, shifting her focus from a concern with white observations of her morality to a concentration on how her children view her. She admits that "her unconscious babe was the ever-present witness of [her] shame."[77] This new form of witnessing transfers power from white women and men who establish the hypocritical rules of propriety to the unblemished eyes of slave babies born into a corrupt system through no fault of their own. These eyes focus not on Brent's exterior slave body but on the slave woman as mother, the inner feelings that define a woman. After her escape, when Brent's daughter, Ellen, absolves her mother of all wrong and repeats "All my love is for you," Jacobs reveals the new terms on which black women should be assessed.[78] In fact, the Picture Book she offers depends on the eyes of black children, a vivid denial of white agency and compromised vision.

Jacobs's visualization of the maternal slave revises and develops Douglass's image of masculine integrity. During her seven-year self-imposed imprisonment in the loophole of retreat, Jacobs acquires an even greater example of a national, holistic vision. Her narrative provides a fitting conclusion to a discussion of the goals of eighteenth- and nineteenth-century black writers. Both Wheatley and the slave narrators acknowledge the insoluble link between written and visual art, thereby facilitating a revitalized attempt to supplant the demeaning picture books established by white writers. The replacements they offer proclaim a purchase on visual veracity that insists on their role as moral arbiters having little in common with the ridiculous servants and entertainers so often portrayed in high and popular art. Their texts, so dependent on moments that define the artistic and moral superiority of African American vision, confirm the crucial nature of their roles as witnesses of an American constitution in desperate need of revision.

CHAPTER 2

Picturing Education and Labor in Washington and Du Bois

The Negro race, like all races, is going to be saved by its exceptional men. The problem of education, then, among Negroes must first of all deal with the Talented Tenth; ... Now the training of men is a difficult and intricate task. Its technique is a matter for educational experts, but its object is for the vision of seers. – W. E. B. Du Bois, 1903[1]

I have just asked Mr. Stewart to ship you 125 of my pictures. ... I am very anxious that they be put not only where the more prosperous and successful colored people live, but in the districts where the ordinary and poorer classes of colored people live, as they are the class I am very anxious to speak to.

– Booker T. Washington, 1909[2]

By the dawn of the twentieth century, the U.S. popular imagination transformed African Americans from slaves dependent on white authority for their morality to free men and women unprepared and undeserving of their lately acquired citizenship. Two extreme notions formed with regard to African American laborers: in addition to being unintelligent, they were either too lazy or too violent to contribute responsibly to the national workforce. If pre-abolition African Americans fell victim to narratives questioning their morality as slaves, postbellum blacks suffered the frontal assault of national questions regarding the value of educating blacks and declaring their unfitness to labor as freeman. Booker T. Washington and W. E. B. Du Bois looked on this perilous landscape and rightly determined that issues of black education and labor lay at its center. Du Bois argued that African American progress would ultimately hinge on the success of its best educated citizens. Although he acknowledged that the structure of their preparation might best be determined by "educational experts," he maintained that the life goals for exceptional black Americans remained an issue for "seers," those imbued with visionary genius. In contrast, Washington focused on educating the "ordinary and poorer classes" of African Americans, and visual media played an important role in his work. Unlike their pre-abolition predecessors who focused on rescuing representations of blackness from bankrupt images of the black servant, slave, and entertainer, these men emphasize black vision in an effort to improve opportunities for black citizens to find better jobs. Their texts feature African Americans who describe their hopes and dreams in visual terms that result from their forthright observation of the world around them.

To combat virulent imagery proclaiming blacks unworthy of full citizenship, Washington's and Du Bois's published works not only document African American preparations for the labor force but also underscore both men's roles as educators. In their hands, the trope of the Picture Book is defined by textual moments that portray black Americans' distinct vision of the education necessary to pave their entrance into the pool of independent laborers. Washington's and Du Bois's most canonical works, *Up from Slavery* (1901) and *The Souls of Black Folk* (1903) respectively, rely on key instances of visual instruction, scenes that emphasize African Americans learning by sight rather than from books alone. Considered with the photographic collections each man sponsors, their written texts alternately complement and complicate themes sounded in the visual images they endorse. By comparing the photographs they promote to their signification on the trope of the Picture Book in their literary projects, this chapter clarifies their philosophical approaches to improving the plight of black Americans. I highlight both men's dependence on tropes of vision to describe academic learning to dramatize their investment in education as a gateway into the U.S. workforce and the national family.

Of course, their shared appeal to visuality is not indicative of a broader agreement concerning black progress.[3] Washington preached the gospel of the Protestant work ethic whereas Du Bois espoused a pragmatic relativism warning against an exclusive focus on material progress. By 1907, both men had repeatedly and meaningfully availed themselves of visual and written art to refine their diverging philosophies. Washington co-authored *A New Negro for a New Century* and published his first autobiography, *The Story of My Life and Work*, in 1900; he published *Up from Slavery* in 1901; produced its sequel, *Working with the Hands*, in 1904; and, in 1907, he authored *The Negro in Business*. Du Bois, meanwhile, published *The Philadelphia Negro* in 1899; presented his photo albums at the 1900 Paris Exposition; published *The Negro Artisan* in 1902; and, compiled *The Souls of Black Folk* in 1903. With this series of public presentations assessing black life, both men sought to replace stereotypical notions of black character with images of a respectable African American citizenry honorably preparing for and contributing to the national welfare. As a crucial part of their projects, their canonical literary texts conspicuously feature visually endowed protagonists who passionately pursue education to prepare for new career opportunities.

Washington and Du Bois shared a deep commitment to improving economic opportunities for African Americans, a dedication reflected in their joint work on the National Negro Business League. As they negotiated the period marking the transition from the Gilded Age to the Progressive Era, these emerging leaders actively sought to revise the country's view of African American character and worked to present black citizens as integral to the national conversation. To this end, both men adapted elements of American exceptionalism to their portrayals of black character at the turn of the century. In *Up from Slavery*, Washington presents a realistic picture of African American ideas of progress, and he emphasizes their capacity to visualize labor and education with an admiration rooted in the hardy lore of American self-reliance. Conversely, in *The Souls of Black Folk*, Du Bois pictures African Americans romantically, portraying black folk as possessors of a vision of American work shaped by the classic idea of the American Dream.

Both men rely on photography to challenge disparaging stereotypes of black citizens inundating the national psyche. At the same moment that antilynching activists turned to photographic art to reassert control over the black body and its post-Emancipation meaning, Washington and Du Bois tilled the visual medium for its potential to reframe notions of African American ambition and work. Their projects seek to revise, in both picture and print, portrayals of respectable black labor just as Ida B. Wells offered a "competing way of 'seeing' lynching" for black and white viewers alike.[4] Their work against the backdrop of the radical attempts to redefine black humanity via lynching reminds us of the enormous challenge African Americans faced in their quest to regain control over visualizations of blackness. Proving black citizens' humanity, morality, and valuable contribution emerged as a life-or-death struggle. At every turn, black leaders faced the daunting task of privileging their vision of African American character alongside and against competing material evidence.

The high profile nature of Du Bois's promotion of photographs – his Georgia Negro Exhibit won a gold medal at the 1900 Paris Exposition – has garnered his photographic work a good deal of scholarly attention. Deborah Willis's excellent scholarship recovers abundant details related to the photographers, sitters, and history reflected in his albums, whereas Shawn Smith reveals the scope, significance, and success of his photographic collections.[5] In contrast, very few critics have examined Washington's investment in pictures and visual practices. Michael Bieze's *Booker T. Washington and the Art of Self-Representation* (2008) stands alone in turning a rigorous eye toward the Tuskegee president's investment in visual media. This scholarly imbalance misses the intriguing ways that Washington depended on visual art and visuality to revise derogatory images of African Americans and recuperate African Americans' instructional power of sight. Overlooking the Tuskegee president's work with photography also neglects to consider how each man's photographic presentations of black identity refines the work they accomplish in their written texts. Thus, while this chapter considers Du Bois's work with photographs to frame my examination of *The Souls of Black Folk*, it also concentrates on Washington's investment in carefully deploying vision – as portrayed in *Up from Slavery* and in photographs – in his drive to achieve racial progress. My focus on the material pictures that complicate and expand Washington's educational philosophy distinguishes this chapter in my study in acknowledgement of the special relationship between his photographic and literary work. The extended contemplation of Tuskegee photographs reveals that both leaders seek to improve the face of the race by training the nation's eyes on African Americans' vision of the ideal black worker and the education necessary for his success.

Du Bois and the Turn-of-the-Century Visual Archive

In *The Souls of Black Folk*, Du Bois showcases African American folk who look toward the future with ambition only to have their optimism stamped out by a society that refuses them opportunity. Du Bois repeatedly describes black aspirations – his own as well as those of the folk masses – in terms of vision, and he particularly focuses on the symbolism of black eyes eager to teach and learn. Yet his cultivation of the trope of the Picture Book parts ways with the positive examples that precede him. Instead of highlighting the confident black vision that augured cultural progress in the nineteenth century, he portrays the lessons taught by disappointed vision. Du Bois declares that "the problem of the Twentieth Century is the problem of the color-line," and this problem, he explains, denies African Americans the ability not only to work to produce goods, but to achieve something more: "to be a co-worker in the kingdom of culture."[6] This denial to participate in labor and culture as equals necessarily transforms the quality of their dreams and signals the birth of black modern identity.

Early in his career, Du Bois faulted poor blacks for their moral failings and declared their flawed character an unfortunate remnant of their slave past. He suggested that the black lower classes lacked the ability to see themselves and their future with discernment, explaining: "The first and greatest step toward settlement of present friction between the races ... lies in correction of immorality, crime, and laziness among Negros themselves, which still remains as heritage of slavery."[7] But as he continued to work in the South, Du Bois grew to understand the intricate nature of black existence in the region, and he adopted a less condemnatory stance.[8] Publications such as *The Philadelphia Negro*, monographs for the U.S. Bureau of Labor (1898–1901), and *The Negro Artisan* capture the ways Du Bois's sociological findings contributed to his developing sense that industrial education alone could not effectively address the challenges facing black workers. *The Negro Artisan* in particular provided him the opportunity to combine the methodological techniques he had implemented in his previous work, and his results produced the first comprehensive research on African American laborers. He began to see African Americans differently, and he reassessed the path forward as he eagerly attempted to reveal their vision of their position in the nation along with their passionate desire for progress.[9]

Du Bois's evolving professional assessment of the African American community first received international attention through the photographic collections he presented at the 1900 Paris Exposition. In some ways, his portrayal of emotionally complex African Americans built on critically acclaimed high art representations and signaled his familiarity with the broader late-nineteenth-century visual archive. For instance, Winslow Homer's masterpieces like *A Visit from the Old Mistress* (1877) and *The Gulf Stream* (1899) attested to African American emotional complexity and highlighted the difficult nature of black existence in the U.S. at the turn of the century. Thomas Eakins also explored black Americans' psychological depth. Paintings such as *Negro Boy Dancing* (1878) and *Negress* (1900) present quiet, contemplative studies of African American character even as Eakins draws on notions of blacks as entertainers and noble savages disconnected from mainstream U.S. experience. Kathleen Foster argues that *Negro Boy Dancing* shows Eakins's tendency "to isolate his models both formally and psychologically," rendering them "islands of interest in a sea of loosely applied strokes."[10] Like Homer, Eakins avoids blatant racism, yet he refuses to advocate strongly for the inclusion of African Americans in the U.S. family. Even Henry Ossawa Tanner, Eakins's student and most acclaimed African American painter of the nineteenth century, failed to portray African Americans in ways that strongly refuted the damaging images of blackness coursing through popular art and print media. Tanner's most famous painting, *The Banjo Lesson* (1893), thoroughly rescues his subject from the eighteenth- and early-nineteenth-century stereotype of the comic black entertainer, but he maintains the impulse to show black life isolated from the heart of U.S. society.

The photographic compositions Du Bois favors do not challenge this tendency to emphasize the segregated nature of black life. Instead, his preference for portraits of middle class success reflects his heightened awareness of the preponderant portrayals of race that exploded across the U.S. as companies began producing branded consumer products en masse by the end of the nineteenth century. The burgeoning U.S. advertising landscape during the 1880s introduced an array of insulting images promoting African Americans in demeaning positions of service and general idiocy. As a result, the eighteenth- and early-nineteenth-century painterly depictions of blacks as servants and entertainers hardened into unassailable truths by the end of the nineteenth century. Elaborate national advertising campaigns accompanying products from soap to cigarettes cast African Americans as comedic Sambos. Blackness in this guise held special allure for white consumers who felt disconnected from unfamiliar commercial products produced in mind-boggling numbers. Enduring figures like Aunt Jemima appeared in 1890 and by 1902 was happily proclaiming "I'se in town, honey!" from grocery stores across the nation while the Cream of Wheat man emerged in 1893.[11] In addition to these iconic figures, Victorian trade cards – postcard-sized cardboard ads that were given out at merchant stores and in mailings – propagated deprecating stereotypes in relation to selling everything from tobacco to stove polish to salad dressing. Stereoviews and postcards also gained newfound popularity during this period while images on sheet music continued proliferating pictures of black absurdity.

Photography further contributed to the formation and reification of stereotypes divorcing African Americans from the national identity. Building on the work of anthropologists and other scientists, magazines like *National Geographic* turned to photographs to define people with dark skin as outside of the U.S. family. First published in 1888, *National Geographic* became renowned for its pictures and reports on exotic places. The photograph of a Zulu bride and groom in South Africa included in the November 1896 issue made history as their first picture of a bare-breasted woman and signaled the magazine's emergent philosophy to "publish photos of indigenous peoples 'as they are.'"[12] In the broader context of World Fairs and Expositions, such images concretized U.S. ideas that African Americans hailed from savage stock. Michael D. Harris, explaining the significance of the 1893 World's Columbian Exposition in Chicago, argues that "the organizers used it as an opportunity to define visually the United States and its relation to the world."[13] In examining the Dahomey Village exhibit, an example of the popularity of native village exhibits from 1889 through 1914, Harris reviews a *Harper's Weekly* cartoon of the Johnson family's experiences at the fair.[14] This demeaning portrayal of a fictional African American family visiting the fair on Colored American Day reports their exploits with offensive images. Harris notes that the shared dialect the cartoon imagined "linked blacks with so-called primitives elsewhere in the world."[15] The Exposition also marked the introduction of Aunt Jemima in the person of Nancy Green.

Du Bois's turn to photography to produce images of African American middle-class prosperity and refinement directly challenges these ubiquitous images of degraded blackness and echoes a broader trend among African Americans. The numbers of black photographers continued to grow, and they added to the foundation laid by early practitioners like Jules Lion, James Presley, and Augustus Washington. By the late nineteenth and early twentieth centuries, black photographers had developed a sophisticated sense of their role in actively asserting a respectful image of black America, and they flexed their photographic muscles in contributing to this "revisionist" cause. Cornelius Marion Battey, Arthur P. Bedou, and Thomas E. Askew are just a few of the men whom Du Bois, and later Washington, depended on to frame their arguments for black progress while documenting and redefining African American citizens and the work they contributed to the growing nation.[16]

The 363 photographs Du Bois displayed at the 1900 Paris Exposition constitute what scholar Shawn Smith describes as a "counterarchive," a collection of photographs that "challenges a long legacy of racist taxonomy, intervening in turn-of-the-century 'race science' by offering competing visual evidence."[17] The majority of the portraits display middle-class black success stories and feature individuals who quietly contest images circulating in the American popular imagination. More than two thirds of the photographs feature proper men and women; in fact, the archive Du Bois constructs offers a rather narrowly conceived rebuttal to derogatory images proliferating in print media and high art. Images of African American polished students, middle-class subjects, impressive property, and successful businessmen comprise the bulk of his representations with pictures of rural inhabitants sparingly interspersed. A comprehensive review of the albums Du Bois presented at the Paris Exposition uncovers precious few images that recall the texture of his presentation of the folk in a written text like *Souls*.[18] Instead, the majority of the portraits feature individuals who appear either to belong to the Talented Tenth or to be well on their way to gaining entrance into this rarefied group.

Du Bois appears acutely aware of what Allan Sekula describes as the complicated practice of pictorially depicting middle class success. In contrast to historical accounts casting photography as a uniformly democratizing technology, Sekula notes that, from its earliest incarnation, photography functioned both "*honorifically* and *repressively*."[19] The development of scientific branches such as physiognomy and phrenology along with advances in police work, established a "*shadow archive*" in the 1840s and 1850s that led to the institution of a photographic archive linked closely to criminology in the 1880s and 1890s.[20] By frankly engaging this photographic work, Du Bois challenges narratives defining African Americans as criminals. Nevertheless, his investment in staid, middle-class visual portraits of individuals, formal pictures from black colleges and universities, and images of church and union groups feels somewhat timid when compared to his written portrayals of the folk. Whereas photographs of Georgia farms and unpaved roads, most of which include no individuals, represent a clear minority in his exhibition collection, *Souls* unflinchingly ponders the less picturesque predicament the black masses face.[21]

The Vision of African American Souls

Du Bois's signification on the trope of the Picture Book in *Souls* interests me as one of the few instances he places his philosophical view of African American experience alongside the vision of the black masses. He not only describes himself as "bone of the bone and flesh of the flesh of them that live within the Veil," but he also portrays his failure to perceive his place in U.S. society as sometimes more pronounced than the struggling vision of rural blacks (*SBF*, 6). Unlike the many photographs he celebrates that locate visionary qualities with the African American upper classes, his most canonical text tightly binds penetrating vision to rural folk. Du Bois intimates that education rather than class remains central to cultivating a progressive sensibility, and he wastes little time in revealing his preoccupation with visuality. His famous description of double consciousness announces his investment in vision as a means of exploring African

American humanity: "the Negro is ... born with a veil and gifted with second-sight in this American world, – a world which yields him no true self-consciousness, but only lets him see himself through the revelation of the other world. It is a peculiar sensation, this double-consciousness, this sense of always looking at one's self through the eyes of others" (*SBF*, 10–11). The fate of viewing oneself through the gaze of others deprives black men and women of "true self-consciousness," and consequently, denies the nation access to honest self-evaluation. To reveal the inner states of the black men and women whom he presents as worthy contributors to the national workforce, Du Bois emphasizes African American emotional complexity as the untold story behind black labor.

He constructs a portrait of black identity that highlights their obstructed vision of success and closely associates African American folk with the less material aspects of American progress. Notwithstanding his sociological training and devotion to statistics, he emphasizes the American right to dream in unrestricted terms. If the ex-slave narrators highlight their morally unencumbered physical vision that allows them to report the depravity sown into the soil of slavery, Du Bois introduces the perils of black American vision deprived of such powers of sight. Indeed, Du Bois insists that even the lowliest worker deserves access to the promise of the Declaration of Independence, the right to the "Pursuit of Happiness," and he casts this right in the rhetoric of vision and American romanticism. In a reading that connects Du Bois to romanticism, Yogita Goyal argues that Du Bois "situates romance at the heart of a deep-rooted cultural nationalism that establishes what is truly distinct about blackness. To do so, Du Bois aligns realism with white America" while he "uses romance to present blackness."[22] Du Bois's ideal African American citizen values imagination and intellect, and these priorities identify him as quintessentially American in ways that white Americans can no longer claim.[23]

This baseline leads to the creation of Josie and John in *Souls*. If the inner seven sociological chapters of Du Bois's text trace the trajectory of the desecration of the American Dream in the Black Belt – the strangulation of those aspiring toward material prosperity – the framing chapters on Josie and John raise the specter of the death of the American Dream that lives in the hearts of black youth. By defining the protagonists of "Of the Meaning of Progress" and "Of the Coming of John" by the quality of their work ethic and ambition, Du Bois extols the quintessentially American vision black folk possess and presents himself as benefitting from their wisdom. His own pedagogical odyssey leads him to Josie, and her vision of progress and success emerges as the standard against which he measures racial advancement. Whereas Du Bois is "haunted by a New England vision of neat little desks and chairs," Josie represents the folk youth who face educational opportunity with "bright eager eyes." In fact, his descriptions of his students focus on their eyes: one of the Dowells looks out of "wondering eyes"; the youngest Burkes is a "haughty-eyed girl"; and "Tildy gazes upon the world with 'starry eyes.'" Together, they look to him with "eyes full of expectation" (*SBF*, 48).

This attention to folk eyes captures the multivalent vision of progress Du Bois hints is most undeniably American, and Josie's heroic morality defines the essence of the striving soul Du Bois sketches. When Du Bois returns to these rural Tennessee climes ten years after his instructional summer sojourns, he finds few signs of advancement. Josie has died. Her death stems directly from the cruel combination of unmitigated labor and a broken heart. When Josie's "vision of schooldays all fled," she continued to toil, but when "some one married another; then Josie crept to her mother like a hurt child, and slept – and sleeps" (*SBF*, 51). Du Bois pulls aside the veil that usually covers the romantic desire of respectable black women, and implies that some form of the dream must be fulfilled to give individuals of any race the perseverance to progress. Josie's sensitive response to emotional pain rejects the stereotypical image of the care-free, childlike African American moving jollily from one life experience to the next. Josie personifies the tragedy of lost hope as she closes her eyes on a world that mocks her dare to dream.

The transformation of the physical school offers material evidence of the emotional wreckage he finds. Du Bois's log schoolhouse has been replaced by "a jaunty board house" with broken windows, a representative of "Progress" (*SBF*, 52). As he returns to Nashville on the Jim Crow car, her wonders, "How shall man measure Progress there where the dark-faced Josie lies? How many heartfuls of sorrow shall balance a bushel of wheat?" (*SBF*, 53). Josie's portrait captures the impossibility of applying the usual measuring tools. As he concludes the chapter, he probes the recesses of life within the veil, admitting the difficulty of wholly grasping this world. He decides that the jury is still out on assessing whether the country is moving forward or backward on improving the prospects of citizens like Josie, and he forces her portrait upon readers as a means of forcing the dilemma of denied desire on those who would refuse African Americans the possession of ambitious vision. He also draws a direct contrast with Washington who concentrated his energy in building schoolhouses throughout the South.[24] The building alone, Du Bois implies, will never accurately gauge success. The folk need the "vision of the seer."

"Of the Coming of John" reveals the impact of the belated falling of the veil and underscores the emotional violence often suffered by the awakening black consciousness. John exemplifies the noble sincerity of the striving black individual in pursuit of the American Dream. If Josie symbolizes individual promise and intellectual curiosity, John represents intellectual accomplishment and artistic appreciation. John Jones's schooling unlocks the deepest recesses of his mind, making him "silent before the vision" or leading him to wander "peering through and beyond the world of men into a world of thought" (*SBF*, 145). John's intellectual expansion propels him further inside for this is the terrain that he has been denied. Only after expending a good deal of energy gazing inward does John direct his eyes outward. And even then, what most moves him is artistic excellence. In the New York opera hall, while the white John chafes at the outrage of sitting next to a black man, John Jones finds himself enraptured by musical poetry. His response attests to the intrinsic artistic appreciation African Americans possess regardless of their economic status:

> A deep longing swelled in all his heart to rise with that clear music out of the dirt and dust of that low life that held him prisoned and befouled. ... He looked thoughtfully across the hall, and wondered why the beautiful gray-haired woman looked so listless, and what the little man could be whispering about. He would not like to be listless and idle, he thought, for he felt with the music the movement of power within him. If he but had some master-work, some life-service, hard, – aye, bitter hard, but without the cringing and sickening servility, without the cruel hurt that hardened his heart and soul. (*SBF*, 147)

Echoing Wheatley's response to Homer, Douglass's lament on the Chesapeake Bay, and untold other African American strivers, John desires that uniquely U.S. promise, the opportunity to accomplish something great. In stark contrast to the privileged white audience members – U.S. citizens who have lost sight of vital aspects of American character – he passionately follows the course of the music as a conduit for life reflection and the impetus for his recommitment to hard work. The sound of the music inspires him to *see* his white counterparts differently: he discovers their apathy and rejects established notions of success. His yearning to serve belies those who would claim that African Americans seek an easy route to progress. John craves a "master-work" unfettered by racial restrictions. Nevertheless, John accepts his fate stripped of any romantic narrative of uplift or self-reliance, and his final concentration on the strains of Wagner's beautiful music, even as he faces the horror of a lynch mob, recognizes the impossibility for a soul like his to find peace in the racist world he inhabits.

Du Bois's portrayal of John and Josie fleshes out the pain of being denied the fullness of the American Dream. These chapters spotlight Du Bois's talent for rendering the subtleties of black life too often ignored or denied by the broader public. He defines African Americans' desire to participate in meaningful labor as representative of their authentic American character. Thus, *Souls* develops the trope of the Picture Book by identifying black interior vision as a crucial factor in determining African American progress. The ability for rural blacks like Josie and John to visualize future success and fulfillment plays a major role in their ability to actualize their desires. Du Bois's photographic collections, however, rarely reflect the same level of emotional texture. In fact, juxtaposing Du Bois's narrative work with his visual collections uncovers the surprising conservatism of his photographic work. Whereas a text such as *Souls* exults in pulling back the veil covering African American life and celebrating black citizens as moored in genuine American-ness, most of the images Du Bois included in his albums for the Paris Exposition hold the metaphorical curtain securely in place. If his written words uncover black complexity, the visual images often strive to deliver an unambiguous verification of black success. Surprisingly, it is his ideological foe who shows a willingness to complicate his development of the trope of the Picture Book with more innovative photographic evidence of black progress in education and labor.

Washington's Pictorial Response to the Popular Image of Black Work

Up from Slavery self-consciously links professional success to the visual appreciation of buildings where educational preparation for work occurs. Early in his autobiography, Washington reveals the most important lesson Hampton taught him: "I not only learned that it was not a disgrace to labour, but I learned to love labour, not alone for its financial value, but for labour's own sake and for the independence and self-reliance which the ability to do something which the world wants done brings."[25] His commitment to labor signals his American character at a time when the traditional idea of the U.S. worker was evolving in the aftermath of the industrial revolution. As labor unions became more powerful and violent conflicts such as the 1886 Haymarket Affair threatened to undermine the image of the honorable working man, Washington presented African

Americans as praiseworthy proponents of the traditional American work ethic. A significant part of his project rested on inserting black workers into the American popular imagination via images generated by literary texts and photographs.

Washington's turn to vision and visual media discloses his awareness of the popular practice of depending on the visual arts to celebrate the American worker. As Melissa Dabakis notes in her study of visualizations of labor in American sculpture during the period of 1880–1935, the visual arts facilitated the production of public memory that celebrated the dignity and honor of labor. Yet neither sculptures, paintings, nor other visual media widely commemorated African American workers. Instead, black laborers struggled to overcome a fine arts legacy that consigned them to the roles of servant or entertainer, representations that influenced pre-abolition writers. As discussed earlier in this chapter, African Americans were sometimes portrayed as emotionally complex, but these painted compositions kept black citizens carefully divorced from the larger American public. Singular examples of powerful plastic depictions of black men at work – such as Daniel Chester French and Edward Clark Potter's sculpture, *Teamster*, which was displayed at the 1893 World's Columbian Exposition in Chicago – made little headway against the deluge of visual art depicting African Americans as incapable of serious work. As idleness accrued new social significance and the word "tramp" entered the national lexicon, African Americans strove to avoid these damning labels.[26] In response to this landscape, Washington not only presented himself as an impressive exhibit of the honorable laborer, he also cast Tuskegee as a direct partner to the growing American factory.

His educational institution, he implied, produced a most desirable U.S. product: the black American laborer who possessed a progressive vision of education and work. But Washington's frank advocacy for industrial education as a boon to white America did not hinder his pursuit of a complex educational philosophy dedicated to improving black life. I want to consider his early publications with an eye toward his support for particular modes of visual art display at Tuskegee. Connecting the pictures that depict the college campus to Washington's literary visualizations of blackness reveals the subtlety inherent in his work, a complexity frequently disregarded in the rush to adopt the narrative defining him as the president of the disparagingly dubbed "Tuskegee Machine."[27] This section places Washington's development of the trope of the Picture Book in *Up from Slavery* in conversation with the photographs that he commissioned at the turn of the century. Such a pairing interjects new possibilities for discerning the nuance in his educational approach and posture toward black advancement.

Washington's literary texts uncover his commitment to portraying African Americans as possessing an independent vision of cultural progress, and his widely read autobiography reveals his self-conscious struggle against a difficult contemporary landscape. As white New Englanders strove to wash their hands of the race problem, Southerners developed multiple lines of attack to strangle black advancement. Playing on the Northern embrace of a noblesse oblige attitude, Southern paternalism joined forces with a revived investment in the rules of free-labor capitalism and new ideas established by Darwinism. The confluence of these concepts led to a mantra demanding that African Americans survive by the sweat of their brows. By the 1890s, virulent racists regained the national megaphone.[28] Extremists like Senator Benjamin R. Tillman seared a new image into the consciousness of the general public as he declared the black man "a fiend, a wild beast, seeking whom he may devour"[29] and branded black workers who crossed strike lines "the club with which your brains were beaten out."[30] John Roach, an AFL (American Federation of Labor) official, affirmed, "[Black strikebreakers are] huge strapping fellows, ignorant and viscous, whose predominating trait [is] animalism."[31] In fact, African American workers who dared to break strike lines were uniformly described in hyperbolic language portraying them as vicious men determined to rob respectable, hard-working white men of their rightful jobs.

Pictures in print media played a crucial role in ensconcing these ideas within the fabric of the nation, and Washington recognized the need to dismantle these ossifying images advanced by news organs. "Yellow journalism," characterized by a greater emphasis on pictures, drew thousands of new readers into the subscriber fold, reaching its height in 1899 and 1900.[32] The birth of the ten-cent magazine increased competition between magazines and newspapers as the quality and quantity of illustrations often distinguished the two media. Many critics disparaged magazines for compromising news quality for pictorial flash. Referring to a magazine competitor, *The Dial* intoned: "In point of illustration they have no superiors anywhere, but much of their text appears to exist only for the sake of the pictures."[33] *Lippincott's Magazine* complained more generally of "The Tyranny of the Pictorial."[34] Bieze notes that even Washington received requests for photos from a newspaper writer in 1897 who assured the Tuskegee president that "[w]e can arrange for an article to be written around the illustrations."[35] Still, as both venues gave rise to a larger, more diverse U.S. reading audience – with many print organs publishing responsible commentary on black suffrage, education, and lynching – the most immediate impact of illustration-driven news media was a pervasive imaging of black stereotypes.

Washington's emphasis on vision in his literary texts also reflects his attention to popular literature of the era. Racist authors like Thomas Nelson Page assured readers that every African American was a "lazy, lying, lustful animal which no conceivable amount of training can transform into a tolerable citizen."[36] The rise of the historical romance featuring the romanticized South drew scores of readers toward Joel Chandler Harris's *Uncle Remus* collections published between 1881 and 1906 while the scandalous celebration of the Klu Klux Klan in Thomas Dixon's *The Leopard's Spots* (1902) and *The Clansman* (1905) enjoyed wild success. *The Clansman*, the second novel in the trilogy that inspired G. W. Griffith's *The Birth of a Nation* (1915), was reported to have sold 40,000 copies in ten days after its 1905 release.

Even children's books contributed to fortifying the popular image of black inferiority. The Bobbsey Twins series launched in 1904 featured the stereotypical Mammy in the character of Dinah, and Helen Bannerman's *The Story of Little Black Sambo* (1899) migrated from Great Britain to the U.S. almost immediately at the turn of the century.[37] Barbara Bader explains that although the official 1900 U.S. version of Bannerman's story published by Frederick Stokes sold well, countless reprints inundated the market and "the majority were reillustrated – with gross, degrading caricatures that set Sambo down on the old plantation or, with equal distortiveness, deposited him in Darkest Africa."[38] In addition to depicting Sambo with outlandishly big red lips and bulging white eyes, the illustrations confirm that when Sambo sheds his clothing for the tigers, he wears a grass skirt as his undergarment, visual certification of his savage roots.

Given this context, it is not surprising that Washington aims to redefine black identity by linking black laborers to the morally upstanding American work ethic and a respectable educational philosophy. He commenced this project in earnest with the publication of *Up from Slavery*. His autobiography outlines how his industrial education philosophy relies on more than physical labor and the accumulation of material goods. Washington vividly demonstrates that only African Americans who possess the gift of vision – the ability to translate the sights one experiences into meaningful understanding – are positioned to advance in the U.S. He assures readers that Tuskegee has no intention of graduating students who fulfill the picture of "an educated Negro, with a high hat, imitation gold eye-glasses, a showy walking-stick, kid gloves, fancy boots, and what not" (*US*, 70). But even as he declares himself wiser than Reconstruction era African Americans who succumbed to "the craze for Greek and Latin learning," he celebrates the importance of cultivating classical cultural appreciation in Tuskegee students (*US*, 47).

In many ways, he seeks to extend the ex-slave narrators' claim for the authority of African American vision of the nation. But in place of their emphasis on morality, Washington underscores African Americans' focus on sites of education as a crucial foundation for maintaining the American work ethic. Amidst a landscape of change, transition, and uncertainty, Washington offers black students' unmitigated vision of traditional educational values as evidence of their importance to the workforce. In fact, his own story depends on the trope of the Picture Book as he connects inspired vision to instructional prowess. Early in his narrative of his life as a slave, Washington riffs on the trope of the Talking Book:

> I had no schooling whatever while I was a slave, though I remember on several occasions I went as far as the schoolhouse door with one of my young mistresses to carry her books. The picture of several dozen boys and girls in a schoolroom engaged in study made a deep impression upon me, and I had the feeling that to get into a schoolhouse and study in this way would be about the same as getting into paradise. (*US*, 4)

In place of the expected discussion of the attainment of literacy, Washington leaves readers to ponder his visual impression of the site of instruction, the schoolhouse. His mistress's books remain closely attached to him as he carries them for her, but he focuses on the "picture of several dozen boys and girls in a schoolroom." The method of their study is left to conjecture, but Washington emphasizes his zeal to enter such a place, equating entering "a schoolhouse" to "getting into paradise." Washington hints that his untutored appreciation of the site where education occurs proves the grounded nature of his desire for an education. Gazing upon the children at work in the classroom impresses him as he identifies the school as the key to self-improvement.

In fact, the "sight" of physical edifices dedicated to education assumes a seminal role in Washington's signification on the trope of the Picture Book. He closely associates the visual impact of school buildings with his future success in constructing such sites, and he ties his disposition to the U.S. philosophy of expansion. When he finally arrives to Hampton after a long and arduous journey, the sight of the school offers valuable instruction:

> [T]he first sight of the large, three-story, brick school building seemed to have rewarded me for all that I had undergone in order to reach the place.

> If the people who gave the money to provide that building could appreci-
> ate the influence the sight of it had upon me, as well as upon thousands of
> youth, they would feel all the more encouraged to make such gifts. ... The
> sight of it seemed to give me new life. I felt that a new existence had now
> begun – that life would now have meaning. I felt that I had reached the
> promised land, and I resolved to let no obstacle prevent me from putting
> forth the highest effort to fit myself to accomplish the most good in the
> world. (*US*, 30)

Washington translates the sight of the school into a religious experience
akin to salvation. If learning to read gave African Americans who became
literate access to the Bible and the opportunity to accept Christ, than
recognizing the spiritual nature of industrial education prepares black
Americans to assume their rightful positions as students ready to develop
skills that prove their inherent American character. Washington emphasizes his ability to see value in the very buildings responsible for producing
laborers, proof of his sturdy character. Unlike many Americans who found
little to admire in factories and other rather unremarkable places of work
and education, he views the red brick buildings of Hampton as the heavenly site where the training for true labor occurs.[39]

Following the lead of pre-abolition writers, Washington extols African
Americans for possessing the ability to see and appreciate – clearly and
without confusion – the role of education as direct preparation for labor.
The Tuskegee president similarly places great faith in the visual power of
the material objects industrial education produces:

> I have found, too, that it is the visible, the tangible, that goes a long ways in
> softening prejudices. The actual sight of a first-class house that a Negro has
> built is ten times more potent than pages of discussion about a house that
> he ought to build or perhaps could build.

> One man may go into a community prepared to supply the people there
> with an analysis of Greek sentences. The community may not at that time
> be prepared for, or feel the need of, Greek analysis, but it may feel its need
> of bricks and houses, and wagons. (*US*, 90–91)

As he explains hypothetical responses to different forms of knowledge,
Washington subtly instructs his readers to value concrete, visible evidence of black progress over intellectual discussions on the topic. This,
he implies, would place the reader on the same plane as the industrial
education student who already looks at the world with such eyes. And his
repeated turn to "Greek" as an unnecessary subject stops short of declaring
it eternally worthless. A community may well need to know something of

Greek literature, and art for that matter, and when they do, the Tuskegee student may be prepared to be of use for both the teaching of Greek and the building of houses.

Washington's focus on the inspirational nature of the material aspect of education makes his interest in photography a natural extension of his literary work. As the second epigraph that opens this chapter reveals, the Tuskegee president understood the power of photographs, and he appealed to them to market the school and promote a textured explanation of his philosophy. Washington's years at the school's helm, from 1881 until 1915, coincide with the years described as "photography's coming-of-age," 1880–1917.[40] To ally black workers with ideas declaring the moral honor of the common laborer, he worked with a number of black and white photographers including Herbert Pinney Tresslar, Harry Shepherd, William E. Benson, Gertrude Kasebier, and after 1903, A. P. Bedou and C. M. Battey.[41] Many of these photographers were employed with the chief responsibility of photographing Washington on his tours throughout the nation. Their pictures substantiate the Tuskegee president's embodiment of the strength of character and progressive outlook he advocated in his speeches and publications. With the help of Frances Benjamin Johnston, however, Washington secured a revealing picture of Tuskegee that both fortifies and extends his conscientious presentation of vision in *Up from Slavery*.

Picturing the Tuskegee Story

When Johnston, a white woman from the North, began her work at Tuskegee in November 1902, she was one of the most highly acclaimed photographers of the era enjoying the distinction of being "chosen by President Teddy Roosevelt to photograph his family" as well as having won a gold prize for her Hampton photographs displayed at the Paris exposition of 1900.[42] Her photographs had been widely hailed a success and deemed "second in importance only to W.E.B. Du Bois's exhibit" of his Georgia albums.[43] Of the 648 photoprints she shot at Tuskegee that are now archived at the Library of Congress, a good number continue her work of articulating a nuanced picture of African American industrial education. Washington clearly employed her with hopes of replicating the success of her Hampton images, for her prize-winning photos confirmed her commitment to portraying a "complex picture" of African American education.[44] In addition to publishing some of her work in *Working with the Hands*, Washington supported Johnston's plan to display a "massive exhibition of Tuskegee photos" in the 1904 St. Louis World's Fair before organizers dropped her submission.[45]

I am most intrigued by the picture galleries Johnston captures on the walls of Tuskegee classrooms, and I want to suggest that her photographs help us amplify the meaning undergirding visually inflected scenes in Washington's autobiography. Given her past success at the 1900 Paris Exposition, Washington unquestionably hoped to garner a good deal of attention from her sweeping portrayal of Tuskegee. As a former slave and man of the South, he remained unyielding to Du Bois's argument that industrial education proved less beneficial than its proponents claimed. As a result of their diverging views, the years from 1894 and 1903 witnessed the relationship between the two men deteriorate drastically. Their interaction changed from a series of friendly exchanges that include Du Bois congratulating Washington on his Atlanta Exposition speech; Washington inviting Du Bois to join Tuskegee's staff; and both men joining together to form the National Negro Business League, to Washington describing Du Bois as "a big dunce" who "was puffed up with insane vanity and jealousy" that deprived him "of common sense."[46] Du Bois, in turn, publicly upbraided Washington in *The Souls of Black Folk*. Their conflicting views on black labor lay at the root of the rupture, and we can tease out the crux of their differing philosophies by considering the divergence documented in their favored photographic subjects and compositions, and by extension, the relationship between their visual images and written texts.

Focusing on Johnston's photographs reveals a more complicated image of Tuskegee than critics have traditionally acknowledged. Whereas scholars like James Guimond disparage her publically displayed photos of African American industrial education in the *Hampton Album* or in Washington's *Working with the Hands*, I am interested in the ways her images visualize Washington's educational philosophy by granting access to interior spaces not widely analyzed. Guimond charges that Johnston's photographs chiefly serve to "document the application of the American Dream of prosperity and progress to the nation's minorities" and the embrace of "the white man's way." He notes that the images decline, however, to show industrial education students "engaging in any cultural activities."[47] Although parts of these claims ring true, such accusations elide the relationship between what might be perceived as "the white man's way" and "culture," and they also fail to consider the complete body of work produced from Johnston's visits to Tuskegee. Drawing from my survey of the complete 648 image archive taken at Tuskegee in 1902, I want to focus on a few images that provide a more textured context for her work.

In contrast to Du Bois who favors single subject portraits, an overview of Johnston's photos suggests that Washington esteems images that celebrate Tuskegee's physical edifices and students. Johnston's pictures convey the honor of the industrial educational model that graduates worthy laborers, and most of her photographs avoid an overtly romantic sensibility. Only the portraits of Washington engaged in outdoor work almost uniformly draw on such romanticism. More broadly, Johnston presents evidence of the social order pervading Tuskegee and its program for training blacks to adopt the work ethic representative of U.S. character. Her photographs of interior campus spaces exhibit displays of high art and substantiate Washington's nuanced sense of how his students should be prepared for their future work. In fact, these classrooms, doubling as mini art galleries, introduce the Greek and classical subjects Washington declared unrelated to the project of preparing rural blacks for the U.S. workforce. The presence of such photographs displayed throughout the campus points to Washington's participation in a broader discussion of the role visual images play in educating African Americans.

A photograph of a history class exhibits Abraham Lincoln and George Washington, as well as printed reproductions of *Laocoön and His Sons* and what looks to be Canova's *Perseus and the Head of Medusa* (see Figure 2.1). The subjects of the reproductions are particularly interesting. Both feature scenes from Greek mythology and broach the issue of facing death heroically. The priest, Laocoön, and his sons pay the ultimate price for attempting to warn the Trojan citizens of impending danger. As he endures the wrath of the gods, Laocoön's expression conveys an elegant pain that Gotthold Lessing applauds as evidence of the sculptor's acknowledgment of the limitations of visual art. Similarly, Canova shows Perseus calmly contemplating the result of his murder of Medusa. The impressive nature of his physical form and regal drapery makes the greatest statement as once again, the moment of death is muted. Medusa does not scream – she sighs. These grand works of Western art relay both a violence and heroism that make them odd decorative choices for an industrial college.

In a second classroom, the art celebrates the birth of Christ. Framed copies of Millet's *The Angelus* and Raphael's *Madonna of the Chair* (see Figure 2.2) portray less audacious narratives than the classical scenes. Millet's painting is one of his most famous celebrations of the divine nature of labor. His depiction of devout peasants pausing to pray and reflect over Gabriel's good news to Mary inspires viewers to contemplate the character

Figure 2.1 Frances Benjamin Johnston, History Class, Tuskegee Normal and Industrial Institute, Tuskegee, Alabama. Prints & Photographs Division, Library of Congress, Washington, DC [LC-USZ62–64712].

of individuals who work the land. Raphael's *Madonna of the Chair*, one of his most popular renditions of his favorite subject, depicts an intimate picture of Mary, baby Jesus, and John the Baptist. Considered with Millet's image of prayer, Raphael's painting appears to advocate maintaining a close

Figure 2.2 Frances Benjamin Johnston, Mathematics Class, Tuskegee Normal and Industrial Institute, Tuskegee, Alabama. Prints & Photographs Division, Library of Congress, Washington, DC [LC-J694–331].

relationship with Christ. A photo of the library interior reveals a similar investment in visual art. Formal busts and framed images of classic pieces grace the bookshelves and decorate the walls (see Figure 2.3).

Figure 2.3 Frances Benjamin Johnston, Library-interior, Tuskegee Normal and Industrial Institute, Tuskegee, Alabama. Prints & Photographs Division, Library of Congress, Washington, DC [LC-J694–344].

The inclusion of such art in the school décor unveils an unexpected portion of Washington's aesthetic philosophy at a time when he carefully stressed the modest aims of his curriculum. For instance, in *Working with the Hands*, when he encourages female students to think of decorating their homes, he avoids naming particular artists. Instead, he encourages them to select "pictures" that are "in good taste."[48] Similarly, in an article in the 1902 *Colored American Magazine*, he praises a "negro home" that displays "pictures on the walls" that "were not of the cheap, 'dawdy,' flashy character, but had been selected with taste and care."[49] These examples attest to Washington's preference for vagueness when he encourages the selection of art in his published work. In direct contrast, the *Colored American Magazine* also includes a 1902 article by W. W. Holland, "Photography for our Young People," in which Holland directs young people to replace poor pictures of relatives and unattractive reprints with "Millet's pictures" and counsels them to learn to appreciate the beauty of "Raphael's masterpieces."[50]

Washington avoids such direct advocacy for European art in his printed texts, but the classroom and library galleries Johnston records with her camera tell a different story.[51] Like Du Bois who retained a lasting appreciation for Western art, Washington finds a role for it at Tuskegee.[52] Johnston's photographs document Washington's participation in what Bieze describes as "aestheticizing black labor," a common tactic during the Progressive Era.[53] Katharine Martinez, focusing on tenement dwellers in the Northeast, offers insight into the broader logic behind such practices. Examining the period from 1880 through 1920, she notes that the confluence of radically improved photomechanical printing techniques – which made copies of all manner of art more widely available – together with the zealousness of cultural tastemakers led to a widespread commitment to improving the public's character. Martinez explains, "Middle-class educators, social reformers, and tastemakers believed that real culture had inherent aesthetic, moral, and social significance. Their aesthetic discrimination centered on beliefs that art uplifted the public's moral and cultural values, by inspiring them through the noble thoughts and great deeds depicted."[54] Despite reformers' best efforts, untutored Americans followed their own sense of taste or the example of trade catalogs which presented "fine art by European and American masters" beside "portraits of presidents ... and views of European cathedrals and Roman monuments."[55]

This description recalls the art displays in Tuskegee's classrooms where the *Laocoön* flanks a picture of Daniel Webster and the *Madonna of the Chair* hangs beside a portrait of Ulysses S. Grant. Yet the beliefs motivating activists like Elizabeth McCracken, who worked tirelessly to refine tenement dwellers' cultural taste by giving them high art reproductions, were less passionately supported in relation to educating African Americans. Bieze touches on the subject when he notes that New England supporters of Tuskegee highly approve of picturesque images of student workspaces and the general testimonials applauding examples of high European art displayed on the school walls. Such championing of high art displays in the industrial classroom was not, however, an attitude embraced by white Southerners. In fact, Kendrick Grandison suggests that the oppositional sentiments of white citizens of Tuskegee even managed to direct Washington's design of the campus.

Grandison contends that Washington intentionally maintained an unassuming appearance for the exterior grounds of the Tuskegee campus.[56]

Taking note of the campus layouts of other southern black colleges, Grandison explains that to comprehend the Tuskegee president's posture toward educating African Americans in Alabama, we must abandon the "college campus as art" theoretical approach that is appropriate for studying "majority college campuses in America."[57] Instead, we must pose alternate questions. In relation to Tuskegee's Carnegie Library, Grandison asks: "Why is so universal a symbol of the academic landscape as the handsome Ionic portico oriented so decisively away from public view? Indeed, why is this pattern repeated by all of the major academic buildings on Tuskegee's campus that were erected adjacent to this public road from the 1880s through the 1930s?"[58]

The answer to this question reminds us of the careful balancing act Washington observed as he worked to empower African American students without antagonizing his Southern neighbors. In the same way that he felt compelled to plan a campus that appears unassuming to those passing by but unveils a more regal air to individuals within its gates, his speeches and articles extolling industrial education did not always divulge the subtleties of his philosophy. In addition to advocating for instruction that would directly prepare students to work in the rural climes many of them called home, Washington sought to remind students of their participation in a broader commitment to demonstrating African Americans' vital position within U.S. society and culture. He clearly saw merit in introducing students to a range of art that included classical examples, but he avoided trumpeting his views where others might take offense. Nevertheless, the classroom exhibits uncover his confidence in his students' abilities to interpret a range of visual art, even in the rural South.

The sophistication with which both Du Bois and Washington approach their written and visual texts underscores the complicated nature of their dueling philosophies. For both men, photographs provide opportunities to portray positive images of African Americans that supplement their portrayals of black characters in their written texts. The celebration of African American visual acuity in their literary works reveals their belief that African American laborers will only find success when they appear in terms that recognize the complexity of their character. To this end, both leaders employ written and visual texts to revise and authenticate respectable images of black American labor. Yet Washington sees the potential of photography for fleshing out less discussed aspects of his educational philosophy, whereas Du Bois turns to photography to strengthen the most conservative ideas of black progress. Together, their work with photographers along with their individual appeals to the trope of the Picture Book solidifies the central role of vision in the turn of the century's development of black literature.

CHAPTER 3

Gazing upon Plastic Art in the Harlem Renaissance

Surely it is more interesting to belong to one's own time, to share its peculiar vision, catch that flying glimpse of the panorama which no subsequent generation can ever recover.
– Nella Larsen, 1925[1]

Once in a while through all of us there flashes some clairvoyance, some clear idea, of what America really is. We who are dark can see America in a way that white Americans cannot. And seeing our country thus, are we satisfied with its present goals and ideals?
– W. E. B. Du Bois, 1926[2]

Blossoming in the aftermath of World War I and amid the upheaval of the Great Migration, the Harlem Renaissance marked a new era of African American artistic productivity. Black writers sought to build on the hard-fought gains achieved by Washington and Du Bois, and they reveled at the prospect of defining literary art on their own terms. For black women, cosmopolitan spaces such as Harlem and Washington, DC provided new opportunities for creative work during the 1920s, the high point of the New Negro Movement. Their participation in progressive artistic communities fostered their evolving sense of modern womanhood and inspired them to challenge traditional conceptions of black identity and African American femininity. Whereas the early years of the twentieth century found Washington and Du Bois focusing primarily on issues related to black education and labor, the jazz age celebrated a renewed interest in an African American culture defined by black music, folk art, and primitivism. Black women, drawing on these rich wells of artistry, actively contributed to molding novel definitions of blackness.

To do so, they signify on the trope of the Picture Book in a strikingly different manner than their predecessors. They, too, focus on visualizations of black experience as the foundation of their sophisticated understanding of American society, but Renaissance women narrow the scope of the sights they feature in their poems and stories. These writers consistently portray

81

encounters defined by economies of visual art. This attention to art pieces reveals their awareness of the long literary practice of defining women as if they are objects of art. By presenting black women poet speakers and fictional protagonists as creators of plastic art – or as individuals possessing a savvy understanding of art objects – New Negro women invert the expected power dynamic of the gaze. And although they are generally less concerned with invoking traditional museum settings, they recognize the power of crafting literary moments around interactions with visual art. They return to earlier notions of the Picture Book trope by connecting interpretations of plastic art to an educational experience even as they advance the discussion of black vision, anticipating the museum focus of the second section of my study. These Renaissance women dramatize the ways African Americans learn from objects of art as they simultaneously teach others to reevaluate the tendency to objectify black citizens, and African American women in particular.

Their increased emphasis on visual art also acknowledges the dominant role of photography which continued to furnish the U.S. popular imagination with new pictures of modern black identity. But for many African American women writers, the time-honored arts of painting and sculpting offered intriguing possibilities for exploring what Larsen identifies as the "peculiar" nature of New Negro vision. Thus, amid the excitement of an artistic movement dedicated to discovering fresh, authentic modes of visualizing blackness, writers discovered what Alain Locke described as "new artistic idioms" rooted in the "plastic and pictorial arts."[3] Poets Anne Spencer, Angelina Grimké, and Gwendolyn Bennett together with fiction writers Nella Larsen, Maude Irwin Owens, and Jessie Fauset incorporate innovative engagements with plastic art objects into their literary works. This creative technique reveals a little discussed practice that shapes their portrayal of black humanity. They appeal to conventional forms of visual art to contest established narratives of black identity. Thus, these women corroborate Du Bois's declaration that black Americans "can see America in a way that white Americans cannot," and they commit their writing to correcting this visual disparity. In fact, the "panorama" Larsen references in the opening epigraph focuses on the highly visual nature of Harlem Renaissance existence and the fulfillment one gains from possessing the wherewithal to appreciate its complexity.

To aid such comprehension, New Negro women craft scenes of instruction conspicuously dependent on visual art. The repeated insertion of paintings and sculptures into their poems and stories – or references to these art forms – links their approach to classical discussions of visual and verbal art and attests to the sophistication of the vision they exhibit. The two sections in this chapter divide according to genre and highlight the ways writers depend on poetry and fiction to instruct dynamic appraisals of plastic art that reveal the intricacy of African American vision and specifically underscore the gendered nature of visuality during the Harlem Renaissance. Along the way, my readings uncover how these women's evolving cultural vision impacts the individual as well as the black community.

In this final chapter of Part I, the writers I analyze anticipate the hurdles later black artists encounter as a result of their more meaningful integration into modern U.S. society. Contrary to black writers of the eighteenth, nineteenth, and early twentieth centuries who confidently announce the superior nature of their moral, political, and philosophical vision, women publishing during the Harlem Renaissance repeatedly depict the difficulty surrounding the maintenance of an independent point of view capable of achieving self-understanding. Although a few poets continue to embody the role of the knowledgeable instructor, most of the works considered in this chapter foreground characters and speakers who lack self-confidence and demonstrate errors in judgment that testify to their increasingly modern identity. By revealing the tenuous grip African Americans maintain on visual clarity, New Negro women uncover a more complicated American racial landscape.

As female writers turned to literature to explore their complicated vision of black womanhood, they enjoyed recognition at the literary dinners hosted by *Opportunity* and the *Crisis*. In fact, the *Opportunity* awards dinner credited with initiating the Harlem Renaissance was ostensibly organized to celebrate the publication of Jessie Fauset's novel, *There is Confusion* (1924). Only when Alain Locke, in the role of master of ceremonies, turned the event into an occasion to articulate his vision of what he termed the "New Negro," did he claim the mantle of philosophical leader of the burgeoning movement. The *Survey Graphic* issue Locke guest-edited soon after the dinner established the major tenets of what came to be called the Harlem Renaissance, and his anthology, *The New Negro* (1925), solidified his ideas. Although Locke included many pieces by female writers, he stopped short of promoting them in revolutionary roles. His conservative portrayals of black women, however, failed to convince the writers I study to cede the stage to the male poets he preferred. Instead, these women boldly showcase a creative identity that anticipates the modern sensibility that emerges more fully in the years following the Harlem Renaissance proper.

The period claimed many new beginnings. Although African American women such as Frances Ellen Watkins Harper and Pauline Hopkins published poetry during the late nineteenth and early years of the twentieth century, the era known as the nadir, the Harlem Renaissance is the first literary period that prominently featured verse by numerous black women. Poetry reigned as the genre of choice during the New Negro Movement, and its position as a high art qualified its practitioners to claim an artistic sophistication not always afforded authors of fiction and drama. Locke, who kept a keen eye trained on the wider world of art, did not miss the seminal position poetry occupied in high modernism or the impact African visual art wielded on European modernists.[4] His efforts to gain greater respect for black art, combined with the growing numbers of African American visual artists contributing to the explosion of illustrated journals, books, and art exhibits, make it easy to understand why women poets of the Renaissance experimented with visual art in their verse. Women publishing novels and stories similarly sought to join the established tradition of referring to plastic art objects in verbal art. Turning to the world of visual aesthetics allowed them to demonstrate the ambition of their work as they acknowledge their radically different visual landscape. If the long period from the 1770s through the turn of the nineteenth century distinguished itself as an era of epic expansion in the world of U.S. painting, advertising, and photography, the short span between 1919 and 1939 emerges as a moment when visual technologies reached new heights and became so ingrained in U.S. society that their impact becomes difficult to measure.

The Ekphrastic Turn

The writers I analyze use their poems to ponder statues, tapestries, still-lifes, and iconic paintings in varied fashion to facilitate their reclamation of the power of ekphrasis. Translated, the Greek term "ekphrasis" means "to speak out," and scholars define it most simply as "that special quality of giving voice and language to a mute art object"[5] or "the poem that addresses a work of art."[6] The most familiar examples include Homer's description of Achilles's shield and the poet speaker's meticulous meditation in Keats's "Ode on a Grecian Urn" (1819). As these works suggest, contemplating an objet d'art requires an extended pause within verse, and this interruption facilitates probing ideas more deeply. The still moment also connects the poet speaker to another artistic form, and thereby launches the project into conversation with other creative ideas. Harlem Renaissance women's active introduction of their verse into contemporary conversations related to art and politics demonstrates their sense of what Elizabeth Loizeaux stresses as the "inherently dialogic" character of ekphrasis: "Ekphrasis is a mode of poetry that, by its very nature, opens out of lyric subjectivity into a social world."[7] An examination of Harlem Renaissance women's poetry published in the 1920s suggests that they employ ekphrasis to participate in sociopolitical debates and to combat conventional images of black humanity permeating American popular culture and restrictively framing their notions of identity. I am particularly interested in their alternating focus on two themes: the incompetent vision of readers who lack racial sympathy or sophisticated powers of interpretation and the anxiety of black female speakers who seek an independent artistic vision. The pieces of plastic art they introduce, or metaphorically create, provide opportunities to access the central dilemma of their poems.

Although these writers generally eschew penning traditional ekphrastic poems like later African American poets ranging from Robert Hayden and Clarence Major to Rita Dove and Natasha Trethewey, New Negro women of the 1920s exploit the gendered tension ekphrasis foregrounds. Their work braids together components from a few core theorizations that reflect a heightened sensitivity to the power of ekphrasis. Their attention to plastic art recalls Murray Krieger's important "*Laokoön* Revisited" which focuses on the impact of writers' introduction of ekphrasis to use an art "object as a symbol of the frozen, stilled world of plastic relationships which must be superimposed on literature's turning world to 'still' it."[8] Other works evoke Wendy Steiner's emphasis on the project of "stilling" literature to emphasize the ways ekphrasis forces readers to ponder the climactic moment in a text, whereas some poets adopt W. J. T. Mitchell's claim that ekphrasis represents a battle for dominance between the image and the word, a duel between male and female gazes. Then again, poets hone in on what Francoise Meltzer terms the ekphrastic "textual portrait," the portrait that never fully allows itself to be "swallowed by the text that invents it." Its insistent autonomy retains and expresses special meaning and thereby "makes knowledge … possible."[9] In this process, they often appeal to paintings in a manner that Hollander describes as "notional ecphrasis," or the representation of an imaginary work of art.[10]

Relying on the language of visual art provided many writers with a means for remaining within the parameters of proper ladylike behavior as they proffered alternative images of black femininity. Most of the women examined in this chapter were extremely well-educated and familiar with the theorization, or at the very least, the history of visual art. For example, before becoming an art instructor at Howard University, Bennett attended Columbia University where she studied fine arts. She graduated from the Pratt Institute and later studied art in Paris.[11] Fauset received her bachelor's from Cornell University, her master's from the University of Pennsylvania, and a certificate from the Sorbonne. She was also the first black woman to be elected to Phi Beta Kappa. Grimké attended the Boston Normal School of Gymnastics, now Wellesley College, and completed summer courses in English at Harvard. With this level of academic finish, it is not surprising that these women incorporate visual representations in their literary work to drape their often polemical contemplations of race and gender in palatable terms.

They also distinguish themselves as one of the earliest groups to confront stereotypes of black identity created by and promulgated by African American power brokers. Thus, although they continue to focus principally on dismantling stereotypes bolstered by white misconceptions, these writers simultaneously challenged definitions of black womanhood propagated by black artists, critics, and leaders. These female poets visualize the creative literary process to picture the black female artist at the center of the New Negro movement, and their turn to ekphrasis seeks to reify racism and sexism, transforming these practices from abstract beliefs into sentiments forthrightly contemplated. Anne Spencer, Angelina Grimké, and Gwendolyn Bennett convert poems about the contemplation of objects of art into opportunities for showcasing black women's innovative conception of black artistry and their readiness to address racial relations. Just as Phillis Wheatley exploits visual art aesthetics to insist on the possibility of black artistry built on moral authority, African American women of the Harlem Renaissance turn to visual art to present a vision that refuses to be circumscribed by social restrictions based on race and gender.

Anne Spencer's Polemical Art Objects

Anne Spencer often situates her poet speakers at the center of difficult political discussions. By penning aggressive calls for reappraisals of African American identity regardless of gender, Spencer uses her verse to compel readers to gaze upon visual objects that give rise to discussions of racism. As an older writer during the Harlem Renaissance, she reveled in her creative daring and deemed it a natural impulse for black women. She declared: "I proudly love being a Negro woman – it's so involved and interesting. *We* are the PROBLEM – the great national game of TABOO."[12] Her bold proclamation of self-pride and confidence highlights her audacious attitude toward her art. Although she lived in Lynchburg, Virginia during the entirety of the Harlem Renaissance, she remained closely connected to writers at the center of the movement and regularly hosted the most famous African American writers publishing at the time.[13] Spencer loved excitement and dedicated many of her letters to encouraging friends to visit her Lynchburg home. Writing to Grace and James Weldon Johnson, she asks: "Can't you plan to stay a few days longer this time? I am weaker than usual, bad case of normality. You are just the transfusion we both need."[14]

But she was quick to shift from joking to addressing serious issues of the day, aiming her sharp tongue and quick wit at political issues. Her letters to Johnson passionately declare her regard for Eleanor Roosevelt whom she professes to "adore," while she keenly upbraids the likes of "the rabid Senator Glass" who "is foaming at his chops" over racial issues. And although she acknowledges the challenges African Americans face as they attempt to withstand the furor of racist scientists and elected officials, she bemoans the ineffective nature of race politics:

> Then, too, kindly tell me why a graceful sentimentalist was elected to joust with such a disgraceful one as Stoddard. Alain as speaks on Oct. "Forum" pages is illogically inane – a kitten rolling catnip during an earthquake. Where were you? Or Pickens, or Kelly, or the merciless, trenchant W.E.B.D.? We Negroes down here are further damned if our champions turn so placidly to Hoyle and the dictionary for rulings on matters of sheer inhumanity.[15]

Never one to mince words, Spencer actively fought for equal rights and criticized ineffectual defenses of racial equality. She approached her poetry as a crucial opportunity to add her voice to the political discussions of the day.

Even so, she often depended on what might be deemed traditional ladylike qualities to press her case as she encouraged women to trumpet their political views and voices unflinchingly. Evie Shockley astutely notes that notwithstanding critical assessments labeling Spencer a poet who aped white writing and avoided political issues, Spencer was both personally and professionally politically active.[16] In many instances, her poetry translates gardening into an occasion for examining racial inequities, sexual passion, poetic accomplishment, and a host of other themes not customarily branded proper feminine topics. In her capable hands, the act of observing a piece of visual art, similarly regarded as a passive, uncontroversial endeavor, becomes an activity wrought with tension. Through ekphrasis and examinations of the practice of viewing, Spencer enlists visual art in her fight for social justice. She accepts the role of instructor and depends heavily on visual art to train her readers to reevaluate their notions of race.

In "The Sévignés," a poem not published during Spencer's lifetime, she demonstrates her wariness of the power that plastic art objects wield in promulgating definitions of African American character. Spencer converts a well-known tourist attraction into a site of instruction as she charges white women with exhibiting an indifference to racism paralleling that of white men, a disposition often revealed by their uncritical acceptance of racially derogatory art objects. Following the erection of what became popularly known as "The Good Darky" statue in Natchitoches, Louisiana in 1927 (see Figure 3.1), Spencer read an article in *National Geographic Magazine* titled "Louisiana, Land of Perpetual Romance" that featured a picture of the statue. Spencer penned the poem to connect the twentieth-century racism in America with the seventeenth-century aristocrat Marquise de Sevigne whose letters revealed a shocking insensitivity to the plight of poor French peasants. Specifically, she draws attention to the danger of uncritical observation. The poet speaker, revealing the irony of the situation, assumes a posture of irate condescension:

> Down in Natchitoches there is a statue in a public square
> A slave replica – not of Uncle Tom, praise God,
> But of Uncle Remus … a big plinth holding a little
>   man bowing humbly to a master-mistress
> This shameless thing set up to the intricate involvement
>   of human slavery.
> Go, see it, read it, with whatever heart you have left.
> No penance, callous beyond belief.
> For these women who had so lately fled from the
>   slavery of Europe to the great wilds of America.[17]

After her sarcastic relief over the subject of the statue, the speaker describes the piece, contrasting its stereotypical appearance – "a little / man bowing humbly" – to the "intricate" nature of American slavery. Spencer dubs the statue "Uncle Remus," stressing the imaginary nature of white America's view of the history of slavery and their desire to concretize the narrative of the happy darky for posterity. The speaker suggests the real awfulness of the American slavery legacy is the failure to acknowledge and understand its horror. Books like *Uncle Tom's Cabin*, ostensibly written in support of abolition, reinforce derogatory stereotypes of black Americans as a result of insufficiently critical readers. Spencer's poet speaker adopts an authoritative tone in the final lines as she orders readers to "Go, see it, read it"

Figure 3.1 Hans Schüler, Sr., *Uncle Jack* (1926). Louisiana State University Rural Life Museum. Courtesy of LSU Trademark Licensing.

and to contemplate the U.S. mindset that has "[n]o penance." The spondees that open these two end-stopped lines underscore the instructional posture the speaker adopts.

J. Lee Greene reports that Spencer drew a distinction between Uncle Remus and Uncle Tom, for she believed that "the twentieth century's connotations of the term *Uncle Tom* had done an injustice to Harriet Beecher Stowe's intentions":

> Every group has been able to survive a lot of epithets, name-calling, and so on but I think Uncle Tom is ... invariably applied by an ignorant nonreader. For instance, in Eleanor Wilson [Randolph] McAdoo's book, *The Priceless Gift* – possibly [Woodrow] Wilson's daughter – she tells of her father saying when she was a kid returning from a visit to the South that she came back "talking like an educated nigger." If her accent had been that of Dear Darky, I'm sure it would have delighted Woodrow Wilson ... Dear Darky and Uncle Remus were slave falsities.[18]

Spencer enjoined African Americans to form their own opinions about race and she was offended by art that propagated false notions of black humanity. By charging readers to "see it, read it," her poet speaker not only emphasizes the intertwined nature of verbal and visual art but encourages observers to generate an independent, informed narrative for the silent statue. In place of a conventional ekphrastic rendering – she assumes readers' familiarity with the statue – Spencer redirects our gaze to the minds of those who countenance such racist symbols. Visual pieces such as the one in Natchitoches demand active interpretation in the same way that novels such as Stowe's need analytical engagement. By taking these issues up in her poem, Spencer cleverly instructs readers on how to approach her poetry and showcases her own sophisticated participation in race politics.

In fact, she strode into an explosive conversation that raged around this statue into the twenty-first century. Originally commissioned by Jackson Lee Bryan, a planter and banker in Natchitoches, the statue was commissioned in 1926 as an acknowledgement of African Americans' contribution to Louisiana's economy. The original plaque affixed to it read: "Erected by the city of Natchitoches in grateful recognition of the arduous and faithful services of the good darkies of Louisiana." It became popularly known as the "Good Darky Statue" after a *National Geographic* article turned it into a landmark that tourists posed with for photographs.[19] By using her poetry to enter the fray, Spencer demonstrates her belief that her verse rightfully belonged in the midst of heated national debates around race.

Some seventy years later, the poet Maya Angelou expressed similar indignation over the statue. After seeking out *Uncle Jack* at Louisiana State University's Rural Life Museum, Angelou compares sculptor Hans Schuller's success with Michelangelo's *David*, noting that Schuller created "the quintessential obsequious Negro servant."[20] She admits, "[V]iewing

the statue of Uncle Jack had wrought a great depression in my spirit"
... for the "sculptor of Uncle Jack had employed the slavocracy's wishful
romance that cast all blacks as congenitally subservient and only too happy
to devote their lives to looking after their white folks."[21] She concludes
her essay by acknowledging the power of the folk museum that unwit-
tingly promotes "the romance of slavery" for its 30,000 annual visitors
while refusing to uncover "our historical truth."[22] Like Spencer, Angelou
recognizes the danger of those who lack the visual acuity and courage to
discover the facts hidden behind obfuscatory objects of art.

"Grapes: Still-Life" (1929) extends Spencer's reliance on ekphrasis to
broach discussions of racism. Greene points out that Spencer draws on
her gardening expertise for the detailed horticultural information about
grapes, thereby adapting her lady-like, apolitical hobby into a vehicle for
engaging the thorny issue of racial bigotry.[23] The poet speaker seems to
gaze upon a still-life painting, but she turns her contemplation into an
occasion for introducing an unexpected discussion of the ridiculous nature
of racism. The speaker, clearly a perceptive viewer of visual art, offers an
incisive reading of the sill life:

> Snugly you rest, sweet globes,
> Aged essence of the sun;
> Copper of the platter
> Like that you lie upon.
>
> Is so well your heritage
> You need feel no change
> From the ringlet of your stem
> To this bright rim's flange;
>
> You, green-white Niagara,
> Cool dull Nordic of your kind, –
> Does your thick meat flinch
> From these ... touch and press your rind?
>
> Caco, there, so close to you,
> Is the beauty of the vine;
> Stamen red and pistil black
> Thru the curving line;
>
> Concord, the too peaceful one,
> Purpling at your side,
> All the colors of his flask
> Holding high in pride...

> This, too, is your heritage,
> You who force the plight;
> Blood and bone you turn to them
> For their root is white.[24]

After presenting the overall painting composition in stanza one, the speaker reflects on the meaning of the static quality of the painting, wondering: "Is so well your heritage / You need feel no change." Her note that the grapes remain held in place by the "bright rim's flange" playfully comments on the double framing by both the copper platter and the painting frame, two rims that hold the pictured grapes in place. She proposes that the grapes' imperviousness to time derives not from these concrete objects; instead, their endurance stems from a knowledge of a rich past, their "heritage." The speaker's lighting upon this idea prompts her individual meditations on the different grape varieties depicted, and she devotes equal energy to crafting verse evoking their appearance as well as the sensibility she associates with each variety.

Separating the grapes from their intermingled cluster, the speaker addresses the Niagara grapes, positioning her remarks for the remainder of the poem in relation to them. In asking whether their "thick meat flinch[es]" from its forced intimacy with the colored grapes and describing the Niagara grapes as "green-white" and "cool dull Nordic," she distinguishes them as unimpressively Caucasian. Spencer's letters confirm the clear connection she intended to draw between the grapes and white racists. Writing to the Johnsons about World War I, she ironically avers: "I favor the wars to <u>come</u> – all Nordics and niggers will then be dead except the <u>good weak</u> ones. ... Nothing wrong about Black except <u>his</u> was not a crime of passion – say like Hitler – hating especial people because he hates <u>people</u>."[25] Turning a satirical eye on the racist science saturating the U.S. and international community, Spencer suggests that if weakness distinguishes a black sensibility from that of Hitler, African Americans can be proud of their lack. Conversely, the green grapes share a strange similarity with such illogical prejudice.

Thus, the red Caco, "the beauty of the vine," and the Concord described as "too peaceful" yet full of "pride," emerge as admirable. These colorful grapes are beautiful and proud of their past without resorting to inane bigotry. In the last stanza, she returns her full attention to the Niagaras, insisting that their investment in addressing the "plight" of existing in close proximity to grapes of other colors does not alter the fact that they share the same "heritage." In the final lines, the speaker contends that the red and purple grapes also have white roots suggesting the common humanity that makes racial bigotry ridiculous. The polemical interpretation of the painting accentuates the penetrating vision of the assumedly black poet speaker and defies what one anticipates from viewing a still life, a genre not associated with forceful social commentary. In fact, the esteemed Sir Joshua Reynolds declared the feminine, mentally weak nature of still-life painting in his *Discourses on Art*. Lord Shaftesbury went further, discouraging men from even engaging such paintings: "So that whilst we look on paintings with the same eyes as we view commonly the ... silks worn by our Ladys, and admired in Dress, Equipage or Furniture, we must of necessity be *effeminate* in our Taste." Explaining Shaftesbury's claim, critic Norman Bryson concludes: "For the male to be drawn away from abstraction towards the mode of female vision is for him to desert his sex: even to *look* at still life, which entails a descent into the particularity of things, is to put manhood at risk."[26] Nevertheless, the viewer of the still life in Spencer's poem transforms her observation into a politically charged discourse that is anything but effeminate.

Spencer's genre choice also reflects the gendered politics of painting during the Harlem Renaissance and early-twentieth-century America more generally. As Kirsten Swinth explains, women were long associated with "still-life and flower paintings" and even after they began participating in the "figure aesthetic," they remained largely excluded from the masculine-dominated area of landscape art and closely aligned with portraiture.[27] Spencer was almost certainly aware of this association and revels in transforming a feminine still life into a canvas for denunciating racial bigotry. Her verse spotlights the educational power inherent in plastic art if viewers are willing to engage visual objects with discerning eyes.

Angelina Grimké and the Erotic Gaze of Ambition

Angelina Grimké, best known for her play *Rachel* (1916) which condemns bringing black babies into a racist world and depends extensively on iconic paintings to dramatize the protagonist's emotional state, turns to ekphrasis to explore African American feminine sexuality. She signifies on the trope of the Picture Book as she demonstrates the educational possibilities – for both viewer and artist – embedded in the interpretation of visual art. Her poem "A Mona Lisa" (1927) empowers an erotic gaze as the speaker passionately considers her desire for lasting poetic achievement. If Spencer declares that African American women legitimately belonged in the heart of political conversations, Grimké adds a claim for the significance of their creative agency and sexual identity. She relies on visual art to broach difficult topics related to black woman's sexual exploration. In the process, she links the act of challenging traditional notions of feminine sexuality to the feat of contesting notions of artistic beauty and accomplishment. Her verse presents the act of a woman gazing passionately and desirously upon a painted woman as both dangerous and exhilarating:

> *1.*
> I should like to creep
> Through the long brown grasses
>   That are your lashes;
> I should like to poise
>   On the very brink
> Of the leaf-brown pools
>   That are your shadowed eyes;
> I should like to cleave
>   Without sound,
> Their glimmering waters;
>   Their unrippled waters;
> I should like to sink down
>   And down
>   And down...
>   And deeply drown.
>
> *2.*
> Would I be more than a bubble breaking?
>   Or an ever-widening circle
>   Ceasing at the marge?
> Would my white bones
>   Be the only white bones
> Wavering back and forth, back and forth
>   In their depths?[28]

By titling the poem "A Mona Lisa," Grimké signals her investment in ekphrasis and suggests that the poet speaker views a painted woman as entrancing as Leonardo da Vinci's High Renaissance masterpiece. The repeated references to the woman's "brown" features underscore her dark appearance and hint that her racial identity shares much in common with her natural surroundings. The "brown grasses" and "pools" also subtly recall the unexpected craggy background of Leonardo's smiling Lisa. But rather than belabor this comparison, the speaker focuses on the painted woman's eyes, likening them to bodies of water. She describes them as "leaf-brown pools," "glimmering waters," and "unrippled waters." Here, the natural imagery assumes an erotic inflection as the speaker hints at her attraction to the woman's unspoiled beauty. As she celebrates the shimmering magnificence of the pictured woman's eyes, even poising "On the very brink" of their allure, her throbbing desire to violate their painted calm overwhelms, emphasized by repetition: "I should like to creep," "I should like to poise," "I should like to cleave," "I should like to sink down." Her yearning to "sink down / And down / And down ... / And deeply drown" anticipates the ecstasy of sexual fulfillment together with Grimké's characteristic contemplation of death.

Interestingly, Grimké echoes the sixth stanza of Du Bois' poem, "The Burden of Black Women" (1914) which reads: "Down with their cheating of childhood, / And drunken orgies of war – / down / down / deep down, / Till the Devil's strength be shorn. / Till some dim, darker Davad a hoeing of his corn, / And married maiden, Mother of God, / Bid the Black Christ be born!"[29] In place of Du Bois's condemnation of white male exploitation and anticipation of black women's spiritual retribution, Grimké's speaker ponders the difficulty of giving oneself completely in a sexual union while maintaining an autonomous existence. She chooses to disregard the common tendency to infuse discussions of black female progress with a redemptive consideration of their potential Madonna status.

Instead, stanza two continues the speaker's musing over the challenge of retaining her individuality in the eyes of the painted woman while acknowledging the possibility of becoming entrapped by the painting itself. The speaker speculates over whether she will be remembered as more than a good orgasm – "Would I be more than a bubble breaking?" – but quickly conflates her sexual insecurity with her uncertainty regarding her creative legacy. Her question of being "the only white bones" foregrounds her concern with longevity as both a lover and artist. The orgasmic language doubly resonates with the rhetoric of ecstatic creative completion and anxiety related to the institution of an artistic legacy. This tension is heightened by the suggestion of lesbian attraction. Grimké makes no effort to suggest the poet speaker is male, and her own letters and diary entries document her attraction to women. As a girl writing to a friend with whom she apparently experienced an intimate relationship, Grimké gushes: "Oh Mamie if you only knew how my heart beats when I think of you and it yearns and pants to gaze, if only for one second upon your lovely face." She also asks her friend to be her "wife."[30] Like the gazing speaker of her poem, the young Grimké invests the act of gazing upon a woman's face with erotic intensity. It is worth noting that Grimké resolves never to bare children after a disastrous lesbian affair. Considering her biography, the poet speaker's rumination over the danger of sexual commitment assumes added significance, and the extended contemplation of artistic accomplishment ponders the consequences for women who refuse traditional molds.

Thus, where Du Bois anticipates a black Madonna to rescue African Americans from a history of abuse and sorrow, Grimké endows artistic creativity and sexual passion with the messianic potential of claiming a space in the annals of great art for the black female writer. The ekphrastic enterprise the first stanza takes up displays the speaker's attempt to employ words to vie with Leonardo's masterpiece, a work of art that transformed painting convention. Grimké's decision to invoke *The Mona Lisa* also recalls Walter Pater's famous recreation of *The Mona Lisa* in *The Renaissance* (1873/1893). Rather than offer a traditional interpretation of the famous portrait, Pater treats it as representative of the Renaissance spirit itself and as such, a worthy symbol of the kind of aestheticism he advocates re-embracing. In Pater's poetic prose, Leonardo's mysteriously smiling woman becomes a repository for his discussion of aesthetic values. In much the same way that Pater's paragraph presents Leonardo's painting as the best representative of High Renaissance ideas, Grimké's poem offers a daring picture of Harlem Renaissance identity. Her celebration of feminine artistic ambition and sexual desire overwrites Locke's notion of the predominantly male Harlem Renaissance artist. In its place, she offers a vision of African American creativity that radically reimagines the character of the female poet.

Gwendolyn Bennett's Discerning Paintbrush

Whereas Spencer and Grimké engage *objets d'art* to contest readers' notions of race and sexuality, Gwendolyn Bennett understood the instructional possibilities associated with visual art in a more fundamental way. Working as an instructor of fine arts at Howard University armed her with direct knowledge of the pedagogical power inherent in creating and viewing plastic art. Her position as a visual artist who published her illustrations in the most popular magazines of the era kept Bennett attuned to the connections between her verse and visual work. She, too, confronts Locke's aesthetic prescriptions in her poetry as she ponders the development of a particularly feminine creative method. Bennett portrays the process of writing a poem as similar to the creation of a visual object, and she uses this comparison to examine the particular challenges facing black women with literary ambitions. But like her peers, she relies on the trope of the Picture Book to emphasize her trenchant visual reading as a necessary skill to preserve her artistic confidence.

In "Advice" (1927), Bennett reflects on her creative odyssey, recalling the challenge of negotiating the expectations of Harlem Renaissance leaders. The work of the female poet is conflated with that of a metaphorical weaver, thereby signaling the need for African American writers to produce work that feels culturally relevant:

> You were a sophist,
> Pale and quite remote,
> As you bade me
> Write poems –
> Brown poems
> Of dark words
> And prehistoric rhythms...
> Your pallor stifled my poesy
> But I remembered a tapestry
> That I would some day weave
> Of dim purples and fine reds
> And blues
> Like night and death –
> The keen precision of your words
> Wove a silver thread
> Through the dusk softness
> Of my dream-stuff...[31]

She almost definitely refers to Alain Locke with her references to a "sophist" who is "pale" with a "stifling pallor," and her poem recreates the challenge of discovering her unique voice.[32] Like Grimké, Bennett elects not to craft a traditionally ekphrastic poem. But the material object at the center of her verse draws on the core principle of ekphrasis. Her poet speaker acknowledges Locke's encouragement to produce verbal objects in color, works so authentically invested in African American experience that they emerge as "[b]rown" and "dark." But she wonders how to achieve this feat under the shadow of Locke's aesthetic notions. She finds inspiration in a womanly folk art, comparing her future poems to "a tapestry" woven of colors indicative of a blackness not necessarily condoned by power brokers who warned against favoring bright colors they deemed uncultured.[33] Locke's advice is subsumed by the poet speaker's aestheticism, a philosophy unafraid of depending on traditionally feminine art forms that boast a substantive, fungible quality. Even the "dusk softness" of the poet speaker's "dream-stuff" recalls her womanliness and authentic feelings of black pride, traits that are enhanced by Locke's erudition without compromising the poet's core creative vision. The tapestry results from her discovery of an independent vision of her artistry, and it is both a past creation she remembers as evidence of her previous success with material art and the inspiration for her to believe in her future success as a poet.

But it is "Quatrains" (1927) that allows Bennett to acquire a firmer sense of what she hopes to achieve in her poetry by relating it to her visual art and its limitations:

> 1.
> Brushes and paints are all I have
> To speak the music in my soul –
> While silently there laughs at me
> A copper jar beside a pale green bowl.
> 2.
> How strange that grass should sing –
> Grass is so still a thing...
> And strange the swift surprise of snow –
> So soft it falls and slow.[34]

In the first quatrain, the poet speaker implicitly compares her creative writing to her painting and wonders about the efficacy of "[b]rushes and paints" as instruments to voice her innermost feelings. She admits feeling mocked by the inadequacy of both her tools and the object she creates. Playing on the impossibility of visual art to "speak ... music," she feels the "copper jar beside a pale green bowl" taunting her with laughter that refuses to acknowledge the individual complexity of her "soul."

The second quatrain, however, suggests that keen visual interpretations of great art potentially overcome perceived limitations of the plastic form. The end-stopped lines, repetition of the "s" in the final word of each line ending with a dash – "soul," "sing," "snow" – together with the preponderant alliteration throughout the second stanza achieves a kind of hush that adds to the sense of quiet Bennett creates through her contemplation of inanimate objects. Yet the speaker discovers the wonder of a painting so masterfully executed as to give voice to "grass." The added "surprise of snow" in motion reveals that the speaker's appreciation of the visual scene conquers the static nature of the painting, thus inspiring the poet that she might pen poems achieving similar feats. The very lyricism of her rendition of the painting attests to the power of the poet speaker's success in transposing her creative vision to her verse, her poetry vouching for her artistic talent. Bennett undermines the premise that still-life paintings lack the agency to make radical statements, and thereby insists on recognizing the potency possible in black women's verse.

Transfiguring Portraits

As Harlem Renaissance women poets offer subtle refutations of Locke's definitions of black artistry, they gesture toward unconventional pictures of the quintessential New Negro female artist. Their reliance on ekphrasis allows them to "speak out" and declare black women's sociopolitical relevance, but the forms their challenges take run the gamut. From Spencer's rejection of the myth of black servility, to Grimké's embrace of lesbian attraction, to Bennett's insistence on black women's creative agency, New Negro women entrust their verse with the responsibility of amending visions of black humanity. In contrast, a number of black women publishing prose works set their sights on a single target as they strive to revise the widely sanctioned portrait of African American womanhood. Authors such as Larsen, Owens, and Fauset take aim at the iconic image of the Madonna.

A peek at Alain Locke's *The New Negro* (1925) suggests why. Locke opens his compendium with a frontispiece of conservative black womanhood in the form of Winold Reiss's *The Brown Madonna* (see Figure 3.2). His choice of this visual work dramatically explains the impetus driving New Negro women to exploit visual art to challenge conventional visualizations of black womanhood in their fiction. Notwithstanding her bobbed hair, Reiss's Madonna defines black women by their maternity and spirituality. Her subdued expression, nondescript blue dress reminiscent of the della robbia blue favored by High Renaissance artists, and downcast eyes offer little in the way of imagining black women as revolutionary artists. Instead, *The Brown Madonna* inserts black women into the long, patriarchal legacy that views women through a traditional rather than radical lens of possibility. African American women writing during the 1920s rely on the trope of the Picture Book to introduce a competing vision of black female productivity and significance.

To be fair, the leading voices of the Harlem Renaissance regarded their pictorial portrayal of black women as the idealized virgin mother a revolutionary move. Like Reiss's well-known picture, the cover of Du Bois's 1924 Children's Number of the *Crisis* updated the black motherhood ideal with an illustration titled "Blowing Bubbles." Anne Stavney notes that Louise Latimer's illustration takes an extra step to proclaim the childlike innocence of black motherhood. By encasing photographs of actual babies inside the bubbles, which the pictured young girl gazes upon, Latimer portrays her enraptured in a childlike dream that symbolizes "undefiled, nonsexual mother love."[35] Notwithstanding the positive intentions behind

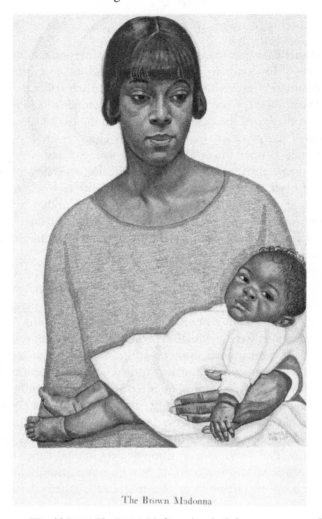

The Brown Madonna

Figure 3.2 Winold Reiss, *The Brown Madonna* (1925). Color transparency, 4"x5".
Courtesy of Fisk University Galleries, Nashville, Tennessee.

such images, the incessant piling on to the Madonna motif threatened to restrict black women to the role of spiritual nurturer rather than artistic contributor as the exciting new era of black artistic production took root. African American women's power of production remained closely circumscribed by gender: the Madonna image celebrates creation divorced from sexuality and agency. Divine intervention is indeed clean.

Black Madonna images offered a strong antidote to less complimentary depictions of black womanhood promulgated since slavery. Although American artists generally avoided depicting the black female nude in work predating the twentieth century, the practice of associating black women with heightened sexuality enjoys a long history in Western painting.[36] Despite this absence in U.S. art, black women continued to represent "exotica and erotica," a legacy established by well-known European paintings like Edouard Manet's *Olympia* (1865) which cast the black maid as both "Jezebel and Mammy, the embodiment of both sexuality and servitude."[37] With analogous portrayals of African American women teeming from world fairs to pancake boxes, the U.S. consigned black women to rigid categories in the American popular imagination. By the early years of the twentieth century, they were firmly codified into three major groups. Scholars alternately describe these types as the Jezebel or erotic primitive, the Mammy or neutered female, and the Madonna or noble black woman.

The Harlem Renaissance was both an heir to and participant in this visual legacy, but the emergence of numerous black artists led to a radical expansion of visual depictions of African American womanhood during the New Negro era. Whereas Tanner stood virtually alone in the late nineteenth and early twentieth centuries, the 1920s welcomed several talented African American artists to the U.S. high art stage. Aaron Douglas, Archibald Motley, Jr., and Richmond Barthé represent just a few of the talented black men who enlisted the paintbrush and chisel to reinterpret black feminine identity. With female artists such as Gwendolyn Bennett and Joyce Carrington also contributing to the reconception of black womanhood, the emerging images portrayed a wide range of interpretations. Most significantly, African American visual artists of the Harlem Renaissance repeatedly vivify black women's ties to Africa and celebrate the strength they derive from this heritage. Spun during the 1920s, this common thread tapped into the fascination with primitivism that fueled the rise of Josephine Baker, the chorus girl turned movie star who took Europe by storm. Photographs of Baker sporting her iconic banana skirt celebrated Baker's embodiment of black woman's jungle sexuality, a stark contrast from the narrative associating black women with the Madonna ideal.

The dichotomy that emerged – associating African American womanhood with the pristine Madonna or sexually unfettered primitive – left many black women writers feeling boxed into untenable options, and they turned to their novels and stories to explore other alternatives. They craft literary scenes that replace or challenge traditional portraits of black womanhood with more progressive notions, thereby releasing African American ladies from the time-worn images ensnaring them. By focusing on their protagonist's failure or success at imagining, pursuing, and accepting complex visions of African American feminine identity, they argue for the necessity of expanding the definition of a respectable black woman. Their engagement of the Madonna theme almost always contests the simplicity associated with the artistic ideal.

Gwendolyn Bennett's visual depiction of a Madonna provides an instructive example. In a letter to Harold Jackman in January 1926, Bennett inquires as to whether he has seen the *Opportunity* "Christmas cover" she drew that was intended for the "December number" (see Figure 3.3). Jackman's response must have been critical, for when she wrote to him from Paris in February 1926, she responds by asking:

> [W]hy should my madonna (and you notice that I spell it with a small letter) be "spiritual," if I dont want her to be? Do you think that immaculate conceptions are such spiritual things as all that? About the swollen jaw I cant say much because I haven't a copy close at hand ... perhaps you are right, I dont know. I hadn't noticed the fact that my mother of Christ needed her teeth looked after. Now, please dont have "the church" on my trail.[38]

Bennett clearly intended to rescue her Mary from a tradition dedicated to celebrating her virginal, spiritual qualities.[39] Her irreverent refusal to capitalize the "m" of Madonna together with her lighthearted remark about the state of Mary's teeth display Bennett's desire to bring her rendition of the mother of Christ down to earth.

In fact, she personally held an uncertain view of motherhood. In an October 1925 letter to Jackman she wonders about the choices of two acquaintances: "Is that the way Llewellyn and Pearl are going to spend the rest of their existence – having children. But then, of course, bringing a Dumas into the world is a thing at which one must not scoff. May descend to that type of thing myself some of these days."[40] Bennett viewed motherhood as beneath artistic accomplishment, and her jesting words suggest that the only redemption for such an act is the possibility of giving birth to a future great artist. Echoing her lighthearted evaluation of her *Opportunity* cover illustration, Bennett's reference to her personal view of motherhood testifies to the uneasy relationship between African American women and the Madonna ideal.

But while artists like Bennett dispute conventional modes of discussing the Virgin Mary, members of the black woman's club movement worked

Figure 3.3 Gwendolyn Bennett, cover of *Opportunity* (January 1926). Courtesy of the Literary Representative for the Works of Gwendolyn B. Bennett, Schomburg Center for Research in Black Culture, New York Public Library, Astor, Lenox and Tilden Foundations.

to fortify African American women's association with the Madonna. These leaders passionately proclaimed the respectable status of modern black women, a status hinging on sexual propriety. Fannie Barrier Williams's work with Booker T. Washington in *A New Negro for a New Century* was trumpeted by a growing chorus of middle class women who extolled black women's devotion to self-improvement and advocated tackling issues related to moral standing through a class-focused lens. They proclaimed the purity and social morality of upper class black women and vowed to instruct the lower classes, implicitly pushing them toward the model mother ideal. For instance, Elise McDougald's essay "The Task of Negro Womanhood" published in *The New Negro* insists, "Sex irregularities are not a matter of race, but of socio-economic conditions."[41] She proceeds to assure readers that "the artist's imagination will find a more inspiring subject in the modern Negro mother – self-directed but as loyal and tender as the much extolled … mammy of slavery days."[42] Thus, McDougald blithely connects the New Negro mother to both the Madonna and mammy revealing a surprising comfort with either icon because both tap into images of moral motherhood.

How then, could middleclass black women writers break the confines of a rigidly imagined feminine sexuality? How could they escape conforming to socially defined expectations without appearing offensively militant? And how could they enlist their pens in the bid to declare black female artistic productivity as effective and important as visual campaigns focused on sexual purity? The answer lies in their turn to the trope of the Picture Book. These writers construct scenes organized around the act of painting portraits or insert characters into settings overflowing with visual art in a bid to reshape the conversation surrounding the creative and political agency of black women's vision. And more often than not, writers use their discussions of visual art objects to reflect back on the black female speaker at the center of their work who doubles as a traditionally silent piece of art. My readings dramatize black women's efforts to carve out a space for reimagining the stakes of their artistry and a complex vision of their modern condition.

New Negro women's aggressive dismantling of conservative visual images of black womanhood recalls earlier political statements by politically attuned women. In Thomas Otten's discussion of the material significance of paintings in Henry James's fiction, he devotes a chapter to contemplating "slashers," suffragists who attacked famous paintings to make a political statement that "uncovers the political nonrepresentation of women that results when women are reduced to embodying an aesthetic ideal."[43] Although African American women writing during the 1920s by no means took up meat choppers in the Metropolitan Museum or shared the radical politics of the suffragists, I want to suggest that they engage in some metaphorical "slashing" of their own. Time and time again, these writers methodically dismantle the Madonna ideal – which was materially multiplied around them in historic and contemporary paintings alike – to reveal the emptiness at the heart of cultural projects seeking to define black women in idyllic terms. African American women writers rely on visual art to defy gendered definitions that obscure the truth of their identity. In the same way that Otten claims that Henry James incorporates paintings into the pages of his fiction to draw our attention to "the social force of painting," I argue for the social stakes of black women's focus on the materiality of paintings that divorce them from the modern identity they strive to embrace.[44]

Untenable Frames in *Quicksand*

Nella Larsen's *Quicksand* (1928) presents Helga Crane as overwhelmed by both the primitive and Madonna stereotypes, extremes exacerbated by visual art portrayals of black women in these roles. Larsen's letter to Gertrude Stein, accompanying a copy of *Quicksand*, suggests that she saw similarities between her project and Stein's much discussed interest in adapting modern art perspectives to her literary presentation of women's complex interior worlds. Writing to Stein in 1928, Larsen confesses,

> I have often talked with our friend Carl Van Vechten about you. Particularly about you and Melanctha, which I have read many times. And always I get from it some new thing. A truly great story. I never cease to wonder how you came to write it and just why you and not some one of us should so accurately have caught the spirit of this race of mine.[45]

Stein claimed that she mentally composed *Three Lives* (1909) during her daily walks to Picasso's studio where she was sitting for her portrait. Picasso's finished portrait of Stein, her mask-like face anticipating his leap into cubism with *Les Demoiselles D'Avignon* (1907), foregrounds Stein's complex sexuality and agency, themes animating *Three Lives*. Although Larsen enjoyed no such illustrious portrait experience, she conspicuously establishes the complexity of her protagonist by emphasizing her failed vision amid a portrait-painting experience. She highlights Helga's inability to visualize modern black womanhood in terms that reject the extremes to which African American women were consigned.

The opening scene of *Quicksand* commences Larsen's contemplation of politically acceptable visualizations of the mixed race female body.[46] Her purposeful portrayal of Helga in portrait-like terms reminds readers of black women's routine objectification, a point scholars such as Pamela Barnett, Cherene Sherrard-Johnson, and Anne Hostetler similarly make. I want to move in a slightly different direction to stress Larsen's specific attention to Madonna and primitive images, icons Barnett insightfully engages but stops short of considering against the contemporary visual landscape. In a vivid contrast to Stein's personal impact on her painted image, Larsen provocatively relates Helga's erasure of strong emotions, her deliberate suppression of feelings that might destabilize the conservative portrait presented in the opening pages. As Helga sits "motionless" in "the room which held her," she notes that her reformer "zest was blotted out" and her "charming personality was smudged out."[47] Larsen's carefully selected painterly terms, "blotted" and "smudged," point to Helga's complicit acceptance – maybe even reinforcement – of her portrait-like status. Whereas Stein's strength of character forced Picasso to erase his realistic painting of her face only to replace it with a forceful mask, Helga alternately enacts and suffers erasures that suppress her individuality.

Helga's quest for peace remains tied to her struggle to visualize herself beyond the conventional options she imagines. In Harlem, she places the African American women she meets into the neat boxes that society prescribes. Anne Grey, who is described as "brownly beautiful" with "the face of a golden Madonna," vividly contrasts the sexually alluring Audrey Denney (*Q*, 47). Although Helga reflexively rejects Anne's hypocritical articulation of racial pride, she views Audrey's frankly seductive example as unacceptable. In the cabaret that pits Anne Grey's Madonna image against Audrey Denney's Josephine Baker persona, Larsen highlights the visual stakes of both icons with the modernist painterly terms she uses to describe Audrey. Her eyebrows are "black smears" on her "alabaster" form, a visualization of modern feminine assurance (*Q*, 62). She represents a bold departure from the High Renaissance depictions of the Madonna often pictured with her mother, St. Anne, a clear reference Larsen invokes through her naming and description of Anne Grey.

Helga's Copenhagen experiences magnify her failure to visualize additional options for defining her sexuality. Larsen appeals to the image of the mask, the primitive object that Picasso engages to vivify Stein's sexual assertiveness, to emphasize Helga's entrapment. Helga surrenders to the social framing that declares her an exotic "other," and her attempts to shield her inner feelings from exposure augment her weakness. From

Olsen's initial appraisal of her where she sits silently under his gaze wearing a smile that "had become a fixed aching mask" to Aunt Katrina's probing questions followed by her "gaz[ing] penetratingly into the masked face of her niece," Helga fails to assert and protect herself (*Q*, 73, 81). In fact, these white gazers simply re-inscribe the position to which various African American communities consign Helga. For instance, when Helga relates her family history to Mrs. Hayes-Rore, the narrator notes that "the faces of the two women, which had been bare, seemed to harden. It was almost as if they had slipped on masks" (*Q*, 42). The African American race-woman demands her young protégé take up a mask that shields both women from discussing difficulties arising from sexual desire. In each of these instances, Helga represents none of the self-assurance and control that inspires Picasso's masked presentation of Stein, a portrait that recognizes and celebrates Stein's confident nonconformist sexual identity. Conversely, Helga passively accepts masks of racial and sexual stereotypes that ultimately invite interpretation and definition rather than self-empowerment.

Helga's unsuccessful manipulation of masks, Larsen's symbol for potential feminine agency, prepares the reader for the tragedy surrounding her portrait experience. In contrast to Stein who ultimately dictates the terms of her portrait, Helga is defined by Axel Olsen's painted visualization. Olsen's portrait represents a complicated combination of truth and falsity that Helga fails to comprehend. Olsen's first proposition that Helga enter a sexual relationship with him depends on the painting: "[H]e had made ... while holding his brush poised for a last, a very last stroke on the portrait, one admirably draped suggestion, speaking seemingly to the pictured face. Had he insinuated marriage, or something less – and easier? ... Helga ... had remained silent, striving to appear unhearing" (*Q*, 86). In place of a long description of Olsen's painting, the text objectifies his language and Helga's response. His "draped suggestion" and her "silent" response transform Helga into the "pictured face." As such, Larsen's numerous descriptions of Helga throughout the novel emerge as preparatory drawings for Olsen's portrait, further implicating Helga's acquiescence to visual objectification as the cause of her powerlessness.

Helga's inability to interpret Olsen's portrait with insight exhibits her lack of self-understanding and inability to visualize black womanhood in modernist terms. The narrator reports: "[S]he had never quite ... forgiven Olsen for that portrait. It wasn't, she contended, herself at all, but some disgusting sensual creature with her features. ... Anyone with half an eye could see that it wasn't, at all, like her." Her Danish maid, Marie, bolsters her interpretation proclaiming the portrait, "bad, wicked" (*Q*, 91). Larsen depicts Helga's failure to assess a visual depiction of herself that does not comply with traditional depictions of black female propriety as a result of Helga's narrow conception of African American women's sexual identity. While Olsen possibly trades on problematic stereotypes, he is right, even prophetic, in declaring Helga's failure to come to terms with her sexual identity "a tragedy" (Q, 91). Helga's concurrence with Marie's assessment showcases her cultural blindness. Upon her arrival in Copenhagen, she catches Marie casting "sly curious glances at her" and concludes that she is likely the first African American Marie has seen "outside the pictured pages of her geography book" (Q, 69). If Helga is the first black American the maid has seen beyond the images of primitive Africans included in juvenile books on world cultures, Helga's agreement with Marie's evaluation of the painting unveils her incapacity to visualize black female sexuality in terms that escape the stereotypes generated by Western picture books.

Helga's ultimate decision to perform her sexuality with abandon upon her return to Harlem uncovers her subconscious acceptance of what she interprets as the painted portrayal of her savage sexuality. Thus, Anderson's kiss actualizes interior desires she fails to understand fully. Her determination to pursue the former Naxos president unfolds before "some examples of African carving" on which Anderson "delivers a long dissertation" before her silence, giving Helga the opportunity to feel "the intentness of his gaze upon her" (Q, 107). She effectively allows Anderson to conflate her with the primitive art objects. Along with Olsen's portrait, the carvings re-inscribe the narrative at the center of the novel, Helga's refusal to acknowledge the legitimacy of her desire, the naturalness of her sexual identity. The setting also closely connects Anderson to Olsen: like his white, European counterpart, he desires to collect Helga and experience what he imagines to be her primitive sexuality for his own selfish pleasure.

Anderson's ultimate choice of Anne, the Madonna, triggers Helga's final fall into the quicksand of Christian doctrine, a temporary cover for the expression of her sexual desires. In fact, her marriage to the Reverend Mr. Pleasant Green provides a kind of Shakespearian "Green World" whose magical correction of her interior conflict can never be sustained beyond the boundaries of her suspended rationality. The physical need her husband fulfills continues to be described by the narrator in terms that reflect Helga's persistent failure to visualize sexual experience in positive terms: "Emotional, palpitating, amorous, all that was living in her sprang like rank weeds at the tingling thought of night, with a vitality so strong that it devoured all shoots of reason" (*Q*, 123). Caught within the suffocating frames of extreme definitions of black female sexuality, Helga remains unable to enjoy the physical intimacy she has long regarded as shameful. What is more, the toll her consecutive pregnancies take on her body reveals the lie inherent in the Madonna ideal. Motherhood for poor black women shares little in common with portraits of Mary calmly inspiring the world with her saintly maternity. Instead, Helga finds that motherhood "used her up" (*Q*, 124). Larsen depends on Helga's quagmire to exhibit the consequences of simplistic portrayals of black femininity that leave no space for formulating complicated attitudes toward black female sexuality.

The religious transfiguration that leads Helga to marry Reverend Pleasant Green ultimately leaves her without access to the Madonna or the uninhibited primitive. Helga's traumatic ending dramatizes the need for black women to establish autonomous definitions of identity that allow them to visualize black sexual desire with pride. By emphasizing Helga's refusal to read visual depictions of blackness affirmatively, Larsen highlights the relationship between black women's struggles with self-perception and their acceptance of definitions, propagated in visual forms, which relegate them to unyielding extremes. In the end, Larsen refuses to provide an easy answer or alternative. Instead, she insists readers recognize the necessity for creating generative notions around sexual identity. The trope of the Picture Book established by Wheatley and expanded by nineteenth-century black writers heralds the positive nature of African American moral and creative vision, an outlook Larsen suggests is in danger of slipping away from women of the Harlem Renaissance.

Maude Irwin Owens and the Messianic Artist

Maude Owens and Jessie Fauset pick up a similar thread in their fiction as their protagonists experience radical changes in the ways they view race and womanhood. Whereas Helga demonstrates an aesthetic sensibility through her investment in fashion, decorating, and love of color, Owens's and Fauset's protagonists emerge as dedicated artists who confidently assess the world around them through their creative work. But even as they exhibit impressive powers of vision that inspire their material creations, until they experience a spiritual transfiguration, they fail to empower the broader black community with a progressive understanding of feminine possibility. In fact, they interpret their artistic vision as proof of personal exceptionality, a conclusion that divides them from the black community. In Owens's short story "Bathesda of Sinners Run" (1928) and Fauset's novel *Plum Bun* (1929), Bathesda and Angela, their respective protagonists, experience religiously inflected conversions that propel them from solitary accomplished artists to activists in their communities. In contrast to Helga's short-lived religious awakening that inspires her brief desire to uplift the rural women of her husband's Southern congregation, Bathesda and Angela make bold political statements that have larger implications. Their transfigurations symbolize the true agency of the black female artist, a potent figure who transforms the lives of other women in a Christ-like, rather than maternal, fashion. As they accept the challenge of slashing stultifying stereotypes, the oversimplified bifurcation of Madonna or Jezebel falls away and these painting protagonists declare the sociopolitical power of female artists. By focusing on their evolving vision, Owens and Fauset liberate their leading ladies from the frames of conventional black womanhood constructed by black and white Americans alike. What is more, they move beyond discussions of feminine agency that rest primarily on sexual activity to probe the consequences faced by artists mainly focused on their creative endeavors.

"Bathesda of Sinner's Run" recounts the development of Bathesda, an artistic woman who is blind to the cultural pain of the African American women living in her provincial community. The story opens with Owens designating Bathesda a kind of wayward Mary, unwilling to follow her mother's footsteps. Although her mixed ethnic and religious heritage explains some of her resistance to Christian theology, her comportment toward her creative talent suggests that Bathesda rejects the traditional Madonna ideal as insufficiently progressive. Yet Owens complicates this characterization by denying Bathesda the full healing power that her mother, Anne, possesses. Even Bathesda's atheist Native-American father sees his wife and daughter as potential icons of holy motherhood. He is delighted by "the yellow gypsy-like Anne in the role of Madonna" when she is pregnant with Bathesda.[48] Repeating Larsen's subtle reference to St. Anne, Owens includes details that recall the apocrypha's scriptural account of St. Anne's experience with the Virgin Mary. According to the apocryphal Book of James, Anne is married to Joachim and they are childless for many years. Owen's Anne is barren until "the age of forty" (*BSR*, 147). After Bathesda is older, the narrator deepens the allusion by describing the two women at work as making "a picture to be remembered" (*BSR*, 148). These words treat Anne and Bathesda as if they replicate iconic paintings of Anne and Mary throughout the ages.

Unlike her mother, whose devout belief in Christ ties her to the common black folk of the town even as she is distinguished by her artistry and healing power, Bathesda vehemently rejects Christianity and the black townspeople's style of worship. She regards the provincial women as representing a duty she will fulfill without compassion or understanding. As Bethesda works to replace the traditional Madonna image with what she deems a progressive alternative, Owens emphasizes her blinkered outlook. The words of a local white girl's Boston fiancé ironically imply that Bathesda's belittling of the black townswomen does not protect her from suffering similar misreading by white eyes. The Boston artist begs "for the privilege of painting Bathesda in all the glory of her little cottage and embroidering frames" and declares her to be like "one of Millet's peasant women" and her home is "[w]orthy of the old Dutch masters" (*BSR*, 154, 155). Notwithstanding the complimentary tone of his words, his descriptions fit her into a prescribed frame that generalizes the hard labor of poor women. Thus, Bathesda's dismissal of the cultural complexity of the black townswomen makes her an unsuspecting accomplice to buttressing white attitudes toward vulnerable women of color.

Unwilling to subject themselves to such disparagement from an African American woman, the black townswomen take matters into their own hands. "[T]en or twelve women" lure Bathesda into the night with a tale of sick people who need her help (*BSR*, 155). "[D]ragging her ... up the sloping hill side" as they brandish "whips, twigs and sticks," the women prepare to teach Bathesda a lesson about what they deem her supercilious attitude and wicked religious practices (*BSR*, 156). An old grandmother, the leader of the women, remains "beswaddled" in the wagon while the younger ones prepare to attack (*BSR*, 156). Yet when the women angrily push Bathesda against a tree and it falls over – they do not realize that it is in the process of being cut down by lumberjacks – the rural ladies run in fear of what they interpret as proof of Bathesda's sinful conjure power. Two white lumberjacks discover Bathesda who suddenly looks her age. In place of the unnatural youthful beauty she had formerly retained, an "ethereal robe of an inner beauty" covers her and attests that "a soul transformation had taken place" (*BSR*, 157). One man's arm is hurt, and as "the men [stand] transfixed," Bathesda heals the injured arm and proclaims, "it is well!" before she walks down the "hill with wide masculine strides" (*BSR*, 157). She testifies:

> Up Calvary's rugged brow did I go, this day with Thee, dear Lord ... To the very foot of the Cross ... and I saw the bloody nails in Thy precious feet ... the cruel thorns ... and the bitter cup was spared me ... but Thou didst drink it to the dregs!" And she went home with a new power – with understanding, tolerance and forgiveness; to be one of her people. (*BSR*, 157–158)

This climactic end demolishes many stereotypes enveloping the town-swomen and Bathesda. Their violent uprising belies Bathesda's disparaging belief that they possess no will to change their lives. More importantly, their refusal to accept Bathesda's scorn leads to Bathesda's discovery of a personal strength she never sought. Owens's heavily symbolic transfiguration connects individual power to an acknowledgement of religiously inspired mercy and grace. Although Owens refuses to explain Bathesda's conversion explicitly as a discovery of her misguided vision of African American women, the symbolic swaddling of Granny Lou, the ringleader of the women, substitutes the elderly black woman for baby Jesus. The hate-filled grandmother represents the horrific effects a racist society wreaks on black female psychology. Granny Lou has been unable to be the salvific nurturer Harlem Renaissance leaders insisted black maternity represents. The townswomen's attempt at a symbolic crucifixion forces Bathesda to see their pain, the poverty of their bleak lives. The transformation of Bathesda's outward appearance confirms the force of her newfound understanding: realizing the truth of these women's lives stamps her with the look of sympathetic long-suffering.

Through coming to understand her community, Bathesda gains a potency that is both Christ-like and womanly. She exchanges the set-apart Madonna position to assume a messianic role reminiscent of Christ who assumes manly form that He might fully experience humanity. Bathesda rediscovers the value of her culture as well as the true purpose of her artistry, and her transfiguration leaves her belonging to no predetermined category, bespeaking the real power of the African American female artist. The fact that the first person who benefits from her newfound power is a white man demonstrates the reach of her new agency. Even her name, itself an echo of the biblical pool of "Bethesda," a bath where people in need of healing waited to enter, suggests the generative nature of black female artistry when properly understood. Owens raises the specter of the Madonna only to replace it with a radically revised portrait of African American womanhood that recuperates the social agency of the female artist. She appeals to the trope of the Picture Book to connect clarity of vision with a crucial moment of instruction, the key to individual and communal healing. Bathesda, however, steps beyond Phillis Wheatley who assumed a similar posture in her poetry. Whereas Wheatley claimed a visual authority that identified her with Christ's sacrificial spirit, Owens links Bathesda to his salvific power.

Political Vision in *Plum Bun*

Angela, the protagonist of Fauset's *Plum Bun*, also initially rejects her mother's model and disassociates herself from the Madonna icon that her younger sister, tellingly named Virginia, represents. A fair-skinned protagonist and painter of portraits, Angela employs her art to explore her vision of black womanhood. Examining Angela's evolving painterly eye – as well as the specific portraits she paints – reveals how her creative transfiguration represents a larger statement on the societal importance of cultivating the vision of the African American female artist. Only in her artwork does Angela appear capable of conceiving of blackness in terms that enable her to appreciate black humanity generally and African American women in particular. Her portrait painting alone leads her to question the legitimacy of the virginal black woman image. Angela depends on her artistic vision to understand African American feminine psychology in terms that penetrate the Madonna stereotype promoted by New Negro leaders.

Angela's favorite painting subject in Philadelphia is Hetty, her family's black maid and chaperone who waxes passionately about her virginal status. As Angela sketches Hetty, the maid declares, "I kept my pearl of great price untarnished. I aimed then and I'm continual to aim to be a verjous woman."[49] While listening to Hetty's regurgitation of the sociocultural gospel of the day, Angela's painterly eye detects the maid's true interior state:

> Her unslaked yearnings gleamed suddenly out of her eyes, transforming her usually rather expressionless face into something wild and avid. The dark brown immobile mask of her skin made an excellent foil for the vividness of an emotion which was so apparent, so palpable that it seemed like something superimposed upon the background of her countenance. (*PB*, 66)

Notwithstanding Hetty's zealous devotion to embodying the image Harlem Renaissance leaders encouraged, her struggle with natural urges rages unabated. The generic frame of religious feminine virtue she uncomfortably inhabits highlights the failure of prescribed identities to stamp out individual nature. Angela dislikes the political discussions of race her black friends tirelessly recap, but for her, the act of painting portraits dismantles stereotypes and offers opportunities for wrestling with the complexity of individual identity.

Yet even this interest is transformed into a debate on race within the space of Angela's art classes in Philadelphia. In fact, Fauset's repeated turn to educational sites to discuss visions of race and humanity reminds us of the persistent need to relate visual dexterity with instruction when writers depend on the trope of the Picture Book. In the purportedly democratic classroom, one of Angela's classmates expresses interest in her sketch of Hetty until Angela reveals the maid's race. The classmate quickly dismisses the possibility of deep emotional pain in "darkies" (*PB*, 70). This introduction of racism into the life art class is especially ironic given the storied history of women's access to such classes at the Philadelphia Academy. When women began entering the school in large numbers in the late nineteenth century, it was deemed improper for them to sketch from scantily clad male models. This view was held so earnestly that when Thomas Eakins allowed a nude male model in his coed life art class in 1886, he was forced to resign. The racial bigotry practiced by Angela's female classmates and teacher flagrantly displays their failure to extend to black women the equality white women fought for and gained at the Academy. It also recalls aspects of Fauset's biography. After earning her bachelor degree, she sought a teaching job in Philadelphia. Like her protagonist, she experienced Philadelphia's biting racism and recalled: "When I graduated from training school, I found the high schools barred to me because of my color. Philadelphia, birthplace of Independence and City of Brotherly Love – I have never quite been able to reconcile theory with fact."[50]

While Angela's experiences in Philadelphia eventually drive her to New York where she passes for white, she remains intrigued by the predicament black women face in a racist society. In New York, Angela repeatedly focuses her gaze on black women, often transforming her eyes into her paintbrush. On her first day in her new drawing class, Angela trains her eyes on the other black woman present: "Her squarish head capped with a mass of unnaturally straight and unnaturally burnished hair possessed a kind of ugly beauty. Angela could not tell whether her features were good but blurred and blunted by the soft night of her skin or really ugly with an ugliness lost and plunged in that skin's deep concealment" (*PB*, 94). Regardless, she determines that none of the students "made the photograph on her mind equal to those made by the coloured girl" (*PB*, 95). Angela's slow consumption of the girl's appearance represents her own attempt to look beyond stereotypes disseminated by both white and black American image makers.[51] The painterly terms she uses such as "blurred and blunted" – recalling Helga Crane's "blotted" and "smudged" – almost imagine that she *is* painting her fellow student.

It is only after Angela's disastrous love affair with a white man that she reappraises her views of women, race, and class. Her sketch titled "Life" features "a mass of lightly indicated figures passing apparently in review before the tall, cloaked form of a woman, thin to emaciation, her hands on her bony hips, slightly bent forward, laughing uproariously yet with a chilling malevolence" (*PB*, 280). Angela's transformation of her sketched pictured woman into a symbol of life highlights her maturing sense of professional seriousness.[52] Fauset was almost certainly familiar with how male portraitists, eager to distinguish themselves from hoards of female "dabblers," began describing their portrait work as suitable for any home and any room. Their paintings did not simply depict an individual, but represented a sensibility, an idea, and the most obvious way many artists asserted this was through their titles. Rather than attach the name of the sitter to the piece, portraits boasted titles like "The Rose."[53] Angela's "Life" goes further, imputing a subversive element to the traditional notion of a woman representing life. Her maliciously laughing lady is a far cry from a serene Madonna.

The ekphrastic rendering of the "Life" portrait and its explosion of the conventional conception of woman as nurturing mother anticipates Angela's reconsideration of Rachel Powell, her black classmate. By deploying descriptive language analogous to Angela's initial observation of Miss Powell, Fauset reveals Angela's revised aesthetic notions of beauty and presents Miss Powell as Angela's final, and most meaningful, portrait study:

> Angela thought she had never seen the girl one half so attractive and exotic. She was wearing a thin silk dress, plainly made but of a flaming red from which the satin blackness of her neck rose, a straight column topped by her squarish, somewhat massive head. Her thin, rather flat dark lips brought into sharp contrast the dazzling perfection of her teeth; her high cheek bones showed a touch of red. To anyone whose ideals of beauty were not already set and sharply limited, she must have made a breathtaking appeal. (*PB*, 342)

Returning to the terms of her initial, ambivalent study of Miss Powell, Angela highlights the extent of her revision. The "squarish" head that previously gave way to her contemplation of her classmate's pressed hair now becomes the foundation for Angela's intense inspection of Miss Powell's face. Her new appreciation for the young lady's appearance sharply contrasts her prior uncertainty as to whether Miss Powell was "really ugly with an ugliness lost and plunged in that skin's deep concealment" (*PB*, 94).

In effect, Angela's newfound appreciation places her in a group "whose ideals of beauty were not already set and sharply limited." She not only articulates a new aesthetic sensibility, her revised gaze impels political action that has real consequences.[54] After consuming Miss Powell as if the young woman is a portrait lacking the means to correct her viewers' misperceptions, Angela takes it upon herself to correct illiterate eyes. In the face of four white journalists hoping to pen stories about Miss Powell's decision to give up her prize scholarship to study in Paris rather than fight the American Committee's racist refusal to fund her ship passage, Angela announces the truth about her racial identity. Her confession becomes both a disavowal of the racist notions the reporters espouse as well as a sensitive interpretation of Miss Powell's unspeaking face. What is more, Angela's revised notions of black beauty, and the agency of her artistic eye in cultivating her political activism, points to the social significance of the black artist, a woman who pierces the facades stifling African American women. Her final trip to Paris, where she receives her love interest, Anthony, as a package delivered on Christmas Day from her Madonna-like sister, Virginia, identifies Angela as a woman able to have it all. She independently seeks her fortune as an artist and reunites with her man, but she needs no child to fulfill her dreams.

Fauset's painting protagonist demonstrates the possibility of devising an artistic philosophy that empowers the broader black community. As a group, many of the black women writing during the Harlem Renaissance struggle to regain a point of view that defines black womanhood in complex terms. The writers examined in this chapter offer new portraits of feminine success and use ekphrasis to model new methods of viewing black identity in visual art. Most basically, they wish to openly acknowledge what African American writers have tacitly accepted throughout literary history: that many readers approach their work with preconceived notions – often founded on visual ideas of blackness. Black women's conspicuous imaging in both high and low art constructs rigid frames which these writers seek to shatter. Introducing ekphrasis and the act of painting portraits facilitates a writer's focus on a character's ability or inability to interpret visual art and distills the issue they confront: They need written art to give voice to black women too often treated like mute objects of visual art. These women do not pull readers into museums, sites of high culture, or spaces that dictate particular modes of observation; instead, they dramatize the force of plastic arts abounding in popular culture. Just as painted images by artists from Manet to Reiss to Motley inspire their writing, pictures of black women on magazine covers, frontispieces, movie ads, and pancake boxes influence their ideas. Their turn to plastic art gives them a means for coming to terms with a society content to designate them as simple spectacles rather than seers. By appealing to still lifes, portraits, sculptures, and folk art, Renaissance women slash restrictive examples and demand new, more accurate pictures of modern black identity. They portray recuperated black feminine vision as indicative of an authority first declared by Wheatley, and in so doing, they testify to the staying power of the trope of the Picture Book.

PART TWO

Lessons from the Museum

CHAPTER 4

Zora Neale Hurston: Seeing by the Rules of the Natural History Museum

The front porch might seem a daring place for the rest of the town, but it was a gallery seat to me.

My favorite place was atop the gate-post.

– Zora Neale Hurston, 1928[1]

I have been amazed by the Anglo-Saxon's lack of curiosity about the internal lives and emotions of the Negroes. ... The question naturally arises as to the why of this indifference. ... The answer lies in what we may call THE AMERICAN MUSEUM OF UNNATURAL HISTORY.

– Zora Neale Hurston, 1950[2]

There are no museums in Hurston's novels. Although my study of her literary work serves as the first chapter of the museum section of this book, I do not probe her fiction for distinct museum sites. Instead, I want to suggest that the philosophy of the early natural history museum shapes Hurston's portrayal of authoritative black vision in her fiction. As the first space dedicated to anthropological collection, display, and education, the museum of natural history provides a foundational logic for Hurston's mature novels. Her turn to museum principles in her portrayal of an evolving African American vision establishes a significant addition to the trope of the Picture Book. Although she does not craft scenes that depict her protagonists visiting museums, she dramatizes observation skills associated with museum behavior that prepare characters to view themselves and their culture with new understanding. As a result, moments of visual instruction reaffirm key aspects of museum conduct and demonstrate how visual education can shape black character. I frame my analysis of her texts by considering specific notions influencing methods of display in the natural history museum. Additionally, I explore how Hurston's portrayal of characters' viewing practices leads her to designate the space of marriage in folk communities as providing a position analogous to that of the participant-observer anthropologist.

Hurston's fiction acknowledges the institutionalization of the museum in U.S. culture, a historical development through which vision accrued new authority as a legitimate path to intelligence. She publishes her major novels between 1934 and 1948, years that follow the 1880–1920 period described as the "Museum Age," and she draws heavily on the importance of vision in discussions of the acquisition of knowledge. The epigraphs highlight Hurston's endeavor to translate her curious spectatorship from a personal trait into a necessary attribute of national character. In her 1928 essay, "How It Feels to Be Colored Me," she recounts her childhood fondness for observing white travelers passing through the all-black town she called home. Her love of the "front porch" and "gate-post," sites of observation defined by Southern customs, establishes her early anthropological inclinations. Unlike her fellow townsmen, or the white people she eagerly surveyed, the young Hurston revels at the prospect of learning more about individuals representing different cultures. In fact, other works show her repeatedly returning to these observation sites.

In her 1924 short story "Drenched in Light," the title character, Isis, replicates the ritual: "The little brown figure perched upon the gate post looked yearningly up the gleaming shell road."[3] And again in *Their Eyes Were Watching God*, Janie "searched as much of the world as she could from the top of the front steps and then went on down to the front gate and leaned over to gaze up and down the road" (*NS*, 184). Finally, in *Dust Tracks on a Road*, Hurston recalls, "I used to take a seat on top of the gate post and watch the world go by" (*FM*, 589). Hurston's repetition of this scene documenting cultural curiosity underscores the importance she places on a questioning disposition as well as her early understanding of effective sites for exercising such inquisitiveness. Her recurring depictions of African American curiosity establish her fascination with pondering visual dexterity, the ability to understand the world through rigorous looking.

This heightened interest in seeing the world beyond one's home hints toward Hurston's investment in designating protagonists as a particular kind of gifted student: they emerge as anthropologists anxious to research folk culture. As early-twentieth-century anthropologists increasingly adopted the role of student of other peoples, Hurston presents the road her characters travel toward greater wisdom as a challenge to readers: she urges her audience to assume the posture encouraged by anthropologists in early natural history museums. By the mid-nineteenth century, museum patrons were forthrightly instructed to take their roles as spectators seriously in an effort to learn about different ethnic groups by viewing scientifically constructed exhibitions. Highlighting this initiative, her novels reveal a dual devotion to portraying protagonists as developing ethnographers while also priming the reader to evaluate a character's visual discoveries. Hurston draws attention to the sights that push protagonists toward visual maturity as well as the sites implicated by anthropological research practices.

Considering these goals, it is no accident that the scene of observation she repeats across texts remains closely aligned with her own biography. Notably, characters such as Isis, Janie, and the young Hurston never remain sequestered on the porch. Although scholars describe the porch as a transitional space, a "liminal place ... where the color barrier could be weakened" and "the sex barrier was also weakened," its architectural connection to the home denies it the freedom of the gatepost.[4] Sue Beckham argues that, like the liminal spaces anthropologists identify in primitive cultures, porches – and particularly those associated with the Southern U.S. home – allow women to participate in rituals between "two cultural states," "between the sanctity of the home and profanity of the marketplace."[5] Nevertheless, Beckham notes that in the Jim Crow South, socialization on the porch continued to observe definite rituals established to regulate intercourse between the races. Considering Hurston's representation of porches, Jocelyn Donlon reads these spaces as both "romantic" and "exclusionary," spaces capable of bringing "communities closer together" while also acting "to separate them."[6] In other words, porches represent a complicated, potentially confining site. By moving her protagonists off the porch, Hurston follows the trajectory of the turn-of-the-century anthropologist no longer willing to perform research from a metaphorical armchair, a site associated with domesticity, convention, and stasis.[7]

But as the second epigraph highlights, even as Hurston stresses her commitment to turning inquiring eyes on the world, she finds black citizens strangely ignored by their white counterparts. Her innate love for research and passion for scrutinizing other people cannot blind her to the unreciprocated nature of interracial exchange. In her 1950 essay, "What White Publishers Won't Print," she laments white Americans' refusal to explore the "internal lives and emotions of the Negroes." Hurston explains that most whites prefer "THE AMERICAN MUSEUM OF UNNATURAL HISTORY," a space where they "may take [non-Anglo-Saxons] in at a glance" (*FM*, 951). Visitors demand "typical" exhibits of blackness that confirm the white majority's conviction that African Americans "don't think." For Hurston, this belief poses real danger prompting her to declare that "for the national welfare, it is urgent to realize that the minorities do think, and think about something other than the race problem" (*FM*, 952). Addressing this crisis is exactly what her fiction sets out to do.

From her earliest stories to her late novels, Hurston celebrates the unique and admirable qualities of rural black culture and ruminates over the best sites for observing and exhibiting this treasure. Examining her anthropological training suggests that she draws on the rules that determine exhibition practices of the natural history museum to display sophisticated African American thinking. What is more, Hurston endows her protagonists with the research methods employed by anthropologists who initially regarded the museum as the proper place to share their discoveries. In stark contrast to the mythical "American Museum of Unnatural History," real natural history museums designated the objects and subjects displayed within their walls as worthy of intellectual attention. Hurston, who studied anthropology under the guidance of Franz Boas, builds narratives around characters whose powers of vision teach them to appreciate African American mental acuity as they simultaneously serve as compelling exhibits of intellectual accomplishment.

Her training in anthropology, one of the "viewing professions" that a number of women entered during the first decades of the twentieth century, prepared her to publish fiction devoted to displaying such cultural sophistication in Southern African American lives.[8] Anthropology extolled the ability for laymen and scientists alike to gain knowledge through visual study, and in complementary fashion, the natural history museum designed exhibits aimed at teaching a broad range of visitors to comprehend science through critical observation. Taking note of both the practices of anthropologists and the museum, this chapter argues that Hurston pens texts that display black citizens' complex interiority. By forcing her protagonists into the role of cultural anthropologists collecting material appropriate for documenting folk culture, Hurston reveals how their superior observation practices facilitate their appreciation of black culture. Furthermore, she presents their mature cultural discernment as the most compelling kind of anthropological exhibit needed to expand her readers' understanding of Southern black experience.

Eyeing Science and Race in the Natural History Museum

The story of Hurston measuring skulls in Harlem remains one of the most enduring anecdotes related to her training as an anthropologist.[9] Armed with a set of calipers on Lenox Avenue, Hurston measured the head of any Harlemite sporting a dome that caught her eye. Her professor, Franz Boas, had long worked to challenge widely accepted research connecting brain size and weight to intellectual ability, and designating blacks intellectually inferior to whites. Under the direction of Melville Herskovits, Hurston collected data for Boas's complicated and sometimes contradictory work in this area. Boas's *The Mind of Primitive Man* (1911) presented his findings and conclusions with regard to the physical evidence of differing brain sizes between black and white men, but he continued to wrestle with this research. Boas acknowledged that, although measurable differences in brain weights persisted, the variability across the masses of both races undermined the idea of any "material inferiority of the Negro race"; instead, his conclusions proposed that although "the Negro race may not produce as many minds of exceptional ability as the white race, there is no evidence for believing in a racial inferiority that would unfit an individual Negro to take his part in modern civilizations."[10] As his first book aimed at a general audience, *The Mind of Primitive Man* captured the complicated nature of nonwhite cultures' thought with particular attention to individual intellectual capacity. Hurston, a budding anthropologist and writer, seems to develop Boas's pronouncements as she draws attention to exceptional black minds in her fiction.

In fact, her persistent investment in tying vision to intellect fuels my contention that her emphasis on observation as a pathway to knowledge echoes the philosophy of the natural history museum. These repositories encouraged visitors to interact with carefully staged exhibits to gain information. In their earliest incarnations, these institutions celebrated the attainment of "natural knowledge" and championed the idea that visitors could leave the museum with a sophisticated grasp of scientific facts. Building on the Renaissance era's cabinets of curiosities often declared the forerunners of modern museums, the natural history museum focused on collecting objects notable for their "visual power."[11] Thus, although the natural history museum remained problematic as an institution that pronounced itself politically and culturally neutral even as its interpretations of objects, cultures, and histories reflected obvious biases, it significantly redefined the value of vision and curiosity as paths to intellectual accomplishment.[12] For Hurston, its legitimization of these activities aided her determination to affirm the analytical sophistication of her protagonists by displaying their visual acquisition of cultural knowledge. The exceptional nature of their minds emerges through their performance of perceptive vision.

The viewing sciences have long esteemed honing intellectual looking as a defining method for establishing intellectual acumen. Recalling Professor Louis Agassiz's pedagogical practice of impressing upon his new graduate students that "looking was the most important skill for aspiring" biological scientists, Carla Yanni recounts that during the mid-nineteenth century, the curator of the Museum of Comparative Zoology forced students to study a pickled fish for a week or longer.[13] Agassiz hoped to demonstrate the complexity of individuals and organisms, a point he sought to make in his museum as well. He strove to prove the importance of using vision as a tool necessary to researchers yet available to laymen. His stature in the field raised vision to a new level of importance in the realm of scientific inquiry.

Hurston's mentor, Franz Boas, also drew heavily from his work in the museum to formulate his anthropological methods. His first job in the U.S. divided his time between teaching at Columbia University and serving as the Assistant Curator of Ethnology and Somatology at the American Museum of Natural History. At the museum, he worked to translate his research into exhibits that successfully represented the different cultures he studied. In a well-known published disagreement, Boas sparred with his museum colleague, Otis T. Mason, over a display titled "Synoptic History of Inventions: Spindles, Shuttles, and Looms." The case exhibiting these tools purported to show the evolution of weaving instruments, but Boas took issue with Mason's complete disregard of the context from which the objects emerged. Boas famously argued that "unlike causes produce like effects," and to demonstrate his thinking, he created exhibits focused on "life-groups" represented by mannequins (see Figure 4.1).[14] He and Mason viewed exhibits from contradictory perspectives: Mason hoped their displays would lead to "the refinement of taste" that would lead the world to become "an unique, comprehensive and undivided home for the whole race," whereas Boas contended that "the main object of ethnological collections should be the dissemination of the fact that civilization is not something absolute, but that it is relative."[15] Boas hoped his displays would help museum goers understand the broader cultural context of the ethnic groups they viewed. In other words, he sought to create in his exhibits what Hurston strives to realize in her texts.[16]

When Hurston began studying with Boas at Barnard in 1925, many of the ideas and methods he fought for during his early career had become standard practice. In 1905, Boas had written to the president of the American Museum of Natural History to clarify the instructional methods of the museum: "I believe it is the educational function of a museum

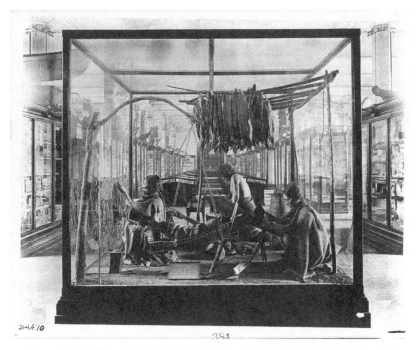

Figure 4.1 Life Group Exhibit Curated by Franz Boas at the American Museum of Natural History (c. 1902). American Museum of Natural History, New York, NY. Photo © American Museum of Natural History Library (Negative 338764).

of the size of the American Museum of Natural History to entertain the masses, to instruct the large number of people who come here to get knowledge, to advance the knowledge of those who possess a higher education, and to help those interested in special studies."[17] Yet as he struggled against opposing views such as those advocated by Mason, Boas moved increasingly away from the museum as the most effective institution for conducting and sharing anthropological work. No matter how sophisticated their displays, the anthropological museum's focus on material objects often left the "psychological and historical relations of cultures" – what Boas termed "the only objects of anthropological inquiry" – woefully unexplored.[18] For Boas, the real importance of anthropological discovery was "'the thoughts that clustered around' the objects, and these could be expressed only inadequately by labels in glass cases."[19] Consequently, Boas channeled his energy into his work at the university where his access to bright graduate students such as Hurston proved one of his best resources. His prolific publications document an evolving philosophy that adapted what he valued in the museum to his work at the university. As Michael Elliot explains, in turning to the university and print culture, Boas began building "a textual museum."[20]

Hurston set out to expand this "textual museum," but she maintained Boas's early sense of the potential value of the philosophy undergirding the natural history museum. Drawing on her academic training with Boas and the rich reality of her experience as a student of anthropology, she introduces museum principles to her fiction, adopting key ideas to instruct readers on African American culture. Of course, Hurston's dependence on anthropology is not without complication. A number of scholars have pointed to the tension inherent in her position. Daphne Lamothe studies several Harlem Renaissance writers' interest in ethnography to argue that they "interrogate and ultimately critique the colonizing gaze on the racialized subject."[21] For Hurston in particular, Lamothe claims that the writer distinguishes her approach by "the extent to which she theorizes specularity, linking ways of seeing to ways of knowing" and by linking "perception and knowledge."[22] I begin with a similar claim linking sight and knowledge in this chapter, and Lamothe's work provides a useful foundation.

Karen Jacobs also addresses the inherent tension within anthropology by arguing that *Their Eyes Were Watching God* "engages with anti-hierarchical fantasy" and ultimately repudiates "the rationalized 'language of visuality' of the anthropological gaze ... in favor of a Romantic idealism that reestablishes Hurston's artistic project on a new, seemingly universalist foundations."[23] Hazel Carby, however, refuses to interpret Hurston's investment in anthropology through a refurbished lens. Focusing on *Their Eyes Were Watching God*, Carby charges Hurston with creating "an antagonistic relationship between Janie and the folk" by casting Janie as the "intellectual" while the "rural black folk become an aesthetic principle, a means by which to embody a rich oral culture."[24] What is more, Carby suggests that by the conclusion of the novel, Hurston evokes "the romantic imagination so characteristic of ethnography in the 1930s" that leaves the "folk as community" as "other."[25]

It is impossible to deny the basic truth in Carby's claims.[26] Not only does Hurston erect a confrontational relationship between Janie and the folk in *Their Eyes Were Watching God*, but eventually, the same antipathy arises between her protagonists and members of their unlearned communities in *Jonah's Gourd Vine* and *Moses, Man of the Mountain*. Protagonists such as Janie, whom Carby describes as the "intellectual" stand-in for Hurston, appear to accept the project of presenting the folk as "other." In fact, one could argue that the distance Hurston maintains between her visionary protagonists and the less discerning folk reenacts the relationship between the museum curator and the objects he displays in the natural history museum. But I want to suggest that a different logic undergirds the relationship between the folk community and visionary protagonists in her fiction.

Hurston was very familiar with the widespread investment in connecting primitive anatomy and physiology to psychology and mental capacity. The persistent interest in displaying primitive people fed the U.S. appetite for visually consuming racial minorities. By tasking her protagonists with the responsibility of visually assessing black culture, Hurston shrewdly indicts readers for depending on stereotypes in place of independent analysis. Her presentation of certain characters as exhibiting exceptional powers of observation and others as lacking such interpretive abilities allows her to picture an intellectual spectrum in rural black communities that is no different from any other ethnic community. Like Boas who recognized a continuum and asserted the value of all cultures, Hurston remained committed to portraying a realistic range of rural individuals in her fiction. Most importantly, she depends on her novels to provide the cultural context that many natural history museum exhibits neglected to provide, and in so doing, she rescues her exceptional and unexceptional characters alike from falling prey to flat stereotypes.

In fleshing out these cultural contexts, she also insists on black Americans' unlimited intellectual capacity. In the same way that the oft-discussed opening of her first ethnography, *Mules and Men* (1938), reveals Hurston's need for the tools of anthropology to analyze rural black culture, she insists that her protagonists refine their power of sight by critically analyzing their experiences. Discussing the importance of her anthropological training, Hurston explains that for some time, she could not understand the significance of the folktales she had grown up with: "[I]t was fitting me like a tight chemise. I couldn't see it for wearing it. It was only when I was off in college, away from my native surroundings, that I could see myself like somebody else and stand off and look at my garment. Then I had to have the spy-glass of Anthropology to look through at that" (*FM*, 9). Critics have insightfully interpreted Hurston's declaration as a subversive critique of white-male-dominated anthropological methods as well as an admission of her own discomfort with the strange position she inhabits when conducting ethnographic research. Hurston tacitly acknowledges the strangeness of being caught under the power of her own skill of observation.

Yet considered with both the letters she writes and the protagonists she develops during the period of her initial fieldwork, Hurston's declaration of her personal profit from her research also reads as an authentic celebration of her scientific and creative ability to analyze rural black communities of the South. Just as she initially failed to understand why white travelers passing through Eatonville thrilled to see her dance and listened to her tales, she needs her anthropological training to comprehend and translate the value of black folklore to herself and to the broader nation. To accomplish this feat, she experiments across artistic genres, inserting folklore into her short stories and novels as well as her autobiography, plays, revues, and essays. Hurston's more traditionally scientific work – such as her ethnographies and documentary films – proves the complexity of her anthropological eye. For example, she not only inserts herself into the text of *Mules and Men*, she includes a visual illustration by Miguel Covarrubias that features her nude body undergoing her hoodoo initiation ceremony.

Even more interesting, the films she takes on her collecting trips during 1928 and 1929, and again in 1940 – footage that scholars describe as "her pioneering contribution to the field of visual anthropology" – take the extraordinary step of including her participation in folk ceremonies.[27] Reviewing footage from Hurston's film work with anthropologist Jane Belo in a South Carolina Seventh Day Church of God, Fatimah Rony explains that Hurston is "both directing the action and taking part in it" to demonstrate the "active *transformation*" that creates "a historical record" capable of transmitting the "ongoing artistry of the highly visual world of black culture."[28] Her willing transition from scientist to rural subject contests the notion that visionary individuals exist in strict opposition to regular folk. Hurston does not establish an impassable divide between the folk subject and intellectual observer; instead, she dramatizes the necessity of active curiosity, an attribute boasted by all of her aspiring ethnographer protagonists. What is more, she slyly hints that her readers also need instruction on how to see African American culture of the South.

Learning to Value African American Culture in Marriage

Hurston's earliest stories reveal her belief that to succeed in declaring the intellectual sophistication of rural blacks, African Americans must first be convinced of their own cultural worth. To illustrate this truth, the protagonists of "John Redding Goes to Sea" (1921) and "Drenched in Light" (1924) – John Redding and Isis respectively – gradually make way for youthful married couples like Missie May and Joe Banks of "The Gilded Six-Bits" (1933). These early works insist that rather than being cowed by racist pronouncements of African American's immature mental state, black Americans must work to maintain the generative elements of their culture. John Redding loses his life as a result of failing to blend his desire to explore the world with a healthy respect for folk wisdom. Similarly, Isis's disregard for her grandmother's admonitions leads her to seek the exploitative acceptance of white outsiders. As young people, they lack the sophisticated sight necessary for successfully negotiating their culture.

At first glance, the protagonists of "The Gilded Six-Bits" appear to be headed down a similar road. Yet, by the time Hurston published this story, she claimed a full arsenal of anthropological fieldwork and orchestrated a different ending for her wayward characters. She pondered with new seriousness the necessity of retaining, respecting, and abiding by black folk values in the face of an invasive white culture, and she points to a strong marriage as a necessity for such preservation. Joe and Missie May Banks's trial forthrightly demonstrates the peril of inaccurately observing worthless objects that lead to the adoption of disparate cultural values and the rejection of black folk wisdom. Hurston correlates the couple's successful reclamation of happiness to their recommitment to black folk values in their marriage. Establishing a plot device that becomes a mainstay in her novels, she portrays marriage as a potential space for cultivating a cultural vision distinct from the mainstream U.S. value system.[29] In turn, her novels serve as the kinds of exhibits with "life groups" that Boas championed in the natural history museum.

"The Gilded Six-Bits" begins by emphasizing Joe and Missie May's blissful marriage. Yet when Joe transfers Missie from the home to Slemmons's ice cream parlor, he unknowingly breaks the marital bank. He transforms his wife's sexual allure, previously characterized in ice-cream-like terms – the narrator describes Missie's "stiff young breasts ... like broad-based cones" – into a commodity. In fact, Joe's introduction of Slemmons, with his "rich white man" physique, implicitly invites incongruous values into their world, and he and Missie May immediately begin to question each other's intelligence. Missie's attempts to open Joe's eyes to the fact that Slemmons is likely lying exasperate Joe: "Good Lawd, Missie! You womens sho is hard to sense into things." Likewise, Joe's excessive admiration for Slemmons forces Missie to lament, "Joe, Ah hates to see you so dumb. Dat stray nigger jes' tell y'all anything and y'all b'lieve it" (*NS*, 989).

Only when Joe acknowledges and claims possession of his wife's pregnancy, physical testimony to their continued commitment, does he begin pushing the pendulum back toward their previous value system. If he had formerly been duped by Slemmons's fake gold, he now regains visual clarity. He tells Missie May, "Ah ain't blind. You makin' feet for shoes" (*NS*, 995). His willful commitment to the baby signals his new agency and progress beyond the couple's momentary endorsement of white society's values figured in the fake gold coin. When Joe returns to making his market, he translates the evolution of his worldview to the white clerk. Borrowing from Slemmons's vocabulary, Joe explains that he has been "round in spots and places" (*NS*, 996). Now, however, his interpretive capacity is back intact for his "spots and places" refers to inner experiences rather than the geographical movement Slemmons recounts and protagonists like Helga Crane pursue.

Joe's new confidence in his cultural vision inspires him to refuse the clerk's suggestion that he buy chocolate bars instead of kisses. The clerk, profoundly ignorant of black life and thought, cannot possibly offer him advice. To stress the clerk's ignorance, the narrator reports that after Joe leaves, the clerk tells a customer that he wished he could be as carefree as "darkies ... [l]aughin' all the time" (*NS*, 996). The depth of his misreading illustrates the impossibility of understanding individuals without comprehending their cultural reality. Joe and Missie May have learned through the pain of their mistaken perception of the gilded coin, but the clerk remains patently uninterested in cultural study. Hurston hints that he needs to adopt the posture of a museum visitor seeking to understand other people's values instead of relying on the narrowness of his own experience. Moreover, she presents the story as a substitute for geographical travel: her exhibition of Joe and Missie May's evolution serves as instruction for readers curious about African American culture.

With these protagonists, Hurston inverts racist science that dismisses African Americans as having childlike minds that make them unfit for responsible citizenship. The long history validating such scientific research reached a crescendo at the turn of the century. In 1907, Stanley Hall, the leading U.S. psychologist of the early twentieth century authoritatively declared: "Most savages in most respects are children, or, because of sexual maturity, more properly adolescents of adult size."[30] Herbert Spencer simply declared: "The intellectual traits of the uncivilized ... are traits recurring in the children of the civilized."[31] The 1908 birth of Alfred Binet's IQ test, the set of criterion that became the standard for measuring intelligence, equipped scientists with an unparalleled method for determining mental age. By 1923, C. C. Brigham appealed to the army mental tests data to publish *A Study of American Intelligence*, a text that boldly claimed:

"The author presents not theories or opinion but facts. It behooves us to consider their reliability and their meaning, for no one of us as a citizen can afford to ignore the menace of race deterioration ... to national progress and welfare."[32] Henry Fairfield Osborn, the president of the American Museum of Natural History, concluded: "we have learned once and for all that the negro is not like us."[33]

Against this backdrop, Hurston creates stories that trace the mental evolution of her characters in ways that reject this science even as she flirts with its flawed premise. Joe and Missie May's childish play within a marriage founded on black folk values announces their cultural independence and maturity as opposed to any intellectual deficiency. Hurston's declaration of this truth reflects her training under Boas. His emphasis on the cultural specificity of any given people or individual – as opposed to numerical measurements of brain size or broad tests determining mental age – placed him at the forefront of a radically different approach to studying human intelligence. As he articulated what he would eventually term the "culture concept," he critiqued those scientists who began from an erroneous starting point. Boas argued: "We must pause before accepting the sweeping assertion that sameness of ethnical phenomena is always due to the sameness of the working of the human mind."[34] For Boas, acknowledging the individuality of the human mind necessitated understanding the specific life ways of different peoples. As he initially proved with regard to the display of evolutionary objects in the anthropological museum, he similarly set out to declare in his published texts. Hurston, his student turned artist and teacher, furthers his logic in her mature novels.

Hurston's Exhibition Books

Hurston's longer texts insist on the necessity of developing a sophisticated vision of folk culture so protagonists might better understand and esteem themselves. The cultural independence she advocates recalls Boas's admonitions. When Du Bois invited Boas to speak at Atlanta University in 1906, the father of anthropology warned against seeking white approval, declaring to the graduates: "[I]f you carry on your work with side glances on your white neighbor, waiting for his recognition and support of your noble work, you are destined to disappointment."[35] For Hurston, he was preaching to the choir. Turning to Boas's specific advocacy for fieldwork as a means of wresting authority away from "armchair anthropologists," Hurston crafts protagonists who move from displaying curiosity about the world around them to striking out on journeys of exploration. In her hands, a childish mental state paves the way toward metaphorical rebirth. Characters must be reborn, or return to a condition of relative innocence, to sharpen their vision of U.S. society and attain real knowledge about themselves and the culture they inhabit.[36]

I want to suggest that Hurston comes to view the participant-observer method as a means for discovering new artistic power.[37] Hurston's long fiction charts the relationship between self-knowledge and intellectual power. These novels emerge as what I term "exhibition books," texts that self-consciously exhibit the folk mind. Like Boas's early ethnographic books – such as *Chinook Texts* (1894), *Kathlamet Texts* (1901), and *Tsimshian Texts* (1902), which are almost completely devoid of explanations of the artifacts he catalogues – Hurston's stories display rural cultures that her protagonists must successfully interpret with minimal assistance. To this end, she portrays her protagonists developing powers of vision that corroborate their intellectual acumen.

The novels that comprise Hurston's mature phase during the 1930s feature protagonists positioned as outsiders. Hurston introduces John Buddy, Janie, and Moses – the protagonists of *Jonah's Gourd Vine* (1934), *Their Eyes Were Watching God* (1937), and *Moses, Man of the Mountain* (1939) respectively – as individuals born outside the inner circles of the folk communities they eventually call home. As a result, they never gain complete insider status and often rely on their marriages for establishing a stable cultural foundation. Hurston further emphasizes their outsider status by identifying their racial identity as atypical from that of their community. John Buddy and Janie are biracial, and their physical appearance plays no small role in their relegation outside of the core sympathies of their neighbors. Similarly, Moses has been raised as an Egyptian prince but finds himself residing among Hebrews. Hurston binds these protagonists more closely by infusing each with the natural curiosity that leads them to seek cultural knowledge through exposure to new experiences and new people. By designating these protagonists intimate members of communities while they also retain a kind of "other" position, Hurston primes them to perform the work of the cultural anthropologist.[38] And although none of these protagonists write ethnographies recording their findings, they all apply their cultural knowledge directly to their comprehension of themselves, an endeavor that reflects Hurston's personal posture toward her anthropological fieldwork.

My readings build on a number of critics who have explored the relationship between Hurston's anthropological work with Boas and her creative writing. In addition to work by Lamothe, Jacobs, and Carby that I have discussed, Houston Baker, Jr., Michael Elliot, Chuck Jackson, and Benigno Sánchez-Eppler have thoughtfully examined the different ways Hurston's anthropological training with Boas impacts her literary texts. Their work provides a fertile foundation for my study of Hurston. But whereas these critics almost always depend on readings of *Their Eyes Were Watching God*, I examine Hurston's wider corpus in an effort to demonstrate the ways her anthropological research fundamentally shapes her creative process and dependence on the visual dexterity demanded by ethnographic work. Thus, this chapter progresses from her early short stories to later novels to argue that Hurston approaches her written texts as exhibits that display African American intellect and cultural authority in ways that vie with, and ultimately surpass, traditional displays in the natural history museum.

Failing to See Past the Shadow of the Gourd Vine

John Buddy Pearson of *Jonah's Gourd Vine* (1934) represents Hurston's first potential ethnographer, but his journey toward personal and cultural understanding is riddled with failure. From the opening of the story, Hurston signals his cultural immaturity by the error of his vision. The novel is based on Hurston's parents' courtship and marriage and follows John's move "across the creek" from life with his mother and stepfather as sharecroppers, to his time working on the plantation of his mother's former slave owner, and on through his three marriages before ending with his untimely death. As an adolescent, the narrator presents John Buddy framed by the doorway of his parents' shack watching "white folks passin' by" to "see whar dey gwine" (*NS*, 4). Hurston's inclusion of this foundational scene to identify John's estimable curiosity connects him to the young Hurston of Eatonville as well as to young protagonists such as John Redding and Isis. Yet John's continued fascination with whiteness suggests a dangerous resemblance to Joe and Missie May Banks. Hurston hints that John Buddy must be wary of admiring white cultural experience to the detriment of seeking greater understanding of black folk culture.[39]

This danger looms larger as John attempts to analyze the culture across the Big Creek and his relationship to it. John struggles to understand Lucy Ann Potts, Hurston's representative of the exceptional black folk mind. He first meets Lucy after crossing the Big Creek, his naked swim symbolizing a baptismal moment that prepares him to see with new eyes. The first sight he encounters on the other side of the creek is the schoolhouse, which he initially mistakes for a church. The image of black children learning to "read and write like white folks" impresses him and recalls a seminal scene in Washington's *Up from Slavery*, but Lucy, described only as a "little girl with bright black eyes," makes a more meaningful imprint on his mind (*NS*, 14). Significantly, Hurston does not use John's discovery of the school as an opportunity to extol the necessity of verbal literacy; instead, she highlights the need for critical observation. She establishes a complicated relationship between traditional educational spaces and visually complex experiences, associating the latter with sophisticated sight that sharpens one's mental ability. In the same way that the natural history museum celebrates learning through astutely viewing cultural exhibits, Hurston implies the need for John Buddy to study his new surroundings with discernment.

Unfortunately, John's love for Lucy suffers under the weight of his confused conflation of her cultural complexity with what he construes as her representation of white intelligence. He repeatedly thinks of her in terms of her white clothing or white speech. The end-of-the-school-year celebration finds Lucy in "[l]acy whiteness" as she delivers her recitation and even her home is overwrought with whiteness: "It was different from every other Negro's place that he had ever seen. Flowers in the yard among whitewashed rocks ... Peanuts drying on white cloth in the sun" (*NS*, 35, 60). This abiding whiteness contributes to his admiration of Lucy, but it also forms the basis for an unhealthy aspect of his love: he gives Lucy the power of knowing him, a power strangely connected to the whiteness in which he swathes her. But even as he offers to be read, he demonstrates precious little self-understanding.

John Buddy both accepts and resents what the black folk in the beginning of *Mules and Men* deny white power and curiosity: access. Hurston describes African Americans as recognizing and resisting the white man's attempt "to know into somebody else's business." To this inquisitiveness, black folk subjects retort: "He can read my writing but he sho' can't read my mind" (*NS*, 10). Hurston acknowledges the tension inherent in the anthropological project of infiltrating the mind of the "other" with the intent to display it for wider consumption. Using her personal position as a guide, she implies that self-knowledge together with an ability to understand white culture makes the presentation of the black mind permissible. In stark distinction to such a disposition, when John proposes marriage to Lucy, he elevates her to an uncomfortable position of authority akin to that of the indifferent white researcher. He tells her, "You knows mah feelings" while she asks, "How Ah know whut you got inside yo' mind?" (*NS*,

65). Although he initially crossed the Big Creek to learn more about the ways of African Americans, his relationship with Lucy shows him abdicating any pretense toward a search for greater folk knowledge in preference for allowing Lucy, whom he deems representative of white intellect, to think for him.

This proves particularly problematic given Hurston's designation of marriage as the space where true learning can occur. In this way, she presents marriage as potentially fostering the position of the participant-observer invested in studying black folk culture. As a relationship that is both within and distinct from the broader community, it offers a generative site for formulating a vision that engenders independent thinking. But in contrast to Joe and Missie May's happy union that stands on their revitalized autonomous value system, John remains a *too*-active participant within the culture of the plantation community after his marriage to Lucy. Even anthropologists who avidly supported field research warned against submerging oneself too deeply into the culture that was the subject of research. Agreeing with Melville Herskovits, Arthur Vidich avers:

> If the participant observer seeks genuine experiences, unqualifiedly immersing and committing himself in the group he is studying, it may become impossible for him to objectify his own experiences for research purposes; in committing his loyalties he develops vested interests which will inevitably enter into his observations.[40]

After Lucy's death, John's marriage to Hattie epitomizes his mistake of "unqualifiedly immersing and committing himself" in the community instead of observing it and participating within limits. This new role interferes with his ability to publish his ideas in the pulpit, the space from which he shares cultural truths that have the potential to impact the community positively.

The painful consequences of his too-close proximity to the folk eventually lead John to recommit to the status of an analytical observer during the uncomfortable spectacle of his divorce trial. From the position of a more responsible participant-observer, the court proceedings strike John as invasive: he *discerns* rather than *desires* white thought patterns and thereby transforms the courtroom into a crucial site of cultural observation. Realizing that the white judge and spectators view the trial as affirmation of black sexual deviancy, John refuses to defend himself against Hattie's accusations. Later, he explains his silence to his friend, saying:

> Ah didn't want de white folks tuh hear 'bout nothin' lak dat. Dey knows too much 'bout us as it is, but dey some things dey ain't tuh know ... Dey

thinks wese all ignorant as it is, and dey thinks wese all alike, and dat dey knows us inside and out, but you know better. Dey wouldn't make no great 'miration if you had uh tole 'em Hattie had all dem mens. Dey spectin' dat. Dey wouldn't zarn 'tween uh woman lak Hattie and one lak Lucy. (*NS*, 140)

John discovers that the white judge and spectators, lazy and disinterested viewers of other cultures, regard his divorce case as a display of the most derogatory aspects of black folk life. Like the clerk at the end of "The Gilded Six-Bits," the white courtroom observers sit ready to fit John and Hattie into the stereotypes they know.

Hurston intimates that the courtroom shares much in common with the ineffective natural history museum exhibit. The presentation of his divorce trial lacks the organizing principles Boas claimed necessary for a successful museum display that included contextualizing elements. As a curator at the American Museum of Natural History, Boas passionately argued for modernizing their exhibition policies to achieve more compelling displays of other cultures. He advocated for staging exhibits that communicated through "a presentational medium, allowing ... cultural connections actually to be *seen*."[41] He insisted that "the Museum maintain the proper atmosphere for viewing collections," and explained that it must be like a "sanctuary."[42] Visitors must be impressed with the magnitude of attempting to understand other people based on cultural terms unlike their own. In the courtroom, John emerges as the sophisticated observer who comprehends the dangerous absence of these exhibition features essential for true education to occur.

John's new perception marks the first time he speaks advisedly on white views of blackness. However, it is his return to gaze upon his parishioners that signals the breadth of his growth. Standing in the pulpit after the spectacle of his divorce trial, he decides to preach on Jesus's wounds. John's sermonic repetition of "I can see Him," ostensibly his proclamation of divine sight, doubles as a testament to a newfound ability to see himself. His capacity to assess the distortions of culturally uninformed vision endows him with enlightening self-knowledge. John's honest assessment of his failings leads to his second rebirth, his necessary return to a childish state. Throughout the night he seeks Lucy, "mewing and crying like a lost child" (*NS*, 153). Though he does not find Lucy, John does discover Sally, his third wife. Before their relationship begins, John divulges all to Sally and finds himself "with his head in her lap sobbing like a boy of four" (*NS*, 158). On their wedding night, he is "as shy as a girl – as Lucy had been" (*NS*, 160). When he fails to remain faithful to Sally, John despises himself. As he drives home overwhelmed by his transgression, he is killed by a train. The narrator reports that John "half-see[s] the railroad from looking inward" (*NS*, 167).

Deborah Clarke insightfully concludes that Hurston uses John's death to construct a "paradigm: Vision must be embodied, one must see outwardly as well as inwardly."[43] By the novel's end, John recognizes that demonstrating visual dexterity in the public church, where he delivers imagistic sermons and offers visually laden prayers, means nothing if he neglects to use such visual acuity when probing the deepest recesses of his mind. By presenting his failure to reconcile his worlds of experience as the cause of his death, Hurston places a new premium on the inside-outside visual dichotomy that signals individual complexity and cultural intelligence in her novels as well as her sense of responsible science. If marriage provides a space for learning to see the world independently, African Americans must take this responsibility seriously. Hurston's construction of Janie brings this idea into sharper focus as she extends the trope of the Picture Book in her creation of a protagonist who achieves cultural understanding through the kind of sophisticated observation enacted by anthropologists and encouraged by the natural history museum.

Janie's Enlightening Fieldwork and Desire to Instruct

Hurston binds her participant-observer protagonists' intellect to their ability to translate cultural knowledge into self-knowledge and their capacity to acquire wisdom through vision. *Their Eyes Were Watching God* presents Janie as the successful ethnographer who not only richly applies her collected cultural knowledge to herself, but also publishes her findings so others might benefit. In terms that anticipate Hurston's celebration of the visionary powers she acquires in *Tell My Horse* (1938), Hurston designates Janie the accomplished cultural anthropologist by emphasizing her increasingly self-reflective vision. Yet within scholarship, if *Jonah's Gourd Vine* is most commonly read with attention to John's failure to realize the greatness of his voice, *Their Eyes* is roundly celebrated as the depiction of Janie asserting her individuality through the triumphant emergence of her voice. Karla Holloway concludes, "Hurston leaves [John's] voice airborne and then brings it back as a wind in *Their Eyes Were Watching God*," and Dolan Hubbard implicitly proclaims Janie an heir to John by defining her story as a "sermon" and studying the "extrachurch modes of expression" in the text.[44]

Within this critical legacy, scholars rightly focus on Janie's dramatic quest. Although my argument draws on the excellent work that identifies Janie as a character working to attain greater interior knowledge through the assertion of her voice, I recover the attendant importance of Hurston's quest to reveal the intimate link between Janie's critical vision and newfound agency. Building on Lamothe's work, I want to suggest that Hurston presents Janie as a questing ethnographer who equates trenchant vision with knowledge. As Janie haltingly begins her narrative, she recognizes the need to make her story readily visible, averring "'tain't no use in me telling you somethin' unless Ah give you de understandin' to go 'long wid it. Unless you see de fur, a mink skin ain't no different from a coon hide" (NS, 180). Stuart Burrows shrewdly notes in reference to the novel: "[I]n order for vision to become knowledge we must not only see but understand what we are seeing. We must see, that is, in terms of something else."[45] Janie is anxious to ensure that Pheoby does not leave her porch as blind as the other porch sitters, so she visualizes her experiences for Pheoby.

At the same time, Hurston encourages readers to emulate Pheoby and repudiate the communal porch. Whereas the porch sitters watch in silent ignorance as Janie returns to town after burying Tea Cake, Pheoby immediately realizes that she needs more information and greater context to understand the sight of Janie returning home in overalls. When Pheoby departs to learn more from Janie, she leaves the other folk sequestered on the porch "pelting her back with unasked questions" and hoping "the answers were cruel and strange" (NS, 177). Pheoby is the ideal museum visitor and student, whereas the porch sitters are the most challenged. Janie identifies the general community's failure to pursue real knowledge as the root of their persistent misapprehension of life, and although she insists that they might learn something from her own wealth of knowledge – "Ah could ... sit down and tell'em things" – she clearly questions their mental capacity (NS, 179). In vivid contrast, Pheoby's potential for supplying a "good thought" inspires Janie's self-revelation (NS, 180).

Janie arrives at this understanding not through her ability to talk but through her extended study of folk culture and her position within it. The famous scene under the pear tree dramatizes her desire to know more about the nature of people and the world beyond her grandmother's home. The deluge of questions she considers as she "gaze[s] on a mystery" echoes the kinds of questions ethnographers generate before embarking on their fieldwork (NS, 183). Significantly, Janie distinguishes the birth of "her conscious life" as beginning at her grandmother's gate, a subtle indictment of Nanny's obstructive position (*NS*, 182). As a representative of the narrow element of the folk community, Nanny's gated yard symbolizes her circumscribed worldview. When she discovers her granddaughter kissing Johnny Taylor, Nanny's "eyes didn't bore and pierce. They diffused and melted Janie, the room and the world into one comprehension" (*NS*, 184). Nanny's indistinct sight sharply contrasts Janie's keen "gaze up and down the road" and her passionate desire to explore, experience, and know (*NS*, 184).

More specifically, Janie's thirst to know more about marriage compared to Nanny's insistence on thrusting her into the institution as defined by white cultural norms signals the radical difference between their views. Nanny warns Janie against the prevailing African American conception of marriage exclaiming, "Lawd have mussy! Dat's de very prong all us black women gits hung on. Dis love!" (*NS*, 193). Her insistence that Janie marry for protection and position, live "lak de white madam," and "[g]it up on uh high chair and sit dere" flies in the face of Janie's desire to "journey to the horizons in search of *people*" (*NS*, 267). Janie seeks the role of collector of ideas and cultural understanding in opposition to her grandmother's desire for her to view the world from a seat of power. Their clashing views epitomize the dueling ideologies of early-twentieth-century anthropologists: Boas forcefully advocated ending the rule of "armchair anthropology," but traditional anthropologists placed little stock in performing fieldwork to understand the subjects they studied.

But before Janie consciously formulates a definition for marriage apart from Nanny's, Joe Starks offers her a different version of an ideal mate consistent with her grandmother's standards. Janie takes pride in his "portly" figure that is "like rich white folks" and overlooks the implications of his declaration that she is "made to sit on de front porch and rock and fan" herself (*NS*, 197). His Nanny-like worldview works to limit her opportunity to participate in or observe the Eatonville community, and the narrator's description of him ominously echoes Joe's initial sketch of Otis Slemmons in "The Gilded Six-Bits." Jody thinks Janie should appreciate his efforts to build "a high chair for her to sit in and overlook the world" whereas Janie wishes to enter and explore the world first hand (*NS*, 224). In fact, her husband conflates an infant highchair and the regressive anthropologist armchair to alarming effect.

She is thirty-five when she begins reading Joe like an accomplished ethnographer: "For the first time she could see a man's head naked of its skull. Saw the cunning thoughts race in and out through the caves and promontories of his mind long before they darted out of the tunnel of his mouth" (*NS*, 237). Trapped in a marriage that denies her the ability to observe and participate actively within her community, Janie turns her powers of perception on her husband and discovers the fullness of his push for power. Joe exchanges the potential for love and true knowledge for the ability to invade and overtake Janie's mind. In her final confrontation with Jody, Janie declares: "[Y]ou wasn't satisfied wid me de way Ah was. Naw! Mah own mind had tuh be squeezed and crowded out tuh make room for yours in me" (*NS*, 244).[46] Janie recognizes that her husband, in many ways representative of white values and power, violated her trusting invitation to see her inside spaces in preference for the power to force her acceptance of his cultural values.

In stark contrast, Tea Cake seems determined to return Janie to the childhood Nanny prematurely ended, implicitly treasuring the immature state that racist scientists deride as proof of black ignorance. The value he places on youthful feelings rejects the legitimacy of such research. On their second meeting, he takes Janie fishing after midnight and she exults in feeling "like a child breaking the rules" (*NS*, 257). In contrast to Joe, Tea Cake revels in her youthful love for him. Tea Cake's declaration, shortly before his death, rings undeniably true: "God made it so you spent yo' ole age first wid somebody else, and saved up yo' young girl days to spend wid me" (*NS*, 322–323). He affects a spiritual rebirth in her life that allows her to recapture her prematurely ended childhood.[47] In fact, he positions her in a student role that she cherishes. She exults to Pheoby: "He done taught me de maiden language" (*NS*, 268). Unlike John, who defiles his born-again state with Sally before he can experience its benefits, Janie returns to Eatonville prepared to translate her lately acquired knowledge into an exhibit for instructing others.

As Janie concludes her story, she encourages Pheoby to ease the curiosity of the porch talkers by sharing her tale, by similarly transitioning from student to teacher. She cautions her friend not to "feel too mean wid de rest of 'em 'cause dey's parched up from not knowin' things," and she maintains, "you got tuh *go* there tuh *know* there" (*NS*, 332). The "there" she refers to is the space of rediscovering values apart from those represented by outside cultural principles, a synonym for the "spots and places" Joe references in "The Gilded Six-Bits." Pheoby, Janie's ideal listener, responds to her friend's revelation in terms very different from the townsfolk. While they gaze upon Janie and wonder whether she has maintained her financial wealth, the standard of worth dictated by majority standards, Pheoby pledges to improve herself: "Ah ain't satisfied wid mahself no mo'. Ah mean tuh make Sam take me fishin' wid him after this" (*NS*, 332).

Pheoby recognizes that Janie's time with Tea Cake transforms marriage into a space for acquiring new knowledge based on individual experiences and rooted in cultural pride.

Janie resembles Hurston in the roles of participant and observer in *Mules and Men*: she shares much in common with the community, but ultimately, she enjoys access to a body of knowledge they do not possess. In embarking on her anthropological fieldwork, Hurston excitedly wrote to friends about finally understanding folk culture through her ability to "look and see."[48] Writing to Langston Hughes while he was finishing his bachelor's degree at Lincoln, she encourages him to "hurry and come out of that knowledge works" and to join her on the road where she is "beginning to *see* really" and hopes that he will "see" as she does.[49] Hurston advocates fieldwork as an antidote to worn-out ideas of the classroom, and she celebrates Janie's realization of Boas's scientific ideal: her protagonist comes to understand her cultural identity through fieldwork and therefore travels a path to individual fulfillment not based on preconceived notions but through cultural discovery acquired from experience. For Boas, the natural history display is successful only to the extent that it presents different cultures on their own terms as opposed to assessing them by Western values. And even then, exhibits require visitors sufficiently perceptive to comprehend them. Hurston designates Janie as capable of both organizing such a display *and* incisively interpreting it. Her exhibition book exhorts readers to achieve a similar level of interpretive sophistication.

Moses and the Steep Climb to Cultural Maturity

Notwithstanding the complex nature of Hurston's appeal to anthropological paradigms to construct her folk protagonists, her novels met with energetic derision leveled by black critics and writers. After a few complimentary remarks about *Their Eyes*, Alain Locke wondered: "[W]hen will the Negro novelist of maturity, who knows how to tell a story convincingly ... come to grips with motive fiction and social document fiction?"[50] Richard Wright was even harsher, effectively using his searing denunciation of Hurston's novel as fuel to launch the protest genre he advocated. He opined: "Her dialogue manages to catch the psychological movements of the Negro folk-mind in their pure simplicity, but that's as far as it goes."[51] Wright condemned Hurston for "*voluntarily*" continuing "the tradition which was *forced* on the Negro in the theatre, that is, the minstrel technique that makes the 'white folks' laugh."[52] Both men determine that *Their Eyes* represents an immature work, a novel that cannot be seriously discussed alongside more radically "progressive" social realist fiction. In fact, their respective misgivings about the "oversimplification" and "simplicity" of her characters implicitly labels Hurston's own artistic mind as equally simplistic.

In many ways, their criticism is fantastic. Although their differing aesthetic philosophies regarding the direction of African American literature understandably leads them to take issue with Hurston's literary style in *Their Eyes*, the attendant suggestion that Hurston lacks artistic maturity ignores her educational background and training. She did not accept their criticism quietly. In response to Locke's review, Hurston penned "The Chick with One Hen" accusing Locke of lacking sufficient knowledge of folk culture or black literature to offer meaningful criticism. Hurston assesses his critique only to conclude that Locke was not worthy of her full engagement. She declared, "I will send my toe-nails to debate him on what he knows about Negroes and Negro life."[53]

Her sharp words remind us that *Moses, Man of the Mountain* emerges out of one of her most politically active moments and might be read as her response to such attacks.[54] Although scholars have compellingly read *Moses* as everything from a political commentary on Nazi Germany to a general rebuke of African Americans' investment in charismatic male leaders, considering Moses as part of a continuum of characters defined as potential anthropologists clarifies Hurston's artistic and political trajectory.[55] In Moses, she crafts a protagonist whose psychological complexity arises from his passionate study of different cultures. In striking opposition to Wright and other black authors invested in portraying black psychology in sociological terms, Hurston dramatizes the force of a fully developed folk mind.[56] As Barbara Johnson explains, Hurston's "project grows out of anthropology" and seeks to answer the question, "How is *culture* transmitted?"[57] I want to suggest that with Moses, Hurston responds to this inquiry by suggesting that culture is transmitted by leaders committed to understanding and promoting folk culture. She signifies on the trope of the Picture Book to argue for the necessity of black leaders who possess a vision of African American progress rooted in cultural maturity. Coming close on the heels of *Tell My Horse*, *Moses* concludes Hurston's mature period with a display of a fully developed cultural anthropologist.

In fact, Hurston's continued reliance on anthropology hints at what really sets detractors like Richard Wright aboil. For Wright, sociology, not anthropology, provided the necessary tools for understanding African American experience in U.S. society in the 1930s. Fleshing out the relationship between these two sciences during this period, Werner Sollors notes,

Anthropologists were more concerned with "culture," "folk," "tradition," and "adaptation," whereas sociologists looked into "civilization," "an urbanized population," "modernization" and "conflict." ... [T]he Boasian anthropologists in the period leaned toward an "internalist approach to the study of human groups – they focused primarily on the group considered in itself, its norms, institutions, and the patterns that gave it coherence." The Parkian sociologists, on the other hand, "highlighted the processes of interaction between groups" that were "being thrown into contact with each other, were reacting to each other, and mutually influencing each other in all sorts of ways." Thus, "folk culture" often suggested the internalist perspective, whereas "urban civilization" summoned the interactionist approach.[58]

Sollors's overview of the main thrust of anthropology and sociology of the late 1930s maps helpfully to the work of Hurston and Wright, respectively. Wright insisted that African American writers confront readers with the dire consequences of interracial conflict, but Hurston focused primarily on intraracial community discord. And notwithstanding the searing critique of contemporaries such as Ellison – who in his rush to boost Wright amazingly lumps Hurston into a group of black writers whom he accuses of "ignoring the folk source of all vital American Negro art" and therefore with *Moses*, produces a novel that "for Negro fiction did nothing" – Hurston tasks her exhibition book with displaying how a strong cultural identity must form the foundation for satisfying black citizenship.[59]

Notwithstanding her abiding interest in anthropological study, *Moses* comes closest to portraying the interaction between groups thrown together in a manner that recalls the issues studied in sociological research on urbanization. The Egyptians stand in for the white majority worldview. The narrator anticipates the coming split between Moses and Pharaoh by explaining that Moses "wanted to go traveling into foreign countries and see how they lived and made war there. But Pharaoh was not interested in the ways of other peoples" (*NS*, 398). Representing a budding ethnographer, Moses sees the value of learning about other cultures while Pharaoh belongs to that complacent majority that resists Boas's anthropological approach. Moses's desire to employ his questioning vision to gain knowledge of other people puts him at odds with his Egyptian family. In discussions with them, Moses appeals to both anthropological as well as sociological ideas. When he advises his brother that it is "a weak spot in any nation to have a large body of disaffected people within its confines," he articulates the logic of the sociologist (*NS*, 394). Yet Hurston carefully associates Moses's hybrid wisdom on such matters with his cultural anthropological devotion to learning from both scholars and priests within traditional educational structures and mysterious religious rites.

Although marriage plays a less prominent role in Moses's development, his childish questioning disposition – "Why was the sky blue? Who bent it up like that? ... Where was the river going and what were the sounds it said? Who made the first day? When? Why?" – recalls Janie's seminal experience under the pear tree (*NS*, 373). But his intimate relationship with Mentu distinguishes his development from Hurston's previous potential anthropologist protagonists. In Mentu, the Hebrew stableman who serves as his folk teacher and echoes "Homer's Mentor," Moses benefits from a knowledgeable teacher who nurtures the brand of knowledge Hurston advocates.[60] When the young Moses expresses admiration for the scholarly priests, Mentu reminds him that the priests "know what is in the books. That is learning, not wisdom. Learning without wisdom is a load of books on a donkey's back. I want *you* to understand" (*NS*, 388). Mentu's insistence that Moses seek understanding that looks beyond conventional books articulates Hurston's notion of how one acquires true knowledge. She encourages black Americans to adopt the predisposition of the museum visitor eager to learn from all that they see.

Hurston hints that protesting a society's unfair power structures without re-instilling cultural pride into a group misses the mark. Like her previous protagonists, Moses's uncertain ethnicity garners a kind of "other" status that affords him an unencumbered view of the Hebrew people as well as of the Egyptians. After spending years leading Goshen, he discovers that the Hebrew leaders suffer from many of the same weaknesses he identified in the Egyptians. Specifically, in Aaron he detects a different version of Ta-Phar, his Egyptian brother: "His face looked like Ta-Phar's. There was the look of weak brains and strong pride" (*NS*, 521). The difference in skin color, background, and rank mean little compared to the two men's shared desire for power and lack of cultural curiosity or understanding. As he attempts to show Aaron the error of his ways, Moses explains: "Your tiny horizon never did get no bigger, so you mistook a spotlight for the sun" (*NS*, 582). This failure to evaluate the Hebrew people and treasure their rich culture leads Moses to proclaim to Aaron: "You are blind" (*NS*, 583). His blindness recalls a line of characters who failed to respect the importance of learning more about the world and their own cultural identity. Like John Redding's mother's "large eyes" that were "watery and weak" or Janie's grandmother's "eyes" that "didn't bore and pierce," Aaron represents poor black vision that must be surpassed for real progress to occur (*NS*, 927, 184).

This compromised vision, this inability to distinguish true knowledge from the false lure of power alone, makes it impossible for Moses to attribute the problems of the Hebrew people solely to their past exploitation by the Egyptians. In fact, his recognition of their shared weakness increases his determination to challenge the Hebrew vision of nationhood. Though a number of scholars question Moses's treatment of Aaron and Miriam, his possible siblings, the narrator identifies them as dangerous examples of individuals enthralled with the majority culture. While Moses is atop Sinai receiving God's sacred law, Aaron goads the people to make a golden calf so they "can worship like [they] did in Egypt" (*NS*, 545). Miriam, eerily reminiscent of Joe Starks, remains fascinated with speechmaking and position, leaving Moses to pity her after she dies and provide her with a Jody-like funeral. In contrast to Aaron, Miriam, and even his wife, Zipporah, Moses refused to "assume the crown" that the Hebrews "were used to" for he "had no wish to impose his will on others" (*NS*, 559). Moses counsels Joshua, his chosen heir not to "let the people take up too many habits from the nations they come in contact with and throw away what they got from God" (*NS*, 586).

Moses's admonition for treasuring one's culture sounds a culminating note for Hurston's trio of mature protagonists. His warning reaffirms Hurston's early declaration of the national need for curiosity and appreciation for other cultures even as one formulates an independent vision of the world. Echoing Janie's words to Pheoby, Moses explains to Joshua that the Hebrew people "don't think. They are trying to go on what they know and that ain't enough" (*NS*, 484). For Hurston, the key to developing active thought remains firmly bound to cultivating the type of vision accumulated through research or fostered by museums and their most effective exhibits. After Moses crosses out of Egypt, he discovers that you "have to go to life to know life," a refrain Hurston repeats in every novel (*NS*, 411). Her fictional representations of protagonists who experience and study the intricacies of folk culture offer rich alternatives to taking up ethnographic fieldwork or heading to institutions devoted to storing and showing such work; in fact, her fiction succeeds in displaying the nuanced context to which Boas aspired in his exhibits for the natural history museum.

A Novel Replacement for the American Museum of Unnatural History

As Boas prepared to leave the American Museum of Natural History, he held onto the hope that anthropologists could organize museum exhibits that "should fulfil (*sic*) the function of a primary objective school for the general public, as well as serve those who strive for higher education and help to train the teacher."[61] Yet, he ended his professional tenure at the museum without feeling that the exhibits he helped construct ever truly succeeded in translating the unique cultures he studied. Even as he advocated for centrally placed large cases holding life groups that offered context for the even larger cases holding the artifacts that represented different aspects of a culture, he acknowledged the many disadvantages of museum display. He attempted to address some drawbacks by designing pamphlets and monographs that followed the organization of the collection and gave museum visitors "a full description of the contents of a case or of several cases."[62] By providing a range of textual formats that spanned from simple labels on cases to detailed monographs intended to contextualize the encased object further, Boas strove to meet the needs of the general visitor as well as the more knowledgeable scholar. But when he transferred his work solely to the Anthropology Department at Columbia University, he faced no such divide: Boas committed himself to producing academic work.

Hurston, however, never completely embraced the ivory walls of the university. As she completed *Mules and Men*, a text she hoped would appeal to a popular audience while also earning respect from the scientific community, she sought professional validation from Boas in the form of a forward. Boas responded to her request in a September 1934 letter:

> A couple of months ago Lippincott wrote to me asking for an introduction to your book and I promised to write one if the manuscript is of a character that would seem to me desirable. They sent me part of the manuscript and said that they would send the rest, which, however, has never come. I think you had better take it up with them.[63]

His insistence that he see the entire manuscript before offering his written endorsement, as well as his stipulation that her book prove to be "a character" that he finds "desirable," reflects his belief that her ethnography should contribute responsibly to the field of anthropology. Hurston walked a fine line as she sought to uncover and share the wealth of Southern black folklore with the world. Even though she succeeded in convincing Boas to pen the forward to *Mules and Men* in addition to obtaining a dust jacket endorsement by Melville Herskovits, her book failed to secure her position in the world of anthropology. In fact, when she applied for a Guggenheim a few months before *Mules and Men* appeared in print, Boas's recommendation letter was less than enthusiastic. He bluntly observed: "On the whole, her methods are more journalistic than scientific and I am not under the impression that she is just the right caliber for a Guggenheim Fellowship."[64]

Hurston might have concurred. She fervently wanted to publish work that would be read widely, but following strict scientific rules of anthropologic research and publication proved a challenge for her. Although she sought grants from the Rosenwald Fund and a Guggenheim Fellowship to aid her documentation of black folklore, she was driven principally by her desire to collect and share her research through art rather than simply file it away in pedantic scientific publications. Even after she published articles in *The Journal of American Folklore* and *The Journal of Negro History*, Hurston remained dedicated to presenting black folk culture as a vibrant, living reality rather than an ethnographic subject to be salvaged. By channeling her energies primarily into her fiction, she found a venue more akin to the natural history museum in its unapologetic appeal to a diverse audience. Unlike her ethnographies that included illustrations or documentary style photographs and seek to present Hurston as the accomplished anthropologist, her novels focus on the visualizing practices of her protagonists, characters who demonstrate the advantages of learning by sight and display the efficacy of developing a sophisticated understanding of their culture. As they move from lacking self-understanding to gaining profound personal and social insight, she builds a paradigm in which sight becomes heavily inflected: Her protagonists' ability "to see" verifies their level of maturity while simultaneously presenting a picture of African American intellectualism. Through her carefully drawn characters, she extends successful museum observation into a posture for assessing life. Thus, the "formal curiosity" that Boas advocated – and Hurston accused white America of lacking when she contemplated the American Museum of Unnatural History – bloomed fully in the forms of her visual-minded protagonists. By the conclusion of her mature period, the exhibition books that catalog her portrayal of rural minds simultaneously display her own intellectual strength. Hurston, like her folk protagonists, accomplishes what Boas strove to do in his early museum work: she makes the folk mind accessible, admirable, and seen.

CHAPTER 5

Melvin Tolson: Gaining Modernist Perspective in the Art Gallery

Practically all the great artists have accepted the influence of others. But the difference lies in the fact that the artist with vision, sees his material, chooses, changes, and by integrating what he has learned with his own experiences, finally molds something distinctly personal. – Romare Bearden, 1934[1]

Melvin Tolson's volumes of poetry begin and end in the art gallery. Whereas Hurston's fiction draws implicitly on methods of observation promoted by the natural history museum, his verse books explicitly engage the lessons in vision administered by the art museum. Tolson's interest in the museum recalls Hurston's relationship to these institutions in that he, too, found spaces for display akin to his primary professional workplace. In the same way that her anthropological training led her to craft novels that model the natural history museum's investment in sight as a means of acquiring knowledge, his career as an English professor impelled him to pen poetry that dramatizes the art exhibition's dedication to challenging a visitor's perspective. After all, Tolson contested different perspectives in the classroom. He maintained a lifelong commitment to college education and prided himself on the pedagogical prowess that kept him popular and respected by students and faculty alike.[2] For him, the collegiate classroom provided a physical space for intellectual inquiry stimulated by diverse texts. By focusing on the two volumes that provide bookends for his career, *A Gallery of Harlem Portraits* (1935) and *Harlem Gallery* (1965), I examine how considering the history of the art gallery together with Tolson's position as a college English professor helps us understand why the gallery becomes an apt metaphor for publication, a space to share ideas. Further signifying on the trope of the Picture Book, Tolson uses his verse to demonstrate how the power to interpret visual art increases one's ability to analyze black culture and individual character. Moreover, by making his most notable speaker an "ex-professor," he particularly emphasizes the importance of instruction.

148

Art Spots: The Jazz Club, Classroom, and Gallery

As a poet, Tolson came of age as the Harlem Renaissance waned. The New Negro movement both fascinated Tolson and helped refine his notions of black artistry. In the concluding paragraph of his master's thesis on Harlem Renaissance writers submitted to the Department of English and Comparative Literature at Columbia University in 1940, he distinguishes the new direction he sees black writing of the 1930s taking: "Most of the members of the Harlem Renaissance portrayed the sensational features of Negro life, which were exploited for the entertainment of white readers. The literature of today is earthy, unromantic, and sociological; and from it emerges Negro characters that are more graphically individualized."[3] Tolson's contemporary literary reputation as an African American poet invested in using Western techniques to secure white critical approval makes his early rejection of an artistic stance calculated to please "white readers" sound ironic.[4] Nevertheless, his assessment of the Harlem Renaissance reveals his awareness of the dangerous underside of white patronage.[5] Tolson proceeds to link the completion of his thesis to his discovery of the need for "a Negro epic in America," and he portrays his evolution from a devotion to "dead classicism" to crafting "word-pictures" of Harlem inhabitants as a natural maturing beyond Harlem Renaissance themes.[6] From his perspective, faithful portrayals of Harlem demanded a new form and an innovative site.

Whereas the jazz club and cabaret epitomize Harlem Renaissance spaces of artistic creation, performance, and criticism, Tolson's first book inserts Harlem dwellers into the art gallery. His relocation hints that the former venues, heralded as integrally connected to authentic verse of the period, eventually left artists exposed to patrons' deadening demands for diversion. Notwithstanding his appreciation for Langston Hughes's trailblazing work in *The Weary Blues* (1926) and *Fine Clothes for the Jew* (1927), Tolson intimates that the blues club lacks crucial ingredients to support the creation of innovative black art.[7] He was well aware of the white pleasure seekers overrunning these locales along with black patrons who grew to expect performances calculated to entertain rather than display artistic virtuosity. As Tolson worked to develop black verse portraying the complexity of African American cultural experience, he contrasted the often exploitative nature of Harlem Renaissance performance with the invigorating possibilities of the art museum.

Unlike the 1920s scene of Harlem night-life, institutions of visual art shared the rigorous expectations and pedagogical impetus of higher learning realms. Tolson felt serious African American art deserved serious criticism and he was famous for sharing this sentiment with readers of his work as well as with his students. Responding to one reader of his verse, he quipped: "My friend, it took me six years to write it. Is it surprising that it takes more than one reading to understand it?"[8] In his passionate rejoinder to J. Saunders Redding's disparaging review of his modernist verse, Tolson exclaimed: "Away with the simple Negro! This is a book to be chewed and digested. If Negro scholars don't get busy on it, white scholars will."[9] A former student recalls Tolson's admonitions in the classroom sounding an identical refrain: "Above and beyond the class assignments, you're going to read and study and dig. Finish *War and Peace* and then go on to his other works. Then I want you to tackle Darwin, Freud, and Marx. Don't just taste them; chew them and digest them. Then we'll get together and argue about them."[10]

The classrooms of historically black colleges and universities (HBCUs), such as Wiley where Tolson began his academic career, offered space for learning about, creating, and challenging art. David Gold explains that private HBCUs supported a program of study reflecting their long-standing commitment to "the classical liberal arts tradition" including "Latin and Greek ... as part of the standard curriculum long after such courses had been dropped from the requirement at elite white schools."[11] Reviewing Tolson's own education, Gold adds that not only was Tolson "trained in the black liberal arts tradition steeped in classics, religion, language, and oratory," but as a teacher, he viewed the classroom as "both a performance space and pulpit" where he integrated "both conservative and radical practices into a pedagogy that serve[d] both students and society."[12] Tolson valued the genuine sense of discovery animating educational spaces even as he exploited the concurrent expectation for professorial performance. One colleague described Tolson's educational posture: "He is a pacing, pounding man, a shouting, screaming man."[13]

His passionate commitment to proclaiming the intricacy of black life led him to demand that readers approach his verse with the kind of earnest interpretive posture afforded texts in a literature class and art objects displayed in museums. In appealing to the general attitude adopted by museum visitors, Tolson's work reflects an awareness of the multiple incarnations of the U.S. museum and the range of goals animating sites of display throughout American history. As he moves from loosely encasing his poetry within the strictures of visual art techniques to drawing meaningfully on the site of display in *Harlem Gallery*, Tolson subscribes to the idea of the gallery as a place of discovery that nonetheless adopts an

educational strategy. Like the version of the college classroom he favored –
a space where democratic analysis periodically gives way to authoritarian
explanation – the art gallery concedes the expertise of curators and direc-
tors responsible for creating the displays that enrich visitors' experiences.[14]
In stark contrast to the sometimes damaging democracy of the jazz club,
institutions of visual display assume a respectful yet less egalitarian relationship with their patrons. As an increasingly sophisticated poet and
old-school professor of literature, Tolson not only valued this mix of principles, he integrated them into his verse.

Accordingly, his aesthetic approach exploits the historical development of the art museum. After completing his master's thesis on Harlem
Renaissance writers, Tolson eagerly began crafting poetry that revealed
the impact urban life wields on African Americans. If Hurston places her
characters into novels structured around the rules of the natural history
museum to display Southern black culture and verify black intelligence,
Tolson inserts his poet speakers into the art museum to explore Northern
African American existence in the city and proclaim the creative potential
of modernist artists. The thirty-year period during which Tolson composed
A Gallery of Harlem Portraits, then set it aside, revised it, reconceived it,
and finally published *Harlem Gallery*, its radically reimagined heir, com-
prises the years in which he developed his aesthetic philosophy for creatively displaying black cultural identity. And this philosophy remained
invested in the site of the American art gallery.

The earliest U.S. museum, Charles Willson Peale's Philadelphia show-
place, began admitting visitors in 1786 and spurred the nineteenth-century rapid growth of American museums. When P. T. Barnum's American
Museum opened in 1842, it established a very different museum experience. Although both Peale and Barnum take a page from natural history *and* art museums, their institutions most significantly signal what
Les Harrison describes as the dueling philosophies shaping the art gallery
as an institution: was it to be a temple or a forum? To refine the logic
undergirding this dichotomy, Harrison quotes Duncan Cameron's definitions of a temple and forum: "As temple, the museum functions as a space
where 'those segments of society with the power to do so … enshrined
those things they held to be significant and valuable.' … The museum
provides opportunity for reaffirmation of the faith."[15] Conversely, a forum
serves as a space for "'confrontation, experimentation, and debate,'" and
"counters the hegemonic influence of the temple through the provision
of an open, alternative cultural site, a site where the values of the temple might be questioned and even contested."[16] Harrison examines Peale's

Philadelphia Museum and Barnum's American Museum as the best examples of Cameron's definitions of the temple and forum philosophies respectively, and his compelling discussion unveils a legacy Tolson indisputably inherits. *Harlem Gallery*, his final volume of poetry, subtly rehashes the nineteenth-century debates Peale and Barnum epitomize, whereas his first volume ponders the very possibility of drawing on urban life for high art subject matter.

Tolson's acknowledgment of this debate and interest in the gallery placed him ahead of the African American museum curve. Unlike mainstream art museums, the first independent African American museums did not appear until the late 1950s. Before then, roughly thirty museums on the campuses of historically black colleges and universities served as the primary spaces for the preservation and display of black art.[17] Although these institutions rarely receive the attention they deserve as significant repositories of African American art, the museums on the campuses of schools such as Hampton, Howard, and Fisk represent the earliest commitments to collecting African American objects of art. Edmund Barry Gaither, director of the Museum of the National Center of Afro-American Artists, notes that HBCU museums also warrant serious consideration for their position as "significant repositories of art and ... critical centers of discussion."[18] HBCUs filled the gap created by segregation laws that, prior to the 1960s, left black artists, scholars, and would-be museum attendees without access to venues where African American art could be displayed, discussed, and enjoyed.

Thus, although Tolson's verse of the 1930s anticipates expanded spaces for appreciating black art, his poetry of the 1950s and 1960s plays on the reality of his contemporary moment. The earliest independent museums devoted to black art include "the African American Museum in Cleveland (1956), Chicago's Ebony Museum of Negro Culture which became the DuSable Museum of African American History in Chicago (1961), and the International Afro American Museum in Detroit (1965)."[19] The history behind the founding of collegiate museums compared to that of independent museums highlights a crucial distinction coloring the philosophy undergirding these institutions. Although college administrators often founded HBCU museums for the express purpose of building racial pride and making great art accessible to students, thereby embodying the temple concept, independent museums arose from more militant sentiments modeled on the forum model.

For example, the official policy Howard adopted as it developed its permanent collection stressed the need for students to interact with excellent art by artists of all races. Conversely, as entities planted in the shadow of the Civil Rights movement and rise of Black Power, the earliest independent museums often sprung from the grassroots efforts of their surrounding communities. These institutions proudly identified themselves as antiestablishment, and they reveled in staging unconventional exhibitions that spoke directly to the needs and interests of the urban centers they called home. Lectures, community specific social programs, and live performances proved integral to their programming and reflected the broader cause they espoused. Christy Coleman notes that for these museums, "there was nothing shameful about doing an exhibit about rats and how to combat them"; on the contrary, displays deemed unrelated to the community ran the risk of being deemed "too 'bourgeois'" and losing the support of surrounding neighborhoods.[20]

The years encapsulating Tolson's reconceptualization of his gallery metaphor as a means for pondering black vision witnessed these developments in the world of the African American art museum, and his verse demonstrates a commitment to championing aspects of both the HBCU and independent museum, the temple and the forum. As he turned to poetry to proffer a new perspective of black urban identity, contemporary African American visual artists likely reminded him of the connection between the museum and the college classroom. Upon arriving to New York in the late 1920s, Tolson could not have missed either the prominence of visual artists in the Harlem Renaissance or the connections many of these artists made with HBCUs. By the early 1930s, the works of black artists were displayed in the galleries of Fisk, Hampton, and Clark. For example, Aaron Douglas, the most well-known visual artist of the Harlem Renaissance, painted his murals, *The Symbolic Negro History Series*, on the walls of Fisk's Cravath Hall in 1930. What is more, Douglas and Hale Woodruff accepted positions of prominence within black colleges and universities. Woodruff's 1931 appointment to the faculty of Atlanta University distinguished him as one of Georgia's first college professors of studio art, and in 1937, Douglas assumed the helm of the Art Department at Fisk where he remained for almost thirty years.

By the 1950s, Tolson enjoyed veteran status as a tenured professor of English at another HBCU, Langston University in Oklahoma. Like Douglas and Woodruff, Tolson viewed his dual position as an artist and instructor as a natural alliance and he continued to pursue pedagogical and creative forms to improve his work. His classroom was home to strains of his radical politics and evolving aesthetic, ideas that mingled seamlessly with his instruction and praise of Western literature. His poetry career continued to mature as he published *Rendezvous with America* in 1944 and the widely acclaimed *Libretto for the Republic of Liberia* in 1953 which showcased his embrace of modernist form. Notwithstanding what many scholars consider Tolson's anachronistic celebration of T. S. Eliot's *The Waste Land* (1922) – his public appreciation for the modernist epic is tied to Eliot's 1948 Nobel Prize – Tolson extolled the modernist idiom as a poetic form suitable for expressing black modern experience. He viewed new modes of expression as the best method for maintaining artistic relevance to one's larger society and culture, and he exulted in the potential the modernist technique held for black poetry.

Contrary to the accusations of his detractors, Tolson's enchantment with modernism remained closely bound to his devotion to portraying African American culture with compelling energy and creativity. Explaining the differences between his appreciation for Eliot and his own poetic technique, Tolson observes:

> My work is certainly difficult in metaphors, symbols and juxtaposed ideas. There the similarity between me and Eliot separates. That is only technique, and any artist must use the technique of his time. ... However, when you look at my ideas and Eliot's, we're as far apart as hell and heaven.[21]

Like the emerging African American independent museums which sought to establish new approaches for representing black culture, Tolson embraced modernist form as a fitting home for unleashing the black artist. The changing cultural landscape wrought by the civil rights movement demanded new spaces and modes for displaying black art to a broader black and white American audience.

Tolson did not, however, believe an eager audience composed of everyday Americans would magically materialize to embrace or even appreciate his difficult verse. In his notebooks, he muses:

> Now, about the little people. Remember "ideas come from above." If you went into the street and said to a ditchdigger in Chi, "Who is Shakespeare?" he'd say, "The greatest writer that ever lived." Now, he wouldn't know a damned thing about *Hamlet* but he might quote some of THE Bard's sayings that he picked up from the boys in the ditch. Ideas sift down. Marx and Lenin and Castro were not of the masses but *for* the masses. What does a Cuban peon know about *Das Kapital*? If you gave him a copy, he'd wipe his behind with it![22]

Tolson ardently supported the notion that artists should strive to create art that could achieve social change, but he steadfastly resisted the idea that artists should anticipate the immediate emergence of an audience composed of "the masses." For that to happen, specialists had to devote themselves to promoting and explaining sophisticated art. The mix of elitism and radicalism revealed in Tolson's words and work persisted throughout his career, and his reliance on the metaphor of the gallery uncovers a strategy for resolving this tension. As museums adapted elements from both the temple and forum philosophies, they provided spaces where complex black art could mingle comfortably with other kinds of performance all the while benefitting from professionals trained to explicate such work. Analyzing his development of the gallery motif from his first volume to his last uncovers Tolson's growing sense that for modern African American art to thrive, artists need audiences encouraged to appreciate demanding art and educated to comprehend it. Although he acknowledged that his literary gallery was "purely imaginary, although some think it's an actual museum," he also averred, the "picture gallery magnetizes me with a potent fascination."[23] This fascination leads to his investment in the trope of the Picture Book and its abiding concentration on honing black visionary practices.

Forms for Curating Black Modernist Vision

Organizationally, *A Gallery of Harlem Portraits* takes a cue from Lee Masters's *Spoon River Anthology* (1915). Yet, in place of Masters's epitaphs and graveyard setting, Tolson describes his individual poems as "portraits" and identifies the art museum as a fitting site for examining African American urban existence. He arranges the 162 portraits comprising *A Gallery* into four sections grouped according to visual art creative methods. The specificity of each technique announces Tolson's interest in artistic forms, the different approaches artists take to heighten the effect of their visual portrayals. In fact, although Harlem Renaissance writers hoping to unveil pictures of modern black identity emphasized fresh themes as opposed to experimenting widely with narrative form, visual artists of the era explored innovative compositional techniques.[24] When Tolson began working on *A Gallery* in the early 1930s, the importance of visual art as a means of redefining African American character was well established. His volume demonstrates how each section is shaped by visual arts methods that contribute to Tolson's project of chiseling away the outer appearances that cover the complexity of urban African Americans. Interior revelation, he suggests, depends on selecting the appropriate form.

The four section titles – Chiaroscuro, Silhouettes, Etchings, and Pastels – do not denote the most well-known graphic techniques or concepts. They also do not conform to the most favored visual art techniques of the New Negro movement. Whereas Aaron Douglas surely revitalized the silhouette, and Winold Reiss favored pastels, when linked with "chiaroscuro" and "etchings," it is difficult to argue that Tolson sought solidarity with popular Harlem Renaissance artists and their preferred painting techniques. Moreover, although critics focus on the new ways artists such as Douglas and Reiss attempt to articulate the primitivism in vogue during the Harlem Renaissance, a cursory consideration of Tolson's selection of art techniques suggests little interest in extending discussions of black Americans' African past. Nor does he appear desirous of simply demonstrating expertise with what Audre Lorde famously deemed the "masters tools" for he selects techniques long employed by diverse artists of low and high art alike. Tolson focuses readers on the pathos, indeed the drama, of his subjects' urban present by draping his portrayal of black modern identity in the folds of older visual forms. He insists that readers reevaluate their tendency to view black Americans in simplistic terms.

The section titles also sidestep an obvious political agenda. Although certain print art forms such as woodcutting were celebrated as intensely democratic and fashionable with leftist artists of the period, Tolson does not restrict his section titles to such techniques.[25] His later work, such as the second section of *Rendezvous with America*, titled "Woodcuts for Americana," makes use of this strategy, but his early impulse suggests different priorities. By including approaches associated with high and low art, Tolson reveals his consistent attraction to celebrating the diverse instruments necessary to make African American identity discernible to an incurious public. Only the final lines of the opening poem, "Harlem," allude to a physical space: "The Curator has hung the likenesses of all / In A Gallery of Harlem Portraits."[26] In place of focusing primarily on the site housing the portraits, Tolson's first book of poetry trains readers' attention on the necessary tools for correctly viewing black urban identity.

Notwithstanding his careful selection of the section titles, critics routinely dismiss their significance. Keith Leonard concludes that the section labels "offer little demonstrable or consistent variation to justify titles of the sections," whereas Craig Werner notes that the headings reveal Tolson's "developing ... interest in visual aesthetics" only to effect an aesthetic disconnect because "its prosody is grounded almost entirely on the oral aesthetic."[27] Although Werner's larger argument helpfully explains Tolson's refusal to erect a dichotomy between oral and visual aesthetics, he glosses *A Gallery* as an inconsequential building block for examining *Harlem Gallery*. But it seems undeniable that in the same way that the musical terms Tolson includes in "Dark Symphony" lead scholars to study his relationship to the broader role of music in 1940s culture and literature, his dependence on visual art terms indicates Tolson's positioning with regard to 1930s visual artists and writers.[28] He clearly imagined the terms functioning as flexible frames highlighting subtle similarities between poems. Taken together, the sections map methods of visual portrayal that execute increasingly frank pictures of black identity. They demonstrate how art techniques might sharpen readers' awareness of African American self-conception.

Each technique also reiterates the necessity for relying on artistic tools capable of uncovering the complexity of modern black identity. Thirty years later, *Harlem Gallery* turns away from the extended contemplation of unveiling the interior world of the urban black community to indulge in an expansive meditation on the modern black artist. Tolson builds on his initial hunch in *A Gallery* that new artistic forms held the secret for crafting successful images of black character; but in *Harlem Gallery*, rather than focusing on visual art methods as a metaphorical contemplation on the significance of form, he concentrates on the form of verse itself.

A Site for Publishing Modern Black Art

A Gallery introduces the character of the Curator, but it is only in *Harlem Gallery* that he claims a central role. His newfound importance transforms the first volume's general interest in the complexity of black identity into the final book's concentrated consideration of black artists, their work, and the most effective means of supporting both. Accordingly, the Curator's lengthy ruminations over his position and the proper pursuits of the Harlem Gallery convert the museum from an ambiguous backdrop tasked with holding together numerous portraits in *A Gallery* to a vital physical site of structural and intellectual significance in *Harlem Gallery*. To this end, Tolson replaces his attention to visual techniques such as chiaroscuro and etching with an ambitious modernist form, thereby foregrounding his advocacy for sophisticated black art through the very form of his ode.

Harlem Gallery's dense allusions, imagist presentation, and epic form garner structural stability from the poem's twenty-four Greek alphabet section divisions. Within these confines, the Curator's circuitous exploration of his own character, his relationship to three black modernist artists, and his role at the Harlem Gallery become a vehicle for examining the dilemma of how those in positions of power might enlarge avenues of publication for black art. His long ode returns to the trope of the Picture

Book by placing the Curator's ability to draw meaning from visual art at the center of his self-exploration. For Tolson, the museum becomes a vibrant metaphor for an expanded notion of "publication": the process by which black art secures the endorsement of established specialists, and over time, gains access to a large, diverse audience. Tolson's contemplation of publication both reflects on and anticipates his struggle to share his work widely, a reality Michael Bérubé considers at length.[29] Tolson never gained a large audience for his work, but he saw promise in the institutional example of the art gallery. Thus, his most ambitious work stresses the importance of teaching African Americans to discern great art and insists that those possessing critical expertise lead the way.

The form of the art museum that Tolson suggests might successfully increase the circulation of black modernist art draws from both the temple and the forum models – the HBCU and the independent museum. Harkening to the atmosphere of the HBCU classroom, the Curator desires a gallery that comfortably exhibits African American art even as he approaches an analysis of these works through a lens tinted with traditional Western ideas. In other words, Tolson recognizes no conflict in celebrating black vernacular art within the confines of visual art display spaces. Although these sites traditionally are viewed as realms devoted to established "high" art, he works to educate audiences on the terms of art deemed complex and worthy of "high" art status. Thus, his most immediate audience appears to be the African American critics who largely rejected his poetry rather than the white scholars who heralded it.[30] He seeks to convince black critics to value modernist black art.

Tolson's point of emphasis reflects the shifting environment for African American artists in the early 1960s and the attendant evolution of publication practices for black art. As the Black Arts movement and Black Power politics gained momentum, African American artists actively spoke against seeking mainstream approval and support. Instead, many black writers, musicians, and visual artists advocated a self-sufficiency and cultural pride defined by creating their own institutions responsible for publishing and celebrating their work. With the rebirth of *Negro Digest* as *Black World* in the 1960s and the founding of Broadside Press (1965), Third World Press (1967), and Lotus Press (1972), black intellectuals and writers enjoyed a wider selection of spaces willing to promote their art on their terms. On the other hand, writers interested in reaching beyond these organs' majority black audiences continued to face an uphill battle.

For Tolson, writing immediately before the birth of these entities, the work to find a larger readership proved particularly daunting. As he grew increasingly committed to exploiting modernist forms to convey the texture of black experience, Tolson became openly desirous of mainstream presses. Writing to his Langston University colleague Horace Mann Bond, Tolson celebrated his success in finding an established press to publish *Libretto*:

> Well the *Libretto for Liberia* is to be published! And we won't have to do it! It has been taken over by the Decker Press, of Belles Lettres, and will be brought out de luxe. The publisher is very enthusiastic, and plans several big occasions in connection with the coming-out. He says it's a natural for critics and the metropolitan press and wire services.[31]

Tolson also grew less wary about seeking support from established white artists. His much discussed courtship of the poet Allen Tate, a prominent poet known for his cultural conservatism, documents Tolson's wish to penetrate literary circles historically closed to blacks. What is more, his passionate embrace of modernism revised his notion that creative art should prove its immediate relevance to a contemporary community. Tolson continued to believe that poets principally strove to impact readers' ideas about society, but he adopted a more aggressive stance in supporting the freedom of the artist to experiment with new forms regardless of his audience's response. A journal entry delineates his evolving philosophy:

> The size of an audience that understands a work of art at the time of its first appearance is no argument against the merit of the work of art. Cultural and civilizational changes produce new ideas and new forms of art. The idiom of old works of art may be esoteric at the farthest remove; and the idiom of a new art may be esoteric at the closest remove.[32]

Farnsworth notes that Tolson's words echo John Ciardi's definition of a "vertical audience," his description of an audience that "consists of everyone, vertically through time, who will ever read a poem" as opposed to a "horizontal audience" which "consists of everybody who is alive at this moment." Ciardi unequivocally declares:, "All good poets write for the vertical audience."[33] Tolson seems to agree wholeheartedly.

But even as Tolson's ideas about audiences evolved, younger African American artists recommitted their work to a distinctly horizontal audience composed of the black masses. This proved particularly true for musicians and visual artists. Bebop, born in the 1940s and reaching maturity in the 1960s, captured the revolutionary sensibility animating black musicians whose work struck a modernist chord. Scott DeVeaux notes that bebop's very form, with its privileging of improvisation, "renounces intention of transmuting creativity into published commodity," thereby facilitating black musicians' "desire for artistic and economic autonomy."[34] A number of African American visual artists espoused similar commitments to producing socially conscious art indifferent to commercial success and dedicated to speaking to black viewers. But these artists took the extra step of addressing institutional limitations to their goal. They called for a radical reassessment of the function of the art museum in the U.S. Although literary groups such as Umbra Workshop founded in 1962 and the later Uptown Writers Movement formed in 1964 espoused equally revolutionary goals, the musicians and visual artists' focus on the physical institutionalization of exclusionary practices gave their struggle added significance.

Taking a page from these artists, Tolson locates his meditation on publication within the museum. The Curator's ruminations on the proper role of the Harlem Gallery engage and anticipate the arguments animating creative contributors to the Black Arts movement.[35] His struggle to open the gallery patrons' eyes to the power coursing through modernist visions of black life exploits the collision of the temple-forum ideals. Nevertheless, most scholars of *Harlem Gallery* treat the art gallery as a basic metaphor not worthy of serious attention. Raymond Nelson, for instance, suggests the error of placing undue significance on Tolson's dependence on the term: "Diehard traditionalists (and others) who ... insist on organizational concepts will be quick to observe that the idea of a gallery suggests a collection of discrete artifacts, separately framed."[36] His following dismissal warns readers against placing undue stress on Tolson's metaphorical use of the gallery. Bérubé emphasizes that "Tolson's gallery is a museum, his protagonist is a curator, and the curator's task concerns the representation of great African-American art," but he proceeds to focus on what he describes as the contrast between "[s]criptural" poetics and oral, "gossip" inflected poetics.[37] This provocative reading misses the possibility of a museum space that comfortably offers a home to both forms.

The scholarly tendency to disregard the specific role of the gallery risks missing the very logic beneath the Curator's musings, the rational for his "autobio-fragment."[38] He seeks to discover whether black artists do indeed produce art worthy of high art status and whether he, as a curator, possesses the personal and professional temerity to display and explicate such pieces. In other words, the Curator's odyssey not only begins and ends at the site of the gallery, but his very purpose is rooted in the endeavor of determining the proper function of the art museum and culturally established spaces of art publication more generally. In facing this dilemma, the Curator reveals his penchant for depending on visual art to shape his view of reality. As he ponders the work of Harlem artists, he agonizes over the prospect of persuading the African American community to recognize the ways black modernist work reframes and elucidates black cultural experience. By focusing on moments in *Harlem Gallery* that showcase the Curator's dependence on visual art to think through personal and cultural quandaries – and placing these episodes in conversation with his evolving discovery of African American art that facilitates similar breakthroughs – I argue that Tolson charges the Curator with demonstrating the potential power of expanding access to sophisticated black art. The linchpin of Tolson's portrayal rests with the Curator's acceptance of the role of erudite critic willing to spotlight his sophisticated vision so as to educate resistant visitors on the merits of black art and modernist black vision.

Reflecting on Paintings in *Harlem Gallery*

Unlike Rita Dove's volume, *Museum* (1983), which scholars note almost surely invokes *Harlem Gallery*, Tolson's ode shows little concern with juxtaposing European and African American art for the purpose of legitimizing the history of black art.[39] Elizabeth Loizeaux convincingly argues that Dove employs ekphrasis to display admired artifacts from Western history next to objects of the African diaspora to recalculate European culture and "simultaneously claim value for African American artifacts by institutionalizing them in a museum."[40] Tolson, however, highlights the Curator's knowledge of renowned visual art to emphasize how his scholarly training empowers him to understand the potential for art to change people's perspective. Time and time again, the Curator's thoughts return to works from the Renaissance to famous artists whose paintings generally belong to the modern art school. The Curator's reflections inspire and strengthen him to lend his interpretive expertise – his visionary power – to support struggling black artists whose creations do not always find an appreciative audience in either the black bourgeois or the African American masses. Like other writers who engage the trope of the Picture Book, Tolson builds his ode around a poet speaker distinguished by his visionary ability and his commitment to helping others develop their power of discernment.

The Curator's dependence on visual art to fortify his critical resolve emerges in the opening canto. As he grapples with his role as a steward and potential advocate for avant-garde black art, he foregrounds the conflict between genuine supporters of art and wealthy patrons who lack a corresponding knowledge and passion. This dilemma lay at the heart of the Harlem Renaissance and reemerged amongst later African American artists who refused to suffer a fate like their 1920s predecessors. The Curator's professional position associates him more closely with the patrons who finance the Harlem Gallery, but he strives to maintain his natural affinity with the artists whom he thinks represent the future of African American art. The opening lines referencing the art of Francisco Goya spell out his anxiety:

> The Harlem Gallery, an Afric pepper bird,
> awakes me at a people's dusk of dawn.
> The age altars its image, a dog's hind leg,
> and hazards the moment of truth in pawn.
> The Lord of the House of Flies,
> jaundice-eyed, synapses purled,
> wries before the tumultuous canvas,
> *The Second of May* –
> by Goya:
> the dagger of Madrid
> vs.
> the scimitar of Murat. (*HG*, 209)

As the Curator prepares to draw on his own experiences to decipher his dilemma, he recognizes the need to depart from past attitudes toward black art. Tolson elects not to provide an exact date for the action of the poem, but the Curator's repeated references to "a people's dust of dawn" suggests that Tolson views the pre-civil rights era as a moment defined by opportunity and new direction.[41] The Curator's notions that the "age altars its image" – the ambiguous spelling suggesting "altars" as in *a place of worship* and *changes its appearance* – heightens his sense of the religious responsibility pervading his role at the gallery.

His uncertain fortitude leads him to seek encouragement from a piece of art, a move that he repeats throughout the ode. Goya's *The Second of May* (see Figure 5.1) depicts the valiant Spanish rising up against the Napoleonic invasion and represents the patriotism and courage a violent attack inspires. Pitting the "dagger of Madrid" against the "scimitar of Murat," Goya's canvas extols the ability of average, principled men to stave off the political tyranny of imperialistic forces. Tellingly, the Curator refrains from mentioning Goya's more popular *The Third of May* (see Figure 5.2), the graphic depiction of Murat's forces executing the Spanish citizenry in retaliation for their uprising on May second. Although both incidents inspired the national revolt that eventually led to pushing back Napoleon, the Curator focuses on the less painful image as a means of steeling his nerve for his task. As he considers joining forces with economically powerless artists, the figurative possessors of "daggers," against the influential regents and

Figure 5.1 Francisco de Goya, *The Second of May 1808 in Madrid* (1808). Museo del Prado, Madrid, Spain. Photo credit: Erich Lessing / Art Resource, NY.

patrons whose positions grant them symbolic "scimitars," he depends on Goya's visual depiction of the triumphant underclass for motivation. Two 1956 versions of the manuscript, however, include no references to Goya's *The Second of May*. This absence suggests that as Tolson sought to flesh out his presentation of the Curator's mindset, references to visual art grew increasingly important.[42] In the published version, he consistently ponders paintings to clarify his vision for his gallery.

In "Gamma," the Curator again evokes visual art to clarify his current dilemma. He not only draws inspiration from paintings but recalls the capacity for great art to shape human perception and memory. After using "Beta" to review his professional trajectory – he is "an ex-professor of Art" who retains "a core / of gas as yet unburnt" even though he lacks the talent of the artist – the Curator returns to extolling the power of art to teach life lessons (*HG*, 214–215). He declares that just as Maurice Utrillo "*trans*figured / a *dis*figured Montmartre street / into a thing of beauty," our own memories, if seen from the proper perspective, possess

Figure 5.2 Francisco de Goya, *The Third of May, 1808* (1814). Museo del Prado, Madrid, Spain. Photo credit: Erich Lessing / Art Resource, NY.

the potential to inspire new strength of character (*HG*, 217). The Curator's turn to Utrillo, the French painter known as a mad alcoholic who transferred the Montmarte streets to canvas with unique perspective, reveals the thrust of his hopes. Utrillo's paintings are renowned for having pleased common men as well as specialists, and art historians applaud his ability to transform the most sordid locales to places of beauty by virtue of his painterly eye. As the Curator dedicates himself to the work of making his gallery a space for applauding African American artists and their creations, examples like Utrillo reify the prospect of success and remind him of how his own experiences and visionary skill fit him for the enterprise.

He concludes the canto by extolling great paintings like Paolo Veronese's *The Flight of Lot and His Family from Sodom* (see Figure 5.3) and Tintoretto's *Paradise* (see Figure 5.4):

Oh hail
Paolo's doomsday *Sodom* that brasses
caricatures of patterns and colors and masses
fluxing away from the cruxing incandescence convulsing

Figure 5.3 Paolo Veronese, (workshop of) *Lot's Family Fleeing Sodom* (1528–1588). Photo by Hervé Lewandowski, Louvre, Paris, France. Photo © RMN-Grand Palais/ Art Resource, NY.

> the engouled town!
> Oh hail
> Tintoretto's *Paradise*,
> lustrous and pulsing
> with blue and silver,
> red and ivory and brown! (*HG*, 218)

Veronese's depiction of Sodom and Gomorrah's fiery demise transforms God's wrath into a picture of grace and beauty, whereas Tintoretto's magnificent rendering of paradise captures the awesome nature of God's promise of the afterlife. The Curator's celebration of these artistic achievements foregrounds his recommitment to artists who transform reality through creative work and the critic who interprets such work. In fact, in the next canto he declares that art is difficult to "*fix*," or define, yet capable of orchestrating an epiphany in the viewer as Keats reveals in "On First Looking into Chapman's Homer" (1816), the sonnet that compares the impact of reading great literature to the experience of seeing great art.

Figure 5.4 Jacopo Tintoretto, *Paradise* (1518–1594). Photo by Jean-Gilles Berizzi, Louvre, Paris, France. Photo © RMN-Grand Palais / Art Resource, NY.

166

The Curator's concurrent contemplation of great art alongside the character of the critic reveals the heart of his struggle. Even as he reaffirms the force of acclaimed visual art, he strains to discover whether an ideal relationship between critics and artists can ever be realized, particularly when he is the critic in question. The roles he played in the past do not bode well for his present attempt to behave heroically: "'Great minds require of us a reading glass; / great souls, a hearing aid.' / But I, / in the shuttle-box world, / again and again, /have both mislaid" (*HG*, 212). Like the Ethiopian eunuch of Acts who asks Phillip to explain the mystery of salvation and baptism, the Curator accepts the truth that the creations of great artists depend on the services of those equipped to explain their work. Having frequented artistic haunts from New York to Paris and considered all manner of painting, he is adept at considering the "pros and cons" of *objets de art*, a description for critical analysis which he will employ repeatedly throughout the poem. In fact, his cyclical contemplation of the critic reveals his refusal to accept a narrow definition for his curatorial role. Even as he insists that black modernist artists maintain the ability to produce great art, he contends that curators, as critics in their own right, must accept the role of providing collaborative explanation and support. They must embrace the responsibility of the educator.

Education In and Out of the Gallery

If the initial cantos serve to strengthen the Curator's resolve by focusing on perspective changing paintings – and commence the process of determining the correct relationship between critics and artists – the remainder of Tolson's ode pursues a deeper understanding of the African American artists behind the modern black art he deems worthy of wider publication. The major obstacle for the Curator, of course, remains the black elites who fail to understand, accept, or champion the avant-garde art of their age. Thus, immediately following his own flight of critical excitement over the command of art in the form of sixteenth-century Venetian School painters, "Epsilon" opens with his recollection of those Harlem patrons who lack visual taste yet insist that their "idols of the tribe" secure space within the gallery: "'We / have heroes! Celebrate them upon our walls!'" (*HG*, 224).

These demands submitted by this artistically immature audience receive legitimacy from the "bulls of Bashan," those powerful, but aesthetically uninformed leaders who share a facile desire to promote themselves and their culture without thought for the accomplishment of the art in question (*HG*, 225). They win by coercing unprincipled critics to adopt and promote their position. The Curator, echoing the psalmist who testifies to Christ's sufferings by beginning Psalm 22 with his lament, "My God, my God, why hast thou forsaken me?", repeats Psalm 22:12: "Many bulls have compassed me: strong bulls of Bashan have beset me round." His reliance on scripture elevates his dilemma to the realm of the divine and compares his suffering to Christ's struggle leading up to his crucifixion, a crucial moment that Ralph Ellison will also contemplate in his unfinished second novel. Although influential men often succeed in shifting critical opinion, the Curator understands the necessity of guarding against such power that seeks to dictate the moral center of men, especially when those wielding authority lack aesthetic or cultural vision.

To withstand such pressure, he reaches out to the African American artists whose works promise answers to his dilemma by challenging his vision and thereby suggesting the proper role for his gallery. The Curator leaves the site of the gallery in search of great art *and* perspective, and he continues to reflect over time-honored visual art for inspiration. His interactions with John Laugart, Hideho Heights, and Mister Starks force him to confront the difficulties black artists face in their efforts to publish art that does not fit squarely within the narrative embraced and promoted by the bulls of Bashan. Additionally, his experiences with these men and the work of locating art objects worthy of display help him perceive his proper role in promoting consequential but technically difficult black art. The three artists need a space to share their art in addition to the support of scholars whose explanations ensure that their creations are properly appreciated and understood. In stark contrast to Ralph Ellison who similarly hoped to depict the vibrancy of Harlem in his effort to complicate his protagonist's worldview yet eventually succumbed to editorial coaxing to reduce the portions of *Invisible Man* set in Harlem, Tolson revels in the urban landscape that dramatically informs the Curator's reassessment of his duty to black art.

By forcing the Curator to begin his journey by confronting the painter, John Laugart, Tolson foregrounds the crucial role sight plays as a means of recognizing artistic accomplishment. Finding Laugart in a sad physical state, the Curator acknowledges the painter's spiritual fineness that propels him to produce meaningful art. He cannot deny the power of Laugart's masterpiece, a testament to African American resilience and native talent commensurate with that of the greatest modernist artists:

> *Here emerges the imago*
> *from the impotence of the chrysalis*
> *in the dusk of a people's dawn –*

> this, this,
> thought I as I gazed at his *Black Bourgeoisie*:
> colors detonating
> fog signals on a railroad track,
> lights and shadows rhythming
> fog images in a negative pack:
> *this*, somehow, a synthesis
> (savage – sanative)
> of Daumier and Gropper and Picasso.
> As a Californian, I thought *Eureka*;
> but as Ulfilas to the dusky Philistines I said,
> "Oh!" (*HG*, 228)

The Curator immediately appreciates the genius of Laugart's canvas and detects its modern visualization of African American strength resulting from the disjointed experiences comprising black history. The power the painting exudes belies "the impotence" associated with black history and celebrates the vigor of African American modern life. But even as he concedes Laugart's skill at translating black existence into a modern visual idiom, the Curator suppresses his reflexive exclamation of praise.

Instead, he resorts to his more customary position of obsequious moderator, devoting more energy to anticipating the responses of the Harlem Gallery Regents than to his own interpretive skill. Returning to Goya as a means for describing the powerful Regents, he likens them to the bride of the etching, *She Says Yes to Anyone* (see Figure 5.5). Figuring the Regents as the bride whose promise to be faithful rings hollow in light of her willingness to marry a hideous man simply because he proposes first, the Curator impugns the Regents' prostitution of their position as artistic patrons. He imagines Laugart's painting inspiring them toward seeking salvation, but he conspicuously fails to ponder the painting's impact on him. His revelation that their "ignorance" leaves his "budget as the / corpse of a chance" ironically hints that his integrity may also be subject to purchase (*HG*, 230). Thus, Laugart's subsequent proclamation of his artistic philosophy – ""A work of art / is an everlasting flower / in kind or unkind hands; / it does not lose its form and color / in native or in alien lands" – subtly indicts both the Curator and Regents (*HG*, 229). The painter insists that meaningful art prevails despite the cowardly postures of those in charge of promoting it.

The Curator's serious response to Guy Delaporte III's outrage over Laugart's bold, modernist painting and its commentary on the black elite underscores his astute vision as opposed to Delaporte's ignorance of visual art. Laugart's modernist masterpiece provides a perfect example of art relevant to its time but difficult for untrained audiences to appreciate. The

Figure 5.5 Francisco de Goya, "Los caprichos," *She Says Yes to Anyone* (1799). Madrid, Spain. Photo credit: Album / Art Resource, NY.

Curator, catholic in his tastes and dedicated to publicizing obscure yet talented artists, has obviously insisted on the inclusion of *Black Bourgeoisie* in the opening exhibit. The four wings of the gallery – conspicuously organized by technique rather than history and clearly taking a page from *A Gallery of Harlem Portraits* – display the Curator's breadth of knowledge and willingness to cater to his patrons' interests. As Raymond Nelson's notes elucidate, the East Wing's "stereochromatic murals" depict "prophetic and ethical tradition"; the West Wing houses primitive art; the North Wing displays portraits celebrating "Negroid diversity"; and, the

South Wing exhibits the revered portraits of "African American ancestors in fresco and secco" (*HG*, 399). The gallery's holdings hint at the Curator's conservative taste, his aversion toward making bold statements with his selections of art. His newfound interest in assuming a stronger critical stance exhibits his emergent devotion to pieces like *Black Bourgeoisie.*

His principled commitment leads to one of the most tension-filled moments in the ode, a conflict that fictionally enacts Tolson's contemporary dilemma. Just as his modernist poetic forms found resistance from black critics, Laugart's painting runs afoul of the Harlem elite. On the evening of the gallery opening, Delaporte assesses the painting:

> Unable to lead his wife
> (with her incurves and outcurves of breasts and hips)
> captive,
> he weeps like Alexander the Fire Burnt Out
> because
> no brand-new \$-world in Harlem gives him pause.
> ....
> Before the *bête noire* of John Laugart's
> *Black Bourgeoisie,*
> Mr. Guy Delaporte III takes his stand,
> a wounded Cape buffalo defying everything and Everyman! (*HG*, 255)

Delaporte's decision to challenge the painting is as much a product of his attempt to recover his ego as it is a response to the work itself. His philandering wife is publically humiliating him, and he needs a means to reassert his masculinity. Even though he lacks the wherewithal to grasp the nuances of Laugart's painting, he reflexively recognizes that the painting challenges the middle class success and values he symbolizes. Tolson does not provide an ekphrastic rendering of the painting, but its title, taken from E. Franklin Frazier's sociological juggernaut, *Black Bourgousie* (1957), suggests that Laugart's modernist masterpiece indeed seeks to question the choices and conduct of the Harlem highbrows. The Curator, observing Delaporte's dim response to the painting, bemoans the state of relations between the black bourgeoisie, visionary artist, and common man. But he concludes the canto by recalling the "elan of Courbet, Cezanne, and Monet" and the resiliency of "Chagall, Matisse, and Picasso" (*HG*, 257). Thus, even as he worries over Guy Delaporte's attack on Laugart's painting, he draws inspiration and assurance from the triumphs of past modern artists who faced down the German conquests of France in 1870 and 1940 with their spiritually edifying work. If great painting helped defeat German armies, surely it can strengthen his resolve.

A Forum for Hideho Heights

While Laugart and Mister Starks remind the Curator of his weaknesses, Hideho Heights – the sole living artist whose work the Curator supports – provides him an opportunity to participate directly in championing the modern black artist. The Curator's incipient recognition of his obligation to encourage trailblazing artists is radically intensified through his interactions with Hideho and his ability to penetrate the poet's public demeanor. Bursting boisterously into the gallery opening, Hideho voices the Curator's confused feelings coarsely but accurately, surprisingly offering the ex-professor of Art relief from his self-imposed intellectual boxing. The poet's defiant assertion, "In the beginning was the Word / ... not the Brush!", both challenges and affirms the Curator's inchoate philosophy regarding the function of the Harlem Gallery (*HG*, 258). As both temple and forum, he wants the gallery to support progressive visual art while additionally providing a site for the kinds of verbal art performances not always deemed appropriate for institutions of high art. Ultimately, Hideho represents the dangerous plight of the gifted African American artist who fails to find the right space of publication and support for his work.

The poet's removal to the Zulu Club underscores Tolson's examination of the tension between designating the gallery a location to try out new art as opposed to serving as an institution dedicated to celebrating established work. After all, Hideho seeks out the jazz club in response to the unenthusiastic welcome he receives at the gallery opening. And although the Zulu Club initially appears to be a serious alternative to the gallery as a space for nurturing the creative spirit of potentially great black artists, Hideho's performance of "John Henry" highlights the underside of its communal nature: its patrons both nourish and consume black artists without much thought about either activity.[43] Although the jazz club of the bebop age continued to inspire artists of all stripes including great painters such as Jackson Pollock, Willem de Kooning, and Franze Kline and famous Beat poets such as Allen Ginsberg, Jack Kerouac, and Robert Frank, it no longer served as a space for communal encouragement. Tolson taps into the modern reality of the jazz club in his depiction of Hideho's performance. After the audience eggs on his alcoholic consumption before co-opting his performance for their own purposes, the evening ends with Hideho's drunken exasperation: "My people, / my people – / they know not what they do" (*HG*, 282). Uniting one of Hurston's favorite expressions of exasperated understanding of African American culture with Jesus's words of forgiveness on the cross, Hideho concedes the dangerous sacrifice demanded by an injudicious audience.

After witnessing Hideho's predicament, the Curator delves more deeply into the quandary facing African American poets unable to find a receptive audience for their modernist art. Unbeknownst to Hideho, the Curator is aware of the poet's secret creation of modernist verse. Hideho appears to kowtow to his urban audience's desires and compromises his artistry in the process. In private, he admits: "*my* fears / of oblivion made me realistic: / with no poems of Hideho's in World Lit – / he'd be a statistic!" (*HG*, 335). Instead of castigating Hideho for acting hypocritically, publicly performing the role of poet for the people while privately penning poems only the elite might decipher, the Curator digs more deeply into the dilemma faced by black artists and examines how his curatorial role relates to their challenges. In fact, focusing on the Curator's professional position insists upon a reading that parts ways with scholars who conclude that the he ultimately scorns Hideho's lack of artistic courage.[44] Since the Curator blames himself for leaving experimental black artists without spaces to share their work, he accepts responsibility for contributing to institutional barriers to Hideho's success.

Doctor Nkomo's return to visual artists directs the Curator's attention back to the accomplishments of modern painters:

> "Remember
> Paul Cézanne,
> the father of modern Art,
> a Toussaint L'Ouverture of Esthetics.
> Remember
> a genius is not a fence-sitter
> with legs wide apart,
>
> . . .
>
> . . . Remember, yes, remember . . .
> Zola, Renoir, Degas, Gauguin, Van Gogh, and Rodin
> hailed Cézanne;
> but *vox poluli* and red-tapedom
> remained as silent as spectators in a court
> when the crier repeats three times, 'Oyez!'"   (*HG*, 291)

Nkomo reminds the Curator that, notwithstanding Cézanne's talent, he was initially not embraced by the general public or "*vox populi*." Their lack of approbation did not, however, dissuade him from his revolutionary artistic vision. Rather than adopt the safe middle position of a "fence-sitter," Cézanne drew inspiration from artists possessing the temerity to applaud his vision. Early in his career, Tolson proved his deep belief in such artistic courage when he defended Langston Hughes's publication of "Goodbye, Christ" (1932). He recalled: "I had defended [Hughes's] constitutional and literary right to write as he pleased ... My defense of free speech in the land of the free almost cost me my job. Writers in the Negro press denounced me as a corrupter of youth."[45] He forces his Curator to consider taking a similar stance.

Earlier drafts document Tolson's evolving sense of the artist's peculiar position. In what would become the ending stanzas of "Pi," the 1956 manuscript reads: "(The Curator was pained to hear / that Doctor Nkomo threw a stinkpot in / the Market Place Gallery / among the Black Muslims and artists and Regents. / 'Life grants the artist / a passport to / the holy of holies or a whorehouse,' he said; / 'but never to the ivory tower.)"[46] Conversely the published version reads:

> (The Harlem Gallery, too, was grieved by Bunyan's
> crabtree cudgel
> when Doctor Nkomo threw a stinkpot into
> the Market Place Gallery,
> among Black Muslims and artists and Good White Friends.
> "The Critics' Circus grants an artist
> a passport to
> the holy of holies," he said, "or a whorehouse;
> but never to
> Harpers Ferry or Babii Yar or Highgate.")   (*HG*, 292)

The change from "The Curator was pained" to "The Harlem Gallery ... was grieved" emphasizes the conflation of the Curator and his gallery, but the more interesting revision emerges in the switch from "Life grants" to "The Critics' Circus grants." Tolson originally planned to accentuate Nkomo's opinion that life experiences directed the artists' highly variegated work. The published version changes its emphasis, highlighting the seminal role played by critical opinion. Although critics may direct an artist in multiple directions, their opinions never result in artistic production that impacts moments of violent revolution. Juxtaposing the published text and draft reveals Tolson's move toward forcing the Curator to contemplate the heightened stakes of his role. He not only influences the determination of which artists gain an audience, but he also contributes to the extent to which the artist prevails in impacting society's most difficult crises. Privately, Tolson hoped black scholars would gain greater power in determining the trajectory of black art. He mused in his notebooks, "Hitherto, white critics have established the reputations of Negro writers—witness Wheatley, Dunbar, Wright—hereafter Negro critics, who are inside, will have perhaps the last say."[47]

Yet the Curator continues to doubt his ability to support principled art. After reading Mister Starks's manuscript, *Harlem Vignettes*, a text reminiscent of Tolson's *A Gallery of Harlem Portraits*, the Curator finds himself disappointed with his lack of integrity. But his sense of failure inspires his contribution to Hideho's final, most impressive artistic performance. In fact, the poet's spontaneous and triumphant delivery of "the sea-turtle and the shark" results from the Curator's willing subordination to Hideho's creative genius. Significantly, the setting for Hideho's performance shifts from the downstairs Zulu cabaret to the upstairs tavern. Like the space of the tavern in Shakespeare's *Henry IV* plays where the local alehouse represents an alternate world to the court that young Hal flees in search of life teachers like Sir John Falstaff, the Zulu tavern distinguishes itself as a social site for male bonding. Within this space, the Curator discovers newfound clarity regarding his role and that of the Harlem Gallery's. He realizes that his own sincere support of Hideho's creative vision yields more than a well-wrought poem; he succeeds in unlocking the artist's inspirational door, that passage through which an audience is invited to experience life more vividly:

> Never before,
> in the tavern of the Zulu Club,
> nor in the cabaret downstairs,
> had Hideho left the cellar door
> of his art ajar, with a Promethean gesture,
> so we could get our penny's worth:
> "Everybody has a private gallery".   (*HG*, 333)

The Curator realizes that he has contributed to Hideho's achievement of creating the kind of art that not only provides the audience with an opportunity to participate in cultural ritual, like Hideho's earlier John Henry recitation, but actually gives voice to his listeners' innermost feelings which they lack the artistry to articulate. The "Promethean gesture" he offers finds acceptance in the Jamaican bartender who passionately applies Hideho's metaphor to his experiences as a black man in the Deep South as well as in the British army of World War II. Seeming to understand his accomplishment, Hideho encourages his listeners to realize that they all possess a "private gallery," a host of experiences that if viewed critically defines their identity.[48] In this moment, Hideho comes closest to realizing Tolson's oft repeated admonition for black art to seek contemporary relevance without compromising artistic autonomy. Hideho's description of imaginative possibility as a gallery drives home Tolson's commitment to the trope of the Picture Book: he closely connects inspired vision to instructing others' cultural progress.

The Curator concludes his introspective questioning by acknowledging that his odyssey as a critic shares much in common with those sojourns of the conflicted artist. Addressing himself to "White Boy and Black Boy," symbolic of an all-inclusive public, he finally achieves some closure regarding the critic and gallery:

> freedom is the oxygen
> of the studio and the gallery.
>
> . . . .
>
> I confess without regret
> in this omega of my education:
> I no longer have the force of a gilbert,
> nor have I ever had the levitation
> to sustain a work of art.
> I have only pilgrimed
> to the cross street
> (a godsend in God's acre)
> where
> curator and creator
> meet – (*HG*, 359–360)

He unapologetically declares that both the artist and the curator thrive on freedom of expression without heed to whether their creations boast obvious, wide-ranging appeal. Although he only discovers this in the "omega" of his educational journey, and he continues to lack artistic skill, his newfound knowledge facilitates a richer meeting with the artist.

Tolson enjoyed a comparable experience on the college campus. A professor of English for more than forty years, he regarded critical expertise highly and viewed the classroom as a space where he unearthed the hidden gems of art for his students to appreciate in new and unexpected ways. His sonnet, "The Gallows," in *Rendezvous with America* offers a striking image of his instructional ideal. The final stanza of the poem connects the gallery to the classroom:

> He dumped the debris of customs on the refuse heap,
> He tore down fences propped with a great Amen,
> He set apart the huddling goats and sheep,
> He let the oxygen of the freedoms in. (*HG*, 60)

Echoing lines the Curator articulates at the end of *Harlem Gallery* to describe his art museum, Tolson's poem reflects the connection he sees between the critic and the teacher: each possess powers of interpretation and explanation. The literary critic transforms the work of unknown names into "gold nuggets" that challenge custom, and with Christ-like power, distinguishes those worthy of the great reward of free thought. At the conclusion of his odyssey, the Curator reaffirms the poet speaker of "The Gallows": the teacher and the curator-critic respectively "let the oxygen of the freedoms in" and acknowledge "freedom is the oxygen / of the studio and the gallery." In fact, the Curator realizes that his reflexive reaction to the majesty of great art makes the case for supporting creative independence and its willing vanguard position. Although it has taken much of his life to arrive at this conclusion, he decides that his position brings him closer to the attitude of the artist.

These discoveries clarify his sense of the Harlem Gallery's purpose. Notwithstanding the onerous nature of the Regents' demands, he declares a renewed faith in his gallery and acknowledges that without the motivation of messianic love, his efforts are for naught. But with proper inspiration and purpose, his curatorial work carries the potential of giving meaning to the present through the lens of the complicated African American cultural past. This discovery not only impels him to seek monetary support more aggressively, it also emboldens his sense of what the Harlem Gallery might achieve: "what if this Harlem Exhibition becomes / a *cause célèbre*?" (*HG*, 363).

> Our public may possess in Art
> a Mantegna figure's arctic rigidity;
> yet – I hazard – yet,
> this allegro of the Harlem Gallery
> is not a chippy fire,
> for here, in focus, are paintings that chronicle
> a people's New World odyssey
> from chattel to Esquire!   (*HG*, 363)

The Curator's cautious optimism stems equally from his renewed personal faith in black art and his growing belief that the African American public was opening up to new perspectives on art. After all, Mantegna not only produced paintings populated with sculpturally rendered subjects; he also experimented boldly with perspective. The Curator hints that the African American audience for art might be cultivating a new appreciation for black art, a new visual sophistication. Appraising the works in his gallery, the Curator triumphantly notes the history of ascendancy the paintings recount. These works are "in focus" under the auspices of the Harlem Gallery: they reap the benefits of his curatorial expertise. With his knowledgeable assistance, viewers will likely find reason to celebrate even the most challengingly wrought depictions of black history. In other words, their publication in the gallery may bear fruit beyond its walls.

Farnsworth reveals that Tolson always believed that one day his poetry would be read and discussed widely. He remained politically radical to the end, a position reiterated in his well-known public clash with Robert Hayden just four months before Tolson's death. As a panelist at a writer's conference at Fisk, Tolson thunderously rejected Hayden's proclamation that he "was a poet who happens to be black." Tolson countered, "I'm a black poet, an African-American poet, a Negro poet. I'm no accident – and I don't give a tinker's damn what you think."[49] Nevertheless, Tolson fully understood that his black pride alone would not ensure his work a wide audience. His success in the classroom suggested a more definite path.

One month after the operation that discovered his terminal cancer, Tolson wrote a short poem to acknowledge the students who organized a special program in his honor:

> How could I miss
> Cleopatra's kiss
> Or a night like this?
> You've heard about me
> And my poetry
> From A to Z.
> As the love feast ends
> A NEW CHAPTER BEGINS.
> So good night dear friends,
> Good night. GOOD NIGHT.[50]

These lines, penned as he sat on the stage undoubtedly touched by the outpouring of love from students who appreciated him as both instructor and artist, reveal Tolson's faith in the power of his work when approached in the right setting. On the Langston campus, students knew him and his work "[f]rom A to Z." The confluence of his reputation as professor and poet protected him from accusations of racial disloyalty. Facing his impending death head-on, Tolson acknowledges that the conclusion of his happy memories at Langston only clears the way for a new chapter, a chapter dependent on his work alone.

Tolson's commitment to a wide notion of publication sprung from a different aesthetic and political sensibility than that which his fellow Oklahoman, Ralph Ellison, espoused. Although both men valued their reputations as writers committed to modernist forms that facilitated their presentation of a complex African American identity, Tolson persistently thought of his work in relationship to other black writers, artists, and ideas. In fact, whereas Ellison, with his protagonist A. Z. Hickman, the bluesman turned preacher in his unfinished novel, attempts to create a character who represents an understanding of the totality of African American experience, Tolson views his public work – in the classroom and in his poetry – as representative of the "A to Z," that all inclusive knowledge his audience need know about black art. Tolson's final unhappy meeting with Ellison left him to conclude, Ellison "is an individualist. I am a social writer."[51] With the help of his exploration of the trope of the Picture Book through his metaphorical public gallery, he strives toward the realization of his self-proclaimed identity as an artist keenly committed to creating art destined to visualize the social upheaval of modern existence.

CHAPTER 6

Ralph Ellison: Engaging Racial Perception beyond Museum Walls

So vital is the part played by the art museum in our approach to works of art today that we ... forget they have imposed on the spectator a wholly new attitude toward the work of art.

...

For a "Museum without Walls" is coming into being, and ... it will carry infinitely farther that revelation of the world of art ... which the "real" museums offer us within their walls.

– André Malraux[1]

In his autobiographical essay, "Hidden Name and Complex Fate," Ellison ruminates over the process of becoming a writer and recalls that during his first days in New York, he "had begun reading the work of André Malraux, not only the fiction but chapters published from his *Psychology of Art*" (*CE*, 204). As Ellison wrestled with the literary form he would embrace, he worked "to grasp [Malraux's] blending of art history, philosophy, and politics."[2] In his passionate response to Irving Howe's attack, Ellison claims that his discovery of Malraux pointed him beyond Richard Wright's aesthetic early in his career, and he demands: "Need my skin blind me to all other values?" (*CE*, 165).[3] For Ellison, Malraux's movement beyond strict Marxism to contemplate the larger world of art unobstructed by political ideology offered a crucial example. In a letter to Wright in 1940, Ellison attempts to refine his notion of the relationship between ideology and art by questioning his friend about Wright's recently published *Native Son*: "How far can the Marxist writer go in presenting a personalized, humanist version of his ideology? Both Gorky and Malraux attempted this and both ran into mysticism and criticism from the politicians and the theoreticians. Then again, does the writer who accepts Marxism have the freedom to expound a personalized philosophy?"[4]

Ultimately, Ellison seems to answer his own question by turning to the founding principles of the public museum. In its earliest incarnation, the public museum emerged as an institution invested in teaching visitors, conceived of in broad terms as a nation's citizenry, to see themselves and their position in society with greater sophistication and cultural refinement. Its guiding philosophy proposed that the act of viewing carefully selected objects in a thoughtfully constructed space would impact the mind and hearts of people. In assessing the aims of liberal governments promoting the nineteenth-century museum, Tony Bennett explains that politicians and advocates of "rational recreations" looked to the public museum as an institution capable of eschewing the increase "of formal regulatory powers of the state" and instead, "achieving its objectives by inscribing these within the self-activating and self-regulating capacities of individuals."[5] To find success, the museum needed to "function as a space of emulation;" arrange its representations not principally to evoke "wonder and surprise" but to "secure the utilization of these for the increase of knowledge and for the culture and enlightenment of the people;" and, finally, to become a "space of observation and regulation in order that the visitor's body might be ... moulded in accordance with ... new norms of public conduct."[6] Throughout *Invisible Man* (1952) and Ellison's unfinished second novel, posthumously published as *Three Days Before the Shooting...* (2010), the many museum spaces and museum-inflected interactions reflect Ellison's attention to the heavily charged ambition of the public museum and the ways the philosophy undergirding these spaces of display extends beyond their walls.

Ellison's novels, then, ponder the stakes of Malraux's assertion that the "Imaginary Art Museum" provides opportunities for much more sophisticated "intellectualization."[7] Although the art gallery succeeds in ministering to a love of beauty and creates a narrative of man's heroic quest, it fails to admit that visitors possess "knowledge" far "more comprehensive than" the holdings of a museum can hope to exhibit.[8] Thus, in stark contrast to Tolson's investment in the private gallery as a space of publication – a metaphor for the larger publishing industry and specialists who determine which works get circulated, analyzed, and actively discussed – Ellison introduces museum culture as a means for evaluating the stakes of integrating the rules of perception dictated by the museum into everyday interactions far beyond its walls.

Ellison's turn to the museum harkens back to his earlier discovery of Marxism. I want to suggest that the museum provides him an alternative to the Marxist ideology that fleetingly underpinned his intellectual philosophy.[9] When he discovered that creative writing could serve as a genuine, innovative channel for political activism, Marxism appealed to him.[10] But although he found the Marxist focus on historical materialism and its relevance to the ongoing class struggle compelling, Ellison quickly recognized the danger Marxist ideas carried for the artist. He regarded the struggle between races in the U.S. as closely linked yet fundamentally distinct from the broader conception of class struggle at the center of Marxist ideology. For Ellison, the exploitation African Americans suffered as a result of their lack of economic and political power related directly to the Marxist focus on the alienation of the working class at the expense of bourgeoisie concerns, but the solution he imagined diverged sharply from the Marxist call for socialist revolution. Instead, Ellison advocated for revolutionizing racial perception. From his point of view, a good deal of racial conflict remained rooted in the inability of both white and black Americans to view the world in sophisticated and honest terms. Achieving such visual clarity necessitates teaching individuals across races to assess each other from a position of greater *knowledge* as opposed to greater *wealth*, and Ellison looked to institutions dedicated to educating rather than governing for the solution to this problem. He repeatedly extols the novel as a powerful educational tool, with or without the assistance of the classroom instructor or critic, and credits it with shaping national identity.

In the museum he discovers an entity connected to governance without being officially implicated in politics proper. This relationship, rarely understood by most museum visitors, lies at the base of the institution's power. In fact, the invisible connection between the bourgeois public museum and the multiple classes that visit it make museum theory a rich foundation for Ellison's fictional representations of individual character's difficulties with understanding race in U.S. society. And although Ellison does not appear to have studied museum theory extensively, his devotion to Malraux's contemplation of the relationship between visual art and modern identity strongly impacted his creative philosophy. In comparison to Hurston's implicit reference to the natural history museum and Tolson's overt allusion to the art museum, Ellison is less invested in a particular iteration of institutions dedicated to the display of art and culture. His novels display the radical extent to which general museum rules – such as the idea that institutions dedicated to displaying plastic art occupy a position of authority and teach visitors to read visually constructed ideas – permeate interactions between U.S. citizens. Consequently, engaging racial perception according to the tenets established by museum culture assumes center stage in Ellison's long fiction.

Ellison's Education in Visual Aesthetics

For Ellison, who had long nursed an interest in the plastic arts, conceiving of racial interaction in terms of viewing objects in museum collections was natural. When he arrived in New York during the summer of 1936, Ellison focused on two passions: music and sculpting. He hoped to supplement his studies in music and music theory at Tuskegee Normal and Industrial Institute and, at the same time, pursue his interest in visual art. As chance would have it, the day after his arrival, Ellison became acquainted with Langston Hughes who introduced him to the world of Harlem artists. With the help of Robert Savion Pious, Ellison met sculptor Richmond Barthé with whom he had corresponded briefly after viewing Barthé's masks.[11] The respected artist accepted Ellison as his first apprentice, and Ellison wrote to Hughes in August 1936, describing his progress as well as his assessment of his instructor:

> I've done two heads and have started my first torso. After seeing the work of several of our so called sculptors, I quite agree with you about Barthé. Not only does his work excel theirs in anatomical truthfulness, but in artistic feeling as well; I think I have been objective in this matter because I waited to study with the person who could give me the most regardless of the opinion of the Negro press.[12]

Ellison admired Barthé's style of integrating African themes with classical forms in his bronze sculptures, but African American critics disparaged the sculptor's work as too conservative and reliant on Western art philosophy.[13] Ellison, with his Oklahoma musical training that embraced such artistic integration, identified with Barthé's aesthetic notions.[14] His early works showed great promise and bore the marks of Barthé's tutelage (see Figure 6.1). The sculptor's declaration that he did not approach his work as commentary on race relations, although he did believe African Americans could "better portray inner feelings of Negro people," resonated deeply with Ellison's budding creative sensibility.[15]

In fact, the artistic inclination that led him to Barthé points to a fundamental aspect of his creative perspective that spawned *Invisible Man* and shaped his work on his second novel. Examining Ellison's interest in visual art and the museum recovers a critical tool for analyzing Invisible Man's journey from idealizing a simple, realistic notion of identity to appreciating a more complicated, abstract definition of African American humanity. In particular, the novel's insistence that Invisible Man display an ability to interpret densely coded interactions as well as decipher plastic art objects – pieces of visual art notable for their multidimensional

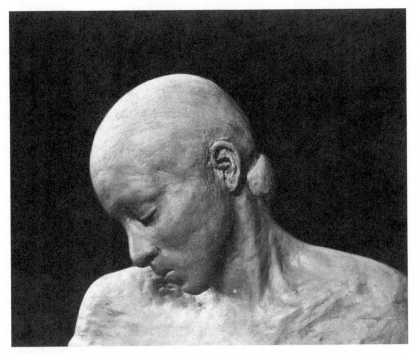

Figure 6.1 Ralph Ellison, Bust of Marie Howard of Tuskegee Institute (c. 1936). Courtesy of The Ralph and Fanny Ellison Charitable Trust. Prints & Photographs Division, Library of Congress, Washington, DC.

presence and malleability, such as framed pictures, sculptures, and handled artifacts – plays a crucial role in this transformation. By focusing on these exchanges and objects, I clarify Ellison's dedication to and advocacy for producing a modernist literary aesthetic capable of celebrating African American visual dexterity that leads to the unveiling of black American interiority. I extend and round out this discussion with a brief analysis of *Three Days* which reveals the way Ellison expands his reliance on visual art to portray the sophisticated interpretive abilities of black folk characters, a central theme in his broader corpus. Ellison's texts foreground the trope of the Picture Book in plots shaped around protagonists who learn to rely on visual literacy to come to terms with U.S. society.

Ellison began solidifying his notion of the utility of visual art for demonstrating African American complexity during his apprenticeship with Barthé. Although Ellison's hands-on work with the sculptor was brief,[16] he remained involved in the visual arts scene for the remainder of his life.

When he traveled to New York from Alabama, following a similar path as Tolson's 1930 journey from Texas to New York, the black visual arts scene bloomed fully.[17] The period marked a moment of experimentation and transition as black artists gained a reputation for their portrayal of the crucial relationship between folk experience and modern existence in African American life. Black artists also began experimenting with abstraction and collage, illustrating black consciousness and rebelling against the social realist genre dominating African American visual and literary art. One such artist, painter Romare Bearden, became a good friend of Ellison's in the 1930s. In "Romie," Ellison discovered a peer equally devoted to creating a multifaceted picture of African American existence.[18] Building on his training with Barthé, Ellison found Bearden's plastic portrayals of African American identity refreshing in their rejection of stereotype and idealization. Additionally, he and Bearden shared a devotion to the blues and jazz, art forms that successfully combine folk culture and modern experience.

In his essay "The Art of Romare Bearden," Ellison describes Bearden's collages as "eloquent of the sharp breaks, leaps in consciousness, distortions, paradoxes, reversals, telescoping of time, and surreal blending of styles, values, hopes, and dreams which characterize much of Negro American history" (*CE*, 693). Ellison also extols Bearden for his ability to "reveal a world long hidden by clichés of sociology and rendered cloudy by the distortions of newsprint and the false continuity imposed upon our conception of Negro life by television and much documentary photography" (*CE*, 690). Bearden's dedication to moving beyond realistic portrayals of African American life agreed with Ellison who "chided visual artists committed to social protest."[19] Yet in 1941 he had responded to Richard Wright's *12 Million Black Voices* (1941), a photographic documentary of black life, in strikingly different terms: "After reading [*12 Million Black Voices*] and experiencing the pictures, the concrete images, I was convinced that we people of emotion shall land the ... destructive-creative blows in the struggle. And we shall do it with books like this!"[20] Ellison valued the intensity of Wright's work, even calling *12 Million Black Voices* "lyrical," but as he grappled with portraying African American consciousness in prose, he sought a literary aesthetic that penetrated the sociologically determined images documentary photography and protest-realist writing often reified (*CE*, 670).

Ellison's shifting assessment of his peer's visual work exposes the evolution of his literary philosophy. Notwithstanding his eventual reservations concerning Wright's naturalist style, Ellison's authorial impulse was motivated by Wright's example and encouragement. Ellison soon concluded that their shared commitment to revitalizing African American literature moved them beyond the realm of mere friendship to the status of "brothers."[21] The two exchanged long letters as Ellison grappled with whether he should commit to writing as a profession. In 1945 he confessed to Wright:

> I have considered the possibility that I may not be a novelist myself. ... Anyway, it isn't the prose, per se, that worries me; it's the form, the learning how to organize my material in order to take the maximum advantage of those psychological and emotional currents within myself and in the reader which endows prose with meaning; and which, in the writer, releases that upsurge of emotion which jells with conceptions and makes prose magical.[22]

Ellison's deliberation over the prose form best suited to his purposes hints toward his growing disenchantment with overt naturalist-realist methods like Wright's. He had breathlessly read the manuscript of *Native Son* as Wright typed it into being, but in the years leading up to his composition of *Invisible Man*, he embraced a more modernist aesthetic. Wright in turn questioned Ellison's potential as a writer. He reflected in his journal, Ralph "writes because he is a Negro; he really wanted to be a sculpture [*sic*], but he found he could not say what was hotly in him to say with stone and marble."[23] In actuality, Ellison was formulating his metaphor of invisibility, a philosophical idea indebted both to Wright and to his interest in visual art.

Invisible Man in manuscript shows Ellison coming to terms with the museum practices he hoped to model. As he secluded himself on a Vermont farm to cultivate his novel, he observed in a letter to Wright: "The cubists, or at least the great cubists such as Picasso, worked through the phase of abstraction only to return to natural objects and events – although they learned through their explorations to present an essence of the real world, the plastic essences of people of human figures."[24] By "plastic essences" he indicates the malleability he sought to capture in his presentation of African American experience. He found himself both working through and discovering the value of "abstraction" in his own work, and his manuscript charts his journey. His seven-year road of composition produced an original manuscript numbering more than eight hundred pages. Countless outlines, elaborate notes, and numerous scenes excised from the published text document the genesis of the novel.[25] The drafts and typescripts also attest to his meticulous revision practices. For example, twelve folders bear the "Brotherhood" designation and several others include pages pertinent to these scenes. Some of these folders boast two hundred pages of typed manuscript including scraps of paper with pencil-scrawled sentences transferred to the published text. Studied in conjunction with his collection of newspaper clippings, art exhibit programs, and various other articles, the manuscript unveils Ellison's composition process. The teeming mass of materials and drafts related to *Three Days* unveils more than forty years of writing that further fleshes out Ellison's evolving artistry. And although he never managed to mold his second novel into a completed, published form, the drafts of this tome shed additional light on his manipulation of museum techniques.

To grasp the essence of Ellison's visual turn, however, I start with *Invisible Man*. His final revisions of the novel focused on the prologue and epilogue, and in reworking these sections, Ellison deftly navigates issues of objectification by replacing realistic examinations of art with a kind of formal modernist packaging of his text.[26] Within this frame, he chronicles his protagonist's journey from a naïve reader of visual images to a critical visual observer. Ellison constructs a relationship between narration and visual culture that redefines traditional perspectives on African American identity as static reality and instead, seeks "plastic essences." In fact, the term "invisible" is itself calculated to challenge narrowly conceived images of black humanity. Expanding Ellison's examination of Invisible Man with a consideration of the Reverend A. Z. Hickman unveils the persistent significance of museum philosophy in his portrayal of sophisticated black identity. Ellison's decision to shift his attention, from his callow protagonist in *Invisible Man* – who until the final pages of the novel lacks the ability to interpret his position in U.S. society – to his jazzman-preacher in *Three Days* who gazes upon the country with keen understanding, allows him to dramatize the full impact of black visual literacy on cultural maturity.

Discarding Traditional Portraits for Modern Complexity

Ellison enlists traditional portraiture to trace Invisible Man's quest for power. He suggests that such portrayals fail to account for the complexity of humanity, and by extension, the protagonist's obsession with emulating such figures displays his shallow understanding of modern existence. As Ellison revised his text, he had to decide how heavily to wield this critique of visual art's representational reliability. He admired authors like Henry James, who connects a character's ability to interpret objects of art to a maturing consciousness, but he doubted that James's aesthetic would be effective for depicting African American individuality.[27] Nevertheless, he clearly shared the sense that traditional portraits, trading on the Grand

Manner with their commitment to conveying a sitter's authority, attractiveness, and historical importance, offer rich opportunities for spotlighting the U.S. fascination with crafting powerful appearances. The attendant refusal of such images to reveal the difficulties of formulating an American identity heightens their danger for individuals like Invisible Man who naively imitate such likenesses.

In the published novel, Invisible Man designates certain characters "men of power," and more often than not, these men appear as portraits and redefine interiors as rooms of display (*IM*, 137). Robert Stepto first labels spaces in the novel as portrait galleries and museums. He contextualizes Ellison's portraits within a larger historical trajectory and imagines him spectacularly building on earlier literary portraiture strategies. Stepto claims the portraits in *Invisible Man* display Ellison's fundamental suspicion of "simple dichotomies" and instead function to "enlarge a fresh narrative space." [28] This claim helpfully positions my approach, though my reading marries contemplating the portraits and artifacts populating the novel with a discussion of plastic art to expand their contribution to Ellison's development of his protagonist.

Ellison was undeniably interested in the theoretical underpinnings of exhibition spaces. By transforming ordinary rooms into these heavily charged places, he acknowledges the growing importance of "high" visual art culture in the early 1950s. The dramatic expansion of African American museums discussed in the previous chapter testifies to the belief that, to present black American history accurately, African Americans needed to take charge of institutions responsible for the task. In conjunction with the growing number of national magazines – such as *Our World*, *Ebony*, *Sepia*, and *Flash* – marketed to black readers and based around the work of African American photojournalists, black American museums countered disparaging images of blacks in popular culture while teaching their constituents the importance of reading, comprehending, and producing positive images of African American life. Ellison's attention to portraits and visual artifact collections reveals his awareness of the power inherent in modes and institutions of display as well as the need to understand principles of visual consumption.

The picture of Invisible Man's grandfather represents the first power portrait and demonstrates the inscrutability of such images. After the battle royal, the protagonist recalls, "I stood beneath his photograph ... and smiled triumphantly into his stolid black peasant's face" (*IM*, 33). His confrontation with his grandfather's portrait vividly dramatizes his psychological confusion. Invisible Man wonders whether his speech of accommodation represents a success or marks him a traitor. His face-to-face meeting with the wall-mounted photographic portrait gives space to his internal quandary. In a manuscript draft, the grandfather reappears in the form of "an old post-card photograph" that falls from a stack of Invisible Man's college books and "lays staring at [him] from the bed."[29] Ellison observes photographic history in choosing the visual format. Following the *carte-de-visite* and the cabinet card, the photo postcard appeared around the turn of the century, and its general availability distinguishes it as the form that made photographs widely accessible. Ellison's deletion of this scene suggests he preferred presenting the grandfather in the visual form most clearly indicating a position of power rather than accessibility. In the published text, the grandfather appears solely in the guise of a wall portrait.

The material specificity also underscores Ellison's attention to the effect of specific pictorial forms in literature. Françoise Meltzer's provocative contemplation of the literary portrait draws on Roland Barthes to explain the unique work of the photograph in novels. Her analysis of Kafka's *Amerika* – in a moment oddly similar to *Invisible Man* as Kafka's protagonist tries "to catch his father's eye" in a photograph – leads her to conclude: "This insistence on trying to bring a picture to life ... is in itself ecphrastic. It is ecphrastic because in stating that such a world cannot be entered ... the text simultaneously does enter that world."[30] This captures what Meltzer describes as "a remarkable property of literature: a text, in its description of an artifact, allows for an entry that hard surfaces otherwise deny us."[31] For Ellison, he repeatedly gives the reader this access to highlight Invisible Man's cluelessness. We understand the possibility of interacting with the grandfather of the photograph in the same way that we experience the grandfather on his deathbed, and this reality makes us increasingly impatient with Invisible Man's naiveté.

Invisible Man's college experiences expand the imposing power of portraiture by introducing museum culture. In fact, after the protagonist recalls the bucolic setting, he introduces the section with a striking example of ekphrasis:

> Then in my mind's eye I see the bronze statue of the college Founder, the cold Father symbol, his hands outstretched in the breathtaking gesture of lifting a veil that flutters in hard, metallic folds above the face of a kneeling slave, and I am standing puzzled, unable to decide whether the veil is really being lifted, or lowered more firmly in place; whether I am witnessing a revelation or more efficient blinding. (*IM*, 36)

Figure 6.2 Charles Keck, Statue of Booker T. Washington "Lifting the Veil of Ignorance" at Tuskegee University in Tuskegee, Alabama (1922). Prints & Photographs Division, Library of Congress, Washington, DC. Photograph by Carol M. Highsmith. [LC-DIG-highsm-05950].

His confused memory of the Founder's statue – a clear invocation of Charles Keck's statue of Booker T. Washington "Lifting the Veil of Ignorance" (see Figure 6.2) – presages his reflection over his tumultuous college years. As he strives to make sense of the sights and events that define his undergraduate experience, he focuses on his inept visual interpretive ability. Yet his reflective confusion also reveals his growing visual acuity: instead of accepting the standard narrative associated with the statue, Invisible Man questions Washington's intentions. He implicitly acknowledges Keck's traditional portrayal of the climactic moment and polemically notes that the Founder may either be removing or replacing the veil.

Invisible Man exhibits no such sophistication during his college days proper. When Bledsoe summons Invisible Man to his office for disciplinary action, the protagonist notes the "framed portrait photographs and relief plaques of presidents and industrialists, men of power – fixed like trophies or heraldic emblems on the walls" (*IM*, 137). His office symbolizes the first site that introduces museum philosophy to the interactions between characters. Yet Invisible Man lacks the necessary knowledge to discern the museum principles defining the college president's office, and thus, he remains virtually blind to the rules of the exhibition space. He determines that the pictures and plaques have been transformed into "trophies or heraldic emblems" by their placement on the wall (*IM*, 137). Although this discovery allows him to classify the pictured individuals as "men of power," he cannot grasp the ordering logic that explains their presence in Bledsoe's office. Ellison's construction of the collection in the office echoes the collection's function in the museum. As Tony Bennett has argued with respect to the formation of museums, the collection manifests an invisible abstraction, the perception of which acts to distinguish the gazer who knows from the gazer who does not. The protagonist, as he stands in Bledsoe's office, is clearly the unknowing gazer. He cannot see through the collected pieces to recognize that they reify Bledsoe's rhetoric of accommodation and hypocrisy. This invisible philosophy explains the visible collection, and the protagonist's inability to penetrate the surface meaning highlights his lack of knowledge, his visual illiteracy.

It is not until his arrival in New York that he begins to comprehend the power dynamic of spaces organized according to museum principles. Upon entering Emerson's office, the protagonist determines that it is "like a museum" (*IM*, 180). Reflecting back on his college campus, the only site in the novel that features a traditional museum, he muses: "There was nothing like this at the college museum." The artifacts in the school museum include slave relics such as "a set of ankle-irons ... an ugly ebony African god ... and a leather whip" (*IM*, 181). Their representation of a past too close to admire leaves Invisible Man unable to fathom the kind of artistic value Ellison later assigns such art objects in essays and interviews. The protagonist, unable to envisage the worth of African American art, misses the irony the college collection conveys by displaying objects of American brutality beside examples of African artistry. Instead, he remains dedicated to converting himself into a traditional figure of power like those he contemplates in Bates's office, the first Wall Street trustee he visits. There he admires pictures of quintessential American power in "three portraits of dignified old gentlemen in winged collars who looked down from their frames with an assurance and arrogance" (*IM*, 167). Bates's gallery reinvigorates Invisible Man's reformative ambition, whereas Emerson's relics complicate his goal by recalling a racial history he misreads. His endorsement of traditional portraits of power and rejection of indigenous artifacts illustrates his denial of his African American heritage as well as the truth of U.S. history.

After merely visiting the spaces of powerful men, Invisible Man finally obtains an office of his own. With a portrait of Frederick Douglass adorning his wall, he imagines he possesses a fuller understanding of visual images. He ruminates over "how magical it was that [Douglass] had talked his way from slavery to a government ministry" and imagines that "something of the kind is happening to" him (*IM*, 381). He places Douglass in the same company as the other portraits representing ideas he cannot follow, but he envisions himself filling a similar frame. The Douglass portrait also recalls Chapter 1's discussion of the aggressive self-imaging the former slave practiced as he sat for countless daguerreotypes, ambrotypes, and painted portraits. The material form of the Douglass portrait is less important than the fact that Douglass, a historical figure, enters the text as a visual object that represents the sophisticated visual legacy he constructed in his effort to establish himself as a visual representative of black America. To return briefly to Meltzer, she reminds us of the literary impulse to introduce history to readers in the form of framed pictures. As we share the experience of contemplating the African American past embodied in the portrait – Ellison assumes readers are familiar with Douglass's image – Meltzer explains that the "icon itself becomes an inscription that the narrator 'translates' into words."[32] Of course, as readers, we remain highly aware of Invisible Man's erroneous interpretation. We recognize the error born of his ignorance of black history.

Both initiatives reinforce Ellison's larger point regarding framed pictures in spaces recalling the museum. He hints at the ideas they represent and questions the ability of average Americans to dissect ideas in visual packaging. By interrogating ideologies ranging from Booker T. Washington's notions of African American education, to corporate America's terms for success, to Douglass's manipulation of his role as a visual symbol of black achievement, Ellison finds cracks in black and white images of accomplishment. Through the flat materiality of the power portraits and the complicated spaces housing them, he suggests that visual presentations of complex philosophies must be dismantled and examined before one can formulate a critical frame for the world. Ellison implicitly recalls Malraux's contention that widespread access to reproductions creates a museum without walls, a society that expects citizens to understand the principles of visual art and the implications of its display. To guide his protagonist to a more sophisticated understanding of the art he confronts, Ellison charts a path riddled with visual images whose representations of race and social power force Invisible Man to reassess his internalized conception of individual success.

Gender, Race, and Shared Frames of Objectification

Starting with his famous battle royal scene, Ellison expands and complicates his protagonist's interaction with plastic imaging by linking the visual objectification of white women and black men. Criticism of *Invisible Man* regularly questions the absence of significant female characters in the text. Drafts of the manuscript, however, reveal Ellison's early intentions of constructing scenes around more developed women. Different versions exhibit Invisible Man engaging in a sexual relationship with a black woman at Mary's house, joining the Brotherhood to pursue a white woman in the organization, experiencing intimacies with Emma, and consistently thinking of his sexual appeal.[33] In contrast, the finished novel contains only ambiguous love scenes with white women. His editors undoubtedly insisted on excising many of these scenes because of their sexually explicit nature (Ellison jokes in a letter to Albert Murray that he had to remove the "sour cream in the vagina" part because "it was too ripe for'em"),[34] but a larger logic seems to order his revisions. Although the drafts dramatize the stereotype of black men's desire for white women, the finished text stresses the social parallel between white women and black men. Ellison's persistent imaging of both groups introduces the traditional paradigm of the gaze and hints at the danger of accepting racial objectification.

The implications of scenes such as the battle royal emerge most forcefully in the context of Ellison's broader appeal to visual culture. Shelly Eversley begins with a similar contention in analyzing the role of women in the text. Her shrewd readings focus on Ellison's use of light, which she notes is integral to producing photographic images, in scenes featuring women as visual artifacts. Although I agree with Eversley's conclusion that these scenes pave the way for the protagonist's realization that invisibility extends beyond black men, I also probe the larger significance of his visually inspired knowledge and his negotiation of heavily freighted display sites.[35] The battle royal, for instance, is held in the "main ballroom of the leading hotel," a description evoking the kind of segregated, off-limits recreational space that offers an interesting parallel to the public museum of the era (*IM*, 17). The powerful white men at the smoker form a circular frame around the dancer dramatizing their authority over her and the boys. After showcasing the stripper's failure to control her frame, Ellison frames and re-frames the boys to symbolize the portraits white men systematically create of black masculinity. The portable fighting ring, replacing the white male faces "ringed around" the blonde, represents a metaphorical frame in which the blindfolded boys cannot see themselves, a foreshadowing of Invisible Man's first speech for the Brotherhood (*IM*, 19).[36] Such framing illustrates what Maurice Wallace describes as the frame's function in the racial gaze's need to fetishize the black male body. Designating the practice as "spectragraphia," a "chronic syndrome of inscripted misrepresentation" that "implies imperfect – indeed, illusory – cultural vision," Wallace concludes that white racialists' "spectragraphic gaze ... cannot see ... their own self-serving blindness."[37] The problem for the protagonist, however, is that he accepts, even endorses, the spectragraphic gaze under which he labors.

Ellison's focus on the canvas of boxing rings provides an inventive background for Invisible Man's emerging portrait.[38] Even when he sees his own blood "glistening and soaking into the soiled gray world of the canvas," the boxing ring canvas substituting for a painting canvas, Invisible Man fails to understand the portrait the men around him create (*IM*, 26). In addition to sharing the same term as the painting material surface, the boxing canvas supplies a focal point for a picture, and it, too, absorbs the color of its subject. That its colors derive from the blood, sweat, and dirt of fighters only intensifies the aptness of the comparison. Like a painting canvas, the boxing ring surface demarcates an off-limits space for viewers: they can observe but should not touch. But at the battle royal, the white men play the roles of spectator and artist. They create the picture on the fight canvas, so they retain rights to violate its space. Ellison underscores this point with the additional framing device of the electrical rug. When the carpet replaces the portable ring, the protagonist wonders whether "he will stand on the rug to deliver [his] speech" (*IM*, 26). He yearns to be framed by the white men, but he fails to understand that the men who choose the frame also control the picture it encases. Moreover, the physical violence unleashed in both spaces illuminates the disjuncture between the fixed quality of portraiture and the volatile nature of racial relations. The protagonist's failed attempt to pass for a picture of African American success and progress animates the irony of this scene.

Invisible Man's interaction with Mr. Norton provides him an additional opportunity to fill a frame a white woman occupies before him. Once again, he misses the implications of his circumstances when the trustee confesses that his philanthropic motivation issues from his devotion to his dead daughter, whom he carries around in the form of a miniature. Primarily created as tokens of mourning, these diminutive portraits popularized in mid-eighteenth-century America commemorated marriages, births, and a general growth of affection for children. Unlike traditional portraits that facilitate "face-to-face" meetings, miniatures add touch to the interaction, injecting an erotic dimension to the images that often made children the "object of an adult gaze."[39] Most scholars attribute such depravity specifically to men who, unlike women who displayed their miniatures on bracelets or necklaces, concealed these tokens in vest pockets. Miniatures also distinguish themselves from traditional portraits in that they have a reverse side: on the back, intricate designs woven with the hair of the pictured person transform them into a wearable "fetish."[40] The history of the diminutive portraits fleshes out the implications of Norton's relationship with his daughter as well as his habit of collecting individuals to expand his collection of curiosities.[41] Additionally, his framed miniature recalls the framing at the battle royal, a point Ellison makes in his notes as he contemplates using the "same symbolism as battle royal" to show that "incest is the ultimate expression of monopoly."[42] Once again, a powerful white man frames and possesses a beautiful white woman whom the protagonist is forced to gaze upon, and in this instance, touch.

In these early scenes, Invisible Man fails to connect the framing of white women with his own visual objectification, and his awareness grows only marginally as he deals with the Brotherhood. After his first speech on the Woman Question, he goes home with a mysterious lady. Her apartment represents another space suffused by museum philosophy. Upon entering the living room he observes "a life-sized painting of a nude, a pink Renoir. Other canvases were hung here and there, and the spacious walls seemed to flash alive with warm, pure color" (*IM*, 411). By designating the painting a Renoir nude, Ellison introduces Renoir's belief that the female nude returns women to a natural, less inhibited state than modern dress imposes. Their natural settings and reflective skin celebrate their earthy natures, but Renoir's classical touches trap them in a traditional heritage of art that objectifies the female body.[43] Like the Renoir nude, the mystery woman is clearly an object bought for her husband's museum. In an earlier draft, Ellison makes this point more clearly. Upon entering the room the protagonist notes: "I suddenly saw a life-sized painting of a pink nude looking out languid-eyed from a dull gold frame. It seemed alive."[44] Here, the detail of a particular artist is removed in favor of emphasizing the connection between the painting and the woman. The protagonist in the published version does not understand that in an attempt to alter her status, the woman seeks to assume the role of collector and add him to her collection.

This becomes strikingly clear when Invisible Man enters her bedroom. The mirror frames reflect images that invoke the impressionist technique of painting scenes that change from moment to moment. Facing each other, the two mirrors create instant portraits. Invisible Man notes that the mirrors toss their "images back and forth, back and forth, furiously multiplying the place and circumstance" (*IM*, 416). This repetition signifies the long tradition of black male sexual exploitation at the hands of white women, but more emphatically, it underscores the significance of framed bodies. When the woman's robe reveals her nakedness, Invisible Man describes her body as if she is the "life-sized" Renoir painting hanging on the wall: "I went breathless at the petite and generously curved nude, framed delicate and firm in the glass" (*IM*, 416). In a preliminary draft, Ellison stresses this point by changing his initial verb, "revealed," to "framed."[45] In fact, the mirrors become frames arresting their images, connecting while juxtaposing their objectified status.

Notwithstanding the numerous incidents linking him to white women, it is not until Sybil unequivocally requests Invisible Man to enter the world of performance that he suspects the full extent of his objectification. He only partially grasps her astute observation acknowledging their mutual subjugation: "[Y]ou're not like other men. We're kind of alike" (*IM*, 520). Similarly, he is unable to extend his reasoning to decipher the attitude of the Brotherhood men. Like the white women who have no interest in his words, the white Brothers use him as a visual example of their inclusiveness. As Jack bluntly states: "You were not hired to think" (*IM*, 469). In truth, he is hired to embody a talking picture within the enervating confines of the Brotherhood frame. Their frame, however, does not announce itself in accordance with traditional museum rules. Invisible Man must use his visual skills to penetrate the meaning of their words and actions that remain encased in visual objects. With the explosion of the museum beyond concrete institutional walls, Ellison's protagonist must develop vision to determine his fate.

Harlem Images in the Street Gallery

As Ellison stages this framing, he also portrays his protagonist's reflection over metaphorical portraits created by and imposed on the Harlem population. In similar fashion, Ellison nurtured his own growing interest in photography, and specifically portraiture, staring at Harlem dwellers from behind his camera lens.[46] Yet even as he fixed Harlem with his increasingly sophisticated cameras, his composition exposes an eagerness to emphasize the mutability of African American life, its unremitting resistance to static imaging. The eviction concretizes the protagonist's endeavor to appreciate the ever evolving nature of black identity forcefully expressed through visual exhibits. Stumbling over the household objects strewn across the snow and listening to the grumbling of the crowd, he muses: "Now I recognized a self-consciousness about them, as though they, we, were ashamed to witness the eviction, as though we were all unwilling intruders on some shameful event; and thus we were careful not to touch or stare too hard at the effects that lined the curb; for we were witnesses of what we did not wish to see" (*IM*, 270). For one of the first times, he realizes that the evicted couple's belongings constitute a heavily burdened display.

With a temporarily awakened sense of cultural pride, he identifies the crowd's, as well as his own, inner response to the outer spectacle. His detection of the collective desire not "to see" announces the crowd's recognition that the artifacts littering the snow epitomize a forced exhibition of private effects. They intuitively comprehend the transgression of forcing a private domestic space to parallel the public museum. The scattered items represent the old couple's knotty life history, their complicated insides pushed outside by the evicting agent, a symbol of white power and injustice.[47] Invisible Man's intense response highlights his incipient status as a reader of visual images: "I turned and stared again at the jumble, no longer looking at what was before my eyes, but inwardly-outwardly, around a corner into the dark, far-away-and-long-ago, not so much my own memory as of remembered words, of linked verbal echoes, images, heard even when not listening at home" (*IM*, 273). He stands on the precipice of realizing a fully formed consciousness that successfully detects personal and communal meaning taking shape through the visual spectacle.

Ellison's careful register of the items displayed in the street includes a number of pictures. Beginning with a "portrait of the old couple when young," the protagonist proceeds to identify "a faded tintype of Abraham Lincoln," an "image of a Hollywood star," a "white man in black-face," and "a yellowing newspaper portrait of a huge black man with the caption: MARCUS GARVEY DEPORTED" (*IM*, 271–272). These visual images, strewn together with a melee of objects, create a collage defined by invisible connections linking the items. In fact, the household articles embody the definition of collage: they form a single image on a shared plane in which their juxtaposition and varying texture interact to achieve an artistic result. The collage chronicles the old couple's life and emblematizes the shared and convoluted history of black Americans. As such, it recalls Ellison's remarks regarding the collages of Romare Bearden.

Like Bearden's art, the eviction collage uncovers the complexity and incongruity of African American experience. In contrast to traditional portrayals of blackness, the collage enables images of African American pride, family and cultural history, and political activism to mingle with images of black self-exploitation and white racism. The old couple embodies the reality Bearden's collages convey, but they lack the corresponding control. To rescue the exhibition of their lives from exploitative chaos and transform it into a collection of African American strength, the protagonist haphazardly asserts control by leading the crowd in dismantling the collage and returning it to the couple's home. Despite his bold actions, he only subconsciously senses the power of the household objects: they represent the vital incongruities characterizing African American life as well as the need to understand the potential strength in a paradoxical past. He does not, however, succeed in accurately decoding the displayed objects.

The "*veil that threatened to lift*" as he contemplates the eviction is firmly resecured by his decision to join the Brotherhood (*IM*, 273). As the leader of the Brotherhood's Harlem district, the protagonist is discouraged from formulating an independent view of the world around him, and he is particularly dissuaded from concentrating on his perception of black experience. Instead, he organizes a placard campaign that trumpets racial diversity with "a color photograph of bright skin texture and smooth contrast" (*IM*, 385). The poster image partakes in the wider campaign to smooth over racial discord by superimposing visual images of harmony. His determination to picture the goal of his Brotherhood work establishes his recommitment to a conventional visual mode of countering racism. In Ellison's manuscript this episode is more explicit in its purpose, and the placard picture includes the protagonist's face. After the placards are posted all over Harlem, they mysteriously begin to disappear. In the draft version, Invisible Man explains his own reaction thoughtfully:

> I was used to seeing Negroes caricatured, and had long identified myself with such things. ... Aunt Jamima, Shoe Shoe Sam, the Cream of Wheat Man and the Ham What Am Man were familiar along with the attitudes that went with them, but this was something new. God, the things that happened to paper and cardboard. What would happen to my image now?[48]

The inclusion of his own face on the poster makes the theft of the placards personally disturbing, and he imagines someone has launched a direct assault on his effort to redefine U.S. race relations. His reflection on African American pictorial stereotypes in popular culture reveals the larger battle he subconsciously wages as well as his desire to escape a legacy of visual derogation by taking the struggle to the street.

Ironically, in this manuscript version, it turns out that the people of Harlem are stealing the placards from public spaces and transferring them to the privacy of their homes. When Invisible Man visits African American Brotherhood members, he sees the poster displayed between "family portraits in cheap ornamental folders." Instead of an assault on his attempt to re-image race relations, the stolen placards disclose the success of the protagonist's plan. Black men and women view the photograph as a hopeful picture of their future, and they display it amongst their personal portraits. One couple informs the protagonist: "Folks we know are crazy about that picture. I know at least four of my friends got them on their walls. Hester Cook and Lizzie Sanders even had their's [*sic*] framed."[49] For Harlem dwellers, the rainbow poster visually combats racist images of their present lives with a realistic image of racial harmony. They self-consciously organize private displays in an attempt to shape the public cultural narrative that defines them.

Still the Brotherhood's ultimate betrayal of the Harlem community, closely modeled after Ellison's evolving view of the Communist Party, highlights the danger of placing too much confidence in such shallow images.[50] Ellison drives this point home in the published novel where the poster features Tod Clifton, the "very black" Brother with "chiseled, marble-like features sometimes found on statues in northern museums," who ends up peddling Sambo dolls, the ultimate image of black degradation (*IM*, 363). Kimberly Lamm argues that Clifton's character exemplifies Ellison's dedication to producing art that challenges "image repertoires" black males "have been historically constituted within."[51] Her ensuing conclusion that, like Bearden's photomontages, Clifton "complicates rigid definitions of race, masculinity, and activism"[52] enforced by institutions like the Brotherhood, not only connects Bearden and Ellison's aesthetic concerns, but pushed further, begins to acknowledge the importance of interpreting visually laden performances and objects.

In early drafts, Clifton attempts to convince Invisible Man of the Brotherhood's duplicitous relationship to the black community by relating his personal odyssey in the organization. He admits that he has been married to a white woman in the Brotherhood, but when he realized that he and his wife would always be viewed as symbols, he bought a sunlamp to make her "a plain, un-symbolic human being" and to rescue himself from the role of "nigger bait."[53] The Sambo doll scene that replaces Clifton's divulgence denies Invisible Man access to the youth leader's decision process. Instead, Clifton forces the protagonist to interpret his actions and the visual object that represents his renouncement. Invisible Man has previously noted moments when the youth leader's "eyes were turned inward," and upon finding Clifton peddling the dolls he observes, "[H]is eyes looked past me deliberately not seeing" (*IM*, 367, 432). He must reconcile his detection of Clifton's introspective vision with the young man's purposeful outward blindness; his "not seeing" eyes redirect the protagonist's gaze to the Sambo doll and its frantic dance. When Invisible Man spits on the doll, a visual confirmation of the stereotypical image he fears society affixes to him, a fat man makes the connection and laughs boisterously "pointing from [the protagonist] to the doll" (*IM*, 433). Invisible Man's failure to escape the image replicates his violent effort to dispose of Mary's Sambo bank and mocks his attempt to subvert a complicated picture of black humanity.

Only Clifton's death prods Invisible Man to begin questioning his resistance to seeking deeper understanding of the individuals and visual exchanges around him. After witnessing the shooting, he gazes upon three African American boys in full zoot suit apparel and recalls the words of his college professor: "You're like one of these African sculptures, distorted in the interest of design."[54] With newfound curiosity, he wonders, "what design and whose?" (*IM*, 440). The boys share the extreme position of the Sambo doll, projecting an image that defies historical containment in an effort to control the terms of their identity. Their existence forces Invisible Man to reassess the accuracy of Brotherhood ideology, and as he delivers Clifton's eulogy, he gains a new perspective of the Harlem residents: "And as I took one last look I saw not a crowd but the set faces of individual men and women" (*IM*, 459). His ability to see individuals comprising the mass signals his growing perception of African American consciousness, and when the Brothers attack his actions, he holds his ground with newfound confidence. To their insistence that Clifton was a traitor, he responds: "He was a man and a Negro; a man and a brother; a man and a traitor, as you say; then he was a dead man, and alive or dead he was jam-full of contradictions" (*IM*, 467). Invisible Man no longer feels compelled to fit Clifton into a flat, uncomplicated frame; instead, he recognizes the fundamental contradictions at the center of his friend's character and determines that his paradoxical actions are not damning but enlivening. Like the Harlem community, he sees Clifton's humanity in his contradictions and declares to Jack: "[T]he political consciousness of Harlem is exactly a thing I know something about" (*IM*, 471). The visual spectacle of the Sambo doll facilitates his comprehension of African American interior life, a consciousness too intricate in its historical experience to accept the Brotherhood frame.

Shattered Pictures and the Novel

As Ellison hammered out his manuscript, his inclination to connect the modern visual art surrounding him to significant scenes assumed varying forms. He saved copies of contemporary paintings such as Eldzier Cortor's *Room No. 5* (1948) in personal folders dedicated to cataloguing visual art. In the same way that Cortor's depiction of a sculptural naked woman reflected in a bureau mirror evokes the novel's bedroom scene between the sensual Brotherhood woman and Invisible Man, the tenor of other paintings Ellison catalogued reverberates with key moments in his text. In the manuscript drafts, directly before Invisible Man witnesses Clifton's death, he enters a bookstore where a white Brother fails to recognize him. Describing the space, he notes: "Paintings flashed upon the walls, Gauguin's; … A phrase, 'the anonymity of the mass' whirled up in my brain. The crowd … cancelled you out. We, he and I, wore the lenses of Brotherhood. We were not blind like the crowd, I thought."[55] In a different version, Invisible Man observes: "Bright reproductions flashed from the walls, Gauguin's, Dufy's, Leger's."[56] Invisible Man's identification of the artwork defining the space in which he begins to suspect Brotherhood hypocrisy frankly advocates learning to read visual art as a means of becoming more discerning interpreters of social reality. His familiarity with the artists responsible for the reproductions also validates Malraux's central contention behind the museum without walls. The explosion of reproductions thrust the museum into everyday life.

Reminiscent of Tolson's Curator, the draft versions also suggest a greater sophistication on the part of Invisible Man. Each of the artists he names depends heavily on the use of vivid color to represent interiority and draws on artistic movements such as expressionism and cubism. Moving forward from the documentary style photographs Ellison extolled in Wright's *12 Million Black Voices*, the visual forms he admired in the late 1940s produce introspective pictures through a range of artistic innovations, often subtle in meaning. But the published novel documents Ellison's decision to emphasize Invisible Man's tortuous path to visual maturity. Unlike the Curator whose expansive knowledge of art history facilitates his rumination over the condition of the modern black artist, Ellison presents Invisible Man in the published text as sorely lacking visual sophistication.

Early manuscript drafts show Ellison depending heavily and clumsily on modern art theory for portraying his protagonist's consciousness. Leroy, a former boarder at Mary's house who is drowned at sea, becomes a potential intellectual guide for the protagonist. When Invisible Man arrives at Mary's, the boarders have just learned of Leroy's death, and he instantly views the dead young man as a competitor. Mary allows him to live in Leroy's room where he peruses the dead sailor's journal. As Invisible Man grapples with the young man's politically radical ideas, he tries to "visualize Leroy" who, despite the journal passages, remains "vague, formless." His desire to see a picture of Leroy promises to be fulfilled when a fellow sailor delivers a portrait of Leroy to Mary. As Treadwell, Leroy's white friend, unwraps the portrait Mary exclaims, "Lawd, I never had no painted picture of nobody before." The boarders intently watch the unveiling of the painted portrait, their interest acknowledging the class difference signaled by the introduction of a painted portrait compared to a photographic representation.

When the portrait is revealed, Invisible Man responds intensely: "I was filled with a sense of repulsion as the baroque geometrical forms of the painting met my eyes, and outraged, for it was more like the plan of a man than a portrait, a plan for a blown assembly chart or disintegration." Treadwell explains that the painter was a "cubist painter" who "felt that by breaking up the details of Leroy's figure and rearranging them ... he would give a stronger impression of Leroy's personality." Invisible Man, confused by the portrayal, admits: "I was annoyed with my own ignorance of painting. I felt that although I disliked the portrait I should have understood it." Later, as Mary prepares to hang the portrait of "the willfully dismembered Leroy," another boarder notices a sketch on the back of the painting that presents a traditional drawing of Leroy's face. Mary decides, however, to display the fractured picture because that is how Leroy "wanted to be remembered."[57] Her fidelity to exhibiting Leroy in the manner he desired celebrates the interpretive capacity of the black folk mind, an issue Ellison eagerly returns to in *Three Days*. Upon hearing Treadwell's explanation of cubism, Mary willingly revises her attachment to realistic imaging and accepts a radically abstract one. On the contrary, the college educated protagonist rejects the modernist painting because he fails to understand it.

By the time of his death, Leroy no longer believes traditional portraiture captures the essence of his being. In turning to cubism, an art style that flattens images onto the canvas to show different sides simultaneously from different angles, the sailor asserts his multifaceted identity. Ellison was enamored with this revolutionary style that gave rise to a radical reassessment of the interaction between form and space, and he considered its implications in his letters, interviews, and essays.[58] He admired Picasso, the painter credited with opening portraiture up to a realm of "psychological experience" through his willingness to break free from traditional portraiture's "fidelity to perceptual experience."[59] Ellison describes Picasso as "the greatest wrestler with forms and techniques" because he "never abandoned the ... symbolic forms of Spanish art ... that allow the artist to speak of complex experiences and to annihilate time with simple lines and curves." He proceeds to aver that Picasso's method allows "the viewer an orientation, both emotional and associative, which goes so deep that a total culture may resound in a simple rhythm, an image" (*CE*, 213–214). Ellison believed the success of black writers depended on a similar approach, and through Leroy's abstract portrait, he forthrightly exploits cubist philosophy.

Yet the published text omits Leroy's portrait and as such, manifests Ellison's increasing focus on portraying Invisible Man's failed vision in less obvious terms.[60] In place of such a forceful representation of his visual naiveté, Ellison returns to the trope of the Picture Book and weaves the culture of viewing art objects – and learning from what one sees – into the very structure of his novel. The numerous portraits and visually constructed scenes carefully placed throughout the narrative comprise a kind of collage that ultimately rejects any parallel to a direct visual representation. We see Invisible Man solely through the lens of his view of the visual objects, voices, and music surrounding him; in turn, he comes to esteem his individuality only as he learns to reject uncomplicated portrait styles that repudiate a chaotic picture of humanity. By becoming attentive to the need for approaching visual images critically, he learns to value the role visual perception plays in understanding African Americans' relation to the founding principles of the country. He no longer seeks to craft a shallow, fixed representation of himself, or consents to being objectified visually; instead, he concludes that the American democratic ideal, in its unperverted form, insists on a sophisticated vision of racial identity. He acknowledges that his "attempt to write" down his experiences facilitates his comprehension of his identity (*IM*, 575).

Ellison's intimation that his protagonist prepares to write by becoming a sophisticated reader of plastic art objects elucidates his view regarding the relationship between U.S. racial interaction and how the philosophy controlling museum conduct influences identity construction beyond museum walls. The invisible portrait he settles on acknowledges his partiality for portrayals of American blackness not dependent on or dedicated to an emphasis on outer appearance. His insistence that his protagonist learn to analyze the visually structured society around him only to represent himself through writing about his past points to Ellison's belief regarding the work of the novel. He explains:

> [T]he novel seeks to communicate a vision of experience. Therefore, whatever else it achieves artistically, it is basically a form of communication. When successful in communicating its vision of experience, that magic thing occurs between the world of the novel and the reader – indeed, between reader and reader in their mutual solitude – which we know as communion ... and it achieves universality, if at all, through accumulating images of reality and arranging them in patterns of universal significance. (*CE*, 696)

By presenting Invisible Man's painful journey to self-knowledge, Ellison imagines himself contributing another stroke to the complex, ever-evolving American portrait not to be contained by any singular frame. His words disclose the ongoing conversation he imagines between his work and his readers, communication empowering his image of black America to escape stasis and simplicity.

The completion of the prologue and epilogue brought Ellison back to his early contemplation of creating prose as magical in meaning as in form. Invisible Man unequivocally declares his invisibility as the result of a state of mind rather than a physical predicament, thereby beginning and ending by directing his audience beyond his outward appearance and toward their interpretive posture. Although the end of the novel finds him in possession of only a budding comprehension of how to look on the world with complex perception, he has traveled a significant road. Just as visitors in a museum must grasp the ordering principles dictating individual collections, Invisible Man's journey suggests that all Americans – especially outside of museum walls – must understand the underlying issues that determine race relations. In composing his novel, Ellison travels a similar trajectory. As he switches lines from the prologue to the epilogue and back again, he tasks the framing sections with turning the text into a kind of verbal portrait, a picture painted with words.

In the years following the publication of *Invisible Man* Ellison remained wary of projects aiming to provide a visual equivalent for his text. After a spread on the novel photographed by his friend Gordon Parks appeared in *Life* magazine, Ellison divulged to Wright: "Being a photographer and a writer, you will appreciate the tremendous difficulty of translating such intensified and heightened prose images into those of photography. At best, the essay turned out to be an excellent ad."[61] He eventually acquiesced to allowing Franklin Library to publish two illustrated versions of *Invisible Man*, but he found the results disappointing.[62] To the several propositions for turning his book into a movie, he steadfastly refused. He wrote to one hopeful producer: "I deeply regret to inform you that my novel, *Invisible Man* is not available for adaptation and never has been." He continues, "I have been consistent in my refusal because I prefer that the book rest on its merits as a novel to be read rather than transposed into a form for which it was not written."[63] A proposition that the novel be adapted into a Marvel comic also met with rejection.[64] In each of these instances, Ellison seems wary of contributing to a concrete picture of blackness. Instead of seeking propitious visual depictions of blackness, Ellison devotes his novel to portraying interior truth, a truth dependent on the cultivation of penetrating vision that vouches for the power of the trope of the Picture Book.

Celebrating the authority of U.S. fiction rose to a refrain in the lectures and essays he presented for the remainder of his life. Although he became increasingly active in the world of visual culture – sitting on museum boards, amassing an impressive collection of African art, and even helping found public television – he grew progressively more invested in the supremacy of the novel as a means for understanding American culture. He insisted that only the word, particularly adapted to modernist forms capable of exploiting visuality, could capture the complexity of American identity. This complexity consisted of the tension arising from the collision of the country's written ideals, as outlined in the founding documents, and the historical and contemporary experiences molding the national consciousness. Invisible Man's very invisibility, a state he embraces after rejecting all forms of visual representation as too restrictive to convey his interiority, demands a concentration on his words, his mental sense of self. His memoir constitutes the ultimate abstract portrait through its power to transform the reality of his experiences into a comprehensive picture of his humanity.

Sights of National Identity in *Three Days Before the Shooting...*

My focus on the significance of visual understanding provides a useful context for analyzing Ellison's unresolved struggle with his second novel. During the forty years that he wrestled with his mammoth work, he altered his emphasis on key characters, shifted the point of view, and revised everything in between. In many ways, *Invisible Man* served as the foundation for his ever evolving second text.[65] But through all his revisions, Ellison remained steadfastly invested in Reverend Alonzo Hickman, God's Trombone, who displays a visual agility Invisible Man never achieves. In Hickman, Ellison crafts an expert of words and music who intimately understands the necessity of transferring his incisive analytical faculty to the motley visual world around him. With Ellison's blessing, Hickman stands on the shoulders of Invisible Man's unresolved battle to discover meaning in visual displays.[66] In stark contrast to his naïve predecessor, Hickman emerges as Ellison's reader par excellence for he is a black man capable of what most Americans of any color cannot accomplish nor desire to try: Hickman is more than willing to deploy his power of perception in multiple museum inflected spaces, and he repeatedly accepts the challenge of decoding the hidden mysteries of U.S. society. As the last purveyor of the national landscape that Ellison examines and that *Visualizing Blackness* considers, Hickman reiterates the centrality of the trope of the Picture Book to the formation of the black literary canon.

Like the manuscript of *Invisible Man*, the drafts of Ellison's second novel disappoint desires for neat conclusions. But with the publication of *Three Days*, we can begin to tackle important narrative strains and compositional strategies. In the computer sequences that editors John Callahan and Adam Bradley title "Hickman in Washington, D.C.," Ellison returns to several scenes "written as early as the 1950s" and revises them completely in July 1993 (*TD*, 499). Together, these scenes comprise Ellison's sustained consideration of Hickman's scrutiny of the U.S. capital as a series of visual displays exhibiting the complexity of U.S. history and national identity. Some of these scenes, such as Hickman and his church members' arrival to DC and trip to the Lincoln Memorial, crop up in virtually every version of Ellison's mercurial text and highlight his investment in portraying Hickman's visual assessment of the U.S. capital city. And in the computer files, Callahan and Bradley note that unlike the typescripts which reveal Ellison's emphasis on a range of character voices, his final revisions "emphasize Hickman's [voice] alone" (*TD*, 490).

These late revisions boast the virtue of returning to scenes from Ellison's earliest work on his second novel even as they simultaneously reflect his final compositional choices. As I trace Hickman's path through what becomes a kind of metaphorical national gallery in the DC section, I draw on unpublished material and published variations of the scenes centered on Hickman's time in DC. But for the sake of continuity and clarity, my reading will focus principally on the published computer files. Their revelation of Ellison's singular focus on Hickman's perambulations around Washington, DC casts the jazzman-preacher's moments of concentrated looking in sharp relief. Together, the repeated examples of ekphrasis celebrate Hickman's rare visual acuity and insist on the necessity of U.S. citizens' willingness to engage in complicated looking. These scenes also present Hickman as descending more probably from Mary Rambo, Ellison's earlier representative of the discerning folk hero, than from the bumbling Invisible Man.

Ellison's intensified reliance on ekphrasis underscores his aim to probe the impact of exported museum culture and to connect Hickman to the interpretive work average Americans must perform. Like the Harlem Renaissance women writing before him, Ellison revels in the ability to "still" his text and display the sophistication of the black reader of visual objects. Even as Hickman's museum-like tour dramatizes his talent for rigorous analysis, Ellison juxtaposes the preacher's interpretive ability with the disinclined or incapable powers of perception exposed by those around him. The scene of Hickman and his parishioners arriving to the U.S. capitol provides a case in point. Ellison seemed disposed to open his novel with their unsuccessful attempt to see Senator Sunraider. The Southern white secretary's response to the arrival of the black church members underscores the danger of refusing to view the world with fresh eyes and active engagement: "As she stood scanning their inscrutable faces she could not recall ever having encountered any of the group before," and "since she could not believe that such as they could ever associate anything having to do with the Senator with patriotic emotion their solemn appearance was simply illogical. ... Therefore, their very presence was enough in itself to arouse suspicion ... and suggested motives that were dark and devious" (*TD*, 507–508). In the earlier Prologue published with Book I, Ellison underscores the museum quality of the Senator's office to highlight the secretary's abdication of civic responsibility: "Suddenly they no longer seemed familiar, and a feeling of dream-like incongruity came over her. They were so many that she could no longer see the large abstract paintings which hung along the paneled wall. Nor the framed facsimiles of State Documents which hung above a bust of Vice President Calhoun." As they depart, she is arrested by Hickman's Grand Style portrait manner as she contemplates "his full height, framed by the doorway" (*TD*, 6).

Both versions emphasize the secretary's need to account for Hickman and his followers according to preestablished standards. In the latter version, her refusal to acknowledge the delegation beyond recognizable categories leaves her no option but to brand them as dangerous and radical, a conclusion also drawn by the naïve guard who stops them as they attempt to exit the capitol. Ellison's earlier conception of the scene contrasts the rich irony of the secretary's sense of "incongruity" arising from her preconceived notions of Southern African American behavior compared to Hickman and his parishioners' demeanor. Her failure to fit Hickman's party into the collection of objects constituting a visual display of national meaning on Sunraider's office walls solidifies her inability to read visual meaning. She exemplifies what Hurston describes as the white American desire to consign African Americans to THE AMERICAN MUSEUM OF UNNATURAL HISTORY. The spectacular nature of her analytical debacle offers a dramatic contrast to Hickman's discerning disposition.

After being bodily removed from the U.S. capitol, Hickman strives to regain his equanimity on the DC streets. But as he stumbles on what he takes to be a storefront church in a basement, Hickman confronts a perplexing sight:

> Then, in a flash, the confusion of brushstrokes and splashes sprang to form, becoming a large, unframed painting.
>
> Then came a chilling shock of surprise. For here, in the last place in the world he would have expected, he was staring at a depiction of Christ marching to Calvary. ... For now, through the clouded glass, he recognized the painting as a type of religious folk art familiar to Negro neighborhoods – an association of style and place immediately confirmed by the heavy symbolism of the scene's faded colors. For while the jeering, spear-wielding soldiers were unquestionably white, the skin of the thorn-crowned, cross-bearing Christ was unmistakably black.
>
> Then, drawn to the impression made in Christ's naked shoulder by the weight of the cross, he began to understand: For some two feet above the point where the rough-hewn upright of the cross knifed into the bruised flesh of Christ's straining shoulder, the artist, suddenly improvising on his theme like a jazzman on a familiar tune, had placed what on first sight had appeared to be the travel-soiled bundle of a hobo. There in the angle where the upright joined the sky-pointing arm of the cross it rested, a bundle consisting of red-white-and-blue cotton which was depicted as having become partially unrolled in the painful march and ended up trailing and distorting the footprints of Christ. And with eyes flying back to the point from which the striped cloth trailed he saw distorted white stars spring into focus and exclaimed, "Good Lord!" And the cloth showed forth as a bundled-up flag... (*TD*, 562–3)

Hickman's deliberate survey of the painting showcases his familiarity with the rendering of particular artistic themes for purposes related to challenging established power structures with unexpected representations of race.

More impressive, however, is his confrontation of the radical inclusion of the disfigured American flag.

The painting initially strikes Hickman as symbolic beyond its most obvious deviations, and he instantly attempts to connect the threads that associate it with related schools of art. The hobo bundle-American flag verifies Hickman's keen gaze, and he immediately comprehends the revolutionary effect of its inclusion. Ellison's insertion of a disfigured painting of Old Glory echoes African American artists of the Black Arts Movement who repeatedly included the American flag in their radical accusations of the nation's broken trust. Although the painting Hickman confronts lacks the biting critique of works like Jeff Donaldson's *Aunt Jemima and the Pillsbury Doughboy* (1963), Faith Ringgold's *Flag for the Moon, Die Nigger* (1969), David Hammons's *Injustice Case* (1970), or Dana Chandler, Jr.'s *American Penal System ... Pan African Concentration Camps and Death Houses* (1971), it unquestionably participates in the critical conversation such works foreground. These artists question, contest, and refuse the neat narrative embodied by the U.S. flag; in fact, they include it in their visual works only to trouble its established meaning with their radical reassessments. Suspecting the inflammatory company the Christ painting keeps, Hickman responds with surprised "outrage" as he rushes "to the door" and gives "it a pounding blow from his shoulder" (*TD*, 563). His violent reaction echoes Invisible Man's response to the storefront windows in Harlem, but Ellison hints that the religious painting requires deeper analysis. Ellison stops short of endorsing the Black Arts artists' rationale for including Old Glory: whereas their paintings disfigure the flag to denote the nation's broken trust with African Americans, Ellison aligns the symbol of democracy with African American's willing sacrifice for U.S. ideals. His example of notional ekphrasis parades black citizens' messianic potential even as he recognizes the fraught nature of African American citizenship.

What took Invisible Man years to resolve, Hickman begins to work through in a single day. In the space of a few hours, he is leading his delegation toward the Lincoln Monument, the sculptural reincarnation of a man of mythic meaning for African Americans. As Hickman gazes upon the sculpture, he focuses on Lincoln's great stone eyes and perceives the complexity of his character and his national meaning. During his extended moment of looking, Hickman discovers sympathy for the man who freed the slaves. Ellison shows Hickman depending on the sculptural monument to acquire new understanding:

> *Yes, with all I know about him and his contradictions – Yes! And with all I have learned about the ways of men, this country, and the world – Yes! And*

with all I know about white men and politicians of all colors, backgrounds and guises – Yes! And with all I know about the things you had to do to be you and remain yourself – Yes! You are one of the few who have ever earned the right to be called "Father."... And though I'm against all the unearned tribute which the weak and lowly are forced to pay to power based on force and false differences and false values – Yes! For you "Father" is all right with me. (*TD*, 576–577)

Hickman's ability to view Lincoln as a legitimate national father even as he acknowledges the president's inconsistencies and contradictions illustrates the preacher's sophisticated measure of the president's humanity. He need not enter the National Gallery organized to establish an official account of U.S. identity. Hickman performs the curatorial work necessary to generate a national narrative that is unafraid to peer beyond the smooth surface of monuments. His determination that Lincoln deserves the title "Father" suggests that his own experience with Bliss provides a lens through which he evaluates the contradictory nature of the man who signed the Emancipation Proclamation. Like Lincoln, Hickman has played a part riddled with inconsistencies and failure. But the sum of his actions, echoing the man whose signature made black slaves' dreams of freedom a reality, attests to his sincere ambition for a greater good. Ellison hints that Hickman requires the sight of Lincoln, rendered in the silent solidity of stark white stone, to make sense of the turbulent national and individual contradictions that constitute U.S. history. The "still" moment enables his folk hero's resolution of the difficult relationships between fathers and sons, nations and men.

Hickman's accomplishment prepares him to grapple with a copy of *Landscape with the Fall of Icarus* (see Figure 6.3), traditionally thought to be by Brueghel. Ellison's introduction of Brueghel's painting inserts Hickman's meditation into the rich history of ekphrasis connected to the famously rendered landscape. The subject of both W. H. Auden's "Musée des Beaux Arts" (1938) and William Carlos Williams's "Landscape with the Fall of Icarus," the second poem in his Pulitzer Prize winning *Pictures from Brueghel and Other Poems* (1962), Brueghel's painting provides Hickman an unexpected occasion to extend his contemplation of the relationship between fathers and sons, Christ's sacrifice, and national identity. Auden's poem opens with a reflection on the visual history of suffering. By its end, the poet speaker presents Brueghel's portrayal as exemplary in its depiction of a world too busy to pause over the tragedy before its eyes or the sound of a forsaken cry. Harkening to Christ's despairing wail, "My God, My God, why hast Thou forsaken Me," from Matthew 27:45–46, Auden

Figure 6.3 Pieter the Elder Brueghel, *Landscape with the Fall of Icarus* (c. 1525–1569). Musee d'Art Ancien, Musees Royaux des Beaux-Arts, Brussels, Belgium. Photo credit: Scala / Art Resource, NY.

reads Brueghel's masterpiece as part of the human tragedy against which even Christ, in the form of man, desperately fought: the pervasive feeling of desertion in a hectic world. Williams's verse intensifies the fact of human obliviousness, his final stanza reporting dispassionately, "a splash quite unnoticed / this was / Icarus drowning."

These modernist poets' engagement of Brueghel's painting gives voice to the confluence of Hickman's feelings and shows Ellison insisting that the black folk hero stands shoulder to shoulder with modernist poet speakers. He has confronted the visualization of African American cultural martyrdom as depicted in the black Christ laboring under the cross of racism; he has made peace with the father figure of Lincoln, a man who authored the freedom of African Americans without a complete investment in the endeavor; and now, he must face the reality that even though his sense of impending tragedy matters little to the world, he must fulfill the role of a true father to Bliss who has transformed himself into Senator Adam Sunraider.

To make this point, Ellison's revised computer files devote untold pages to Hickman's perusal of the tapestry in the Longview Hotel, and he wrestles with the scene through numerous revisions, too. In each case, he painstakingly recreates Hickman's growing awareness of the details of the painted scene as he intersperses this discovery with Hickman's translation of the image into the black vernacular, the complexity of Hickman's Southern-black-Christian-jazzman experience. Hickman's natural sense of the need to read the Brueghal scene in relation to his fresh discovery of the painting of the black Christ's flag-laden march to Calvary announces his artistic sophistication.[67] After initially mistaking the tapestry for an "abstract painting, of which he was ignorant," Hickman comfortably contemplates the scene at length, feeling at ease with his ability to interpret its meaning (*TD*, 592). It is only when he recalls the rules of the museum exhibit, the necessity of relating one work to the next, that he becomes wary: "Then, recalling the shock at discovering a picture of Christ abandoned in a basement window he tensed, suddenly suspicious that what he had taken for a peaceful landscape might conceal similar details of shocking distaste" (*TD*, 594). This incitement toward closer looking celebrates Hickman's reliance on African American artistic vocabulary. Hickman echoes the work of the museum as he muses that "the goal of both jazz musician and weaver was one of using their skills to arouse pleasure and wonder. And both did so by drawing on that which was left carefully understated or concealed as a means for achieving a transcendent goal" (*TD*, 595). Drawing from his own artistic experience, Hickman exemplifies the ideal museum visitor. His patient analysis is rewarded by the discovery of the "lonely legs ... of someone who appeared to have plunged headfirst out of nowhere and into the wind-ruffled sea"; moreover, he immediately recognizes a "vague sense of connection between the sprawling legs and the danger that had prompted his flight to Washington" (*TD*, 597).

Hickman's analytical acumen and insight places him in a radically different league from Ellison's first purveyor of visual art, Invisible Man. His mastery of visual interpretations girds him with the confidence to analyze his role in U.S. society with a cultural sophistication and flexibility that Ellison connects inextricably to museum culture. As an African American jazzman turned preacher, Hickman's visual analyses bring new meaning to well-known objects. He channels Mary Rambo in fully developed, uncut form even as he develops her initial strengths as a folk hero gifted with extraordinary interpretive powers. In fact, the jazz playing preacher's authoritative reading connecting disparate visual objects reveals Ellison's insistence that readers' confront his protagonist's intellectual prowess on the terms he initiates, the logic he ordains. In the vein of Mary Rambo, Reverend A. Z. embodies the analytical power of the folk grounded in confident blackness. His appeal to a range of visual objects in an effort to make sense of the contradictory nature of American history and of African American experience demonstrates Ellison's belief in a democratic pluralism that affords individuals of all backgrounds legitimate access to interpreting U.S. identity.

In fact, Hickman's DC study of the black Christ painting, Lincoln Memorial, and *The Fall of Icarus* argues for the necessity of diverse interpretations of national and cultural experiences to develop a nuanced understanding of U.S. identity. The distinctness of Hickman's visual reading relies on a history of racial subjugation and exploitation that inspires rather than embitters him, and his willingness to draw on his interpretive skill to explain the world to his parishioners points to Ellison's faith in the agency and political potency of artistic knowledge. In the person of Hickman, Ellison combines the common man with the critic and insists on the legitimacy of his blend. From his point of view, when the African American folk mind relies unabashedly on the utility of black cultural experience, it deserves special acclaim for demonstrating a power of vision that reaches far beyond the walls of the museum. Thus, he moves beyond Tolson's Curator who is left hoping that his gallery will influence a broad African American audience's response to modern art. In the person of Hickman, Ellison exhibits the power of a black reader of visual art who confidently translates his interpretation of visual displays into a deeper understanding of American identity.

Coda: Redefining the Look of American Character

Ellison's focus on African American visual prowess in *Three Days Before the Shooting…* brings my study of the trope of the Picture Book full circle. With a protagonist like Hickman, Ellison displays how the modern black U.S. citizen can reclaim the capacity for self-definition by visualizing exemplary citizenship and embracing the responsibility of defining the nation as well. Hickman's incisive vision propels him beyond Invisible Man whose final discovery of his position in the country emphasizes Ellison's unwavering, almost religious belief in America's founding ideals without giving his fumbling protagonist the opportunity to put his newfound understanding to use. In fact, Invisible Man's confused journey argues for the necessity of African Americans' contribution to the realization of the country's most hallowed principles. As Invisible Man learns to visualize blackness on his own terms, he discovers the source of the pluralistic democracy Ellison so passionately promotes. Invisible Man's final astute, frank, and uncompromising vision of American democracy represents the best possibility of leading the country to rediscover and recommit to its fundamental values. This, ultimately, is what black writers pursue through their investment in and signification on the trope of the Picture Book: they portray black vision as a necessary component of recovering an honest sense of American self-conception *and* an honorable practice of racial perception. To demonstrate their capacity for visualizing blackness in sophisticated terms, they craft protagonists and poet speakers whose performance of keen vision vouches for the complexity of black humanity.

Ellison's unfinished second novel provides a concluding case in point. In contrast to most of the protagonists and poet speakers who precede Hickman, Ellison invites readers to witness his preacher putting his visual knowledge to good purpose. *Three Days* not only boasts the most visually sophisticated character in my study, it also provides a cast of clever supporting actors. With their help, Ellison displays the need for black Americans to build on their shared interpretations of the country to influence the larger American citizenry. For a final reflection that both looks back on the inception of the trope of the Picture Book and distinguishes the writers of this study from the general posture assumed by black writers to come, I want to focus briefly on the "Hickman in Georgia & Oklahoma" section of *Three Days*, an episode that provides additional background about Bliss, the child whom Hickman raised from birth until he ran away as an adolescent.

In many ways, this episode represents the nucleus of Ellison's second novel. As early as 1953, Ellison announced to Albert Murray, "I've got *one* Okl. book in me I do believe."[1] This section begins with Hickman attempting to piece together the mystery of Bliss's disappearance by returning to a report from Walker Millsap. Millsap is an old acquaintance whom Hickman had asked to keep an eye out for the long lost Bliss, and his report details his discovery of a young man who fits Bliss's description and is currently connected to an African American trickster known as Missippy Brown. In a somewhat bizarre digression, Millsap admits that the white-looking Bliss and brown-skinned "Sippy" remind him of two paintings featuring George Washington and his slave, William Lee. Millsap describes both paintings ekphrastically:

> In the first the General stands before a field tent holding a scroll of papers as he strikes a pose, á la Napoleon, with his left hand stuck in the breast of his jacket; while in the background, wearing a plumed turban, his round-cheeked, white-toothed young servant holds the bridle of his master's horse and grins as he looks knowingly at its docked, high-lifted tail. Incidentally, the portrait was done by a Frenchman. ...

> The second painting is actually a family scene in which, resplendent in dress uniform and boots with spurs, General Washington sits crossed-legged beside a table upon which his hat and the hilt of his sword rest upon a large military map. The map covers most of the table but the General appears to be staring far into the future as, to the right of the table, his young grandson stands close by with a hand resting on a globe of the world which sits on a convenient stand. And as the boy looks on, his willowy young lady of a sister (who sits across the table) is holding a furled end of the map in her delicate fingers so that Mrs. Washington (who sits beside her, richly bedecked in a ribboned bonnet, lacy scarf, and silken dress) may trace what appears to have been the course of one of the General's battles. ... The General stares from the canvas as though contemplating the invisible viewers who would inherit it, and if so, he was right on target.

> Because across the table and in a corner behind the elegant ladies there hovers a shadow of the past – and that shadow is the point of all my bumbling attempt at description.

Because the embodiment of that "shadow" is none other than the man who had been the young boy who appears in the first painting. Presented in semi-profile, he stands erect and attentive with his left hand thrust into the bosom of his vest and his eyes properly averted. His name was William Lee.

(*TD*, 687–688)

These passages capture the startling detail with which Ellison recreates two visual images. Millsap clearly refers to an engraving, *George Washington holding the Declaration of Independence and the Treaty of Alliance with France* (see Figure C.1) by Noël Le Mire, and a painting, *The Washington Family* (see Figure C.2) by American portraitist Edward Savage. Both eighteenth-century works contribute to establishing George Washington's mythic character, and they draw on the relationship between white and black vision to do so.

Thus, these images unexpectedly return to Wheatley's frontispiece. As I discuss in Chapter 1, Moorhead's innovative portrayal of Wheatley begins the work of rescuing the African American poet from depending on white authority for her moral integrity. Her upturned eyes remind readers of her spiritual and creative independence as her gaze finds no pictured white subject to contemplate; instead, she seeks the heavens for moral and artistic inspiration, and only the words encircling the portrait reassert her enslavement. The portrait forcefully proclaims Wheatley's independent vision and vividly contrasts her with contemporary painted portrayals of African Americans. Ellison, however, takes a bolder step that reflects the grand strides made over the two hundred year period African American writers invest in the trope of the Picture Book. He elects not to create a scene in which his black character ponders a painting that removes or demotes a white subject. Instead, he spotlights two eighteenth-century portraits featuring the ultimate figure of U.S. authority and mythic morality. The pictures of George Washington and William Lee that Millsap recalls seem to display African American vision in the traditional terms intended to convey reverence for white inviolability.

But Millsap's musings illustrate Ellison's decision to evoke this established narrative only to upend it. Rather than remove white authority, Ellison trumpets Millsap's radical reinterpretation of Washington's presence, his redefinition of the president's relationship to his slave. Referring to the engraving, Millsap translates William Lee's smile into a puckish recognition of the irony pervading the scene. The engraving shows Washington, holding the Declaration of Independence and the Treaty of Alliance with France, in the field during the American Revolutionary War.

Figure C.1 Noël Le Mire, *Portrait of George Washington*, engraving (1780). National Portrait Gallery, Smithsonian Institution, Washington, DC. Photo credit: National Portrait Gallery, Smithsonian Institution / Art Resource, NY.

Figure C.2 Edward Savage, *The Washington Family* (1789–1796). Andrew W. Mellon Collection, National Gallery of Art, Washington, DC. (1940.1.2).

As the sole observer of Washington performing his commitment to liberty, Lee bears the responsibility of offering the first sign of approval for U.S. republican government. Millsap's emphasis on Lee's "white-toothed" grin and knowing gaze hints that he discerns the contradiction the presence of his black body parades: How can Washington magnanimously embody freedom pictured beside his African American slave?

Implicitly noting this paradox, Millsap reminds Hickman:

> Black William Lee was with George Washington for thirty-one years, during which time an undeclared independence of observation was, perhaps, his only self-defining area of freedom. But don't forget that although a slave he was still privy to many matters having to do with affairs of family, state, and politics. And if interested he might well have used his shadowy position as unsurveyed landscape for self-exploration (*TD*, 688–689).

Millsap converts William Lee from a powerless slave and symbolic contributor to the creation of mythic American character into a witness of U.S. potential who refuses to overlook the hypocrisies separating American ideals from their realization. He also defines Lee's uninhibited vision as "freedom" leading to deeper self-understanding. In contrast to the scholarly focus on Douglass's well-known contention that verbal literacy provided the path to freedom, Ellison argues that an unencumbered vision of American character epitomized one of the earliest realizations of emotional autonomy. The "freedom" Millsap discerns concentrates on "self-exploration," the ability to formulate an independent definition of black humanity and U.S. citizenship.

Turning to the family portrait, Millsap speculates that in addition to keeping Washington grounded and humble, William Lee "deepen[ed] the painting's historical perspective" even as he "foreshadows other 'shadows' to come." Unable to refrain from riffing, Millsap concludes,

> [I]f I know anything about our people, old Bill has his eyes and ears wide open to what's going down, and *nobody*, not even the surveyor, slave-master, general and father of our country, knew what the hell he was *thinking* – much less the influence for good or evil that he might have been having on the first family's grandchildren. And here you might recall that the father of our country fathered no children of his own. (*TD*, 688)

This passage captures the extreme nature of Ellison's signification on the trope of the Picture Book. Millsap not only insists on the slave's liberated vision and thoughts, but he also claims for William Lee agency and culpability, unusual intimacy together with a peculiar opportunity to betray the first U.S. president. Millsap appeals to the painting of the national family not so much to celebrate the importance of African American contributions to the early republic – in the vein, say, of Crispus Attucks who is honored as the first man to spill blood in the fight for independence – as to hint at black Americans' power to influence their masters and master's children in self-serving ways. At the same moment that he confers the status of a son on Lee, he imagines him capable of transgression. And Ellison seemed particularly invested in stressing the father-son relationship, adding the sentence that notes Washington "fathered no children of his own" after drafting many versions of the scene.[2]

Ellison's selection of these visual pieces to initiate an argument about black complicity in U.S. moral compromise is astounding. Millsap's interpretive musings suggest that African Americans have been shaping the most powerful white men in politics for more than 150 years. Ellison introduces the engraving and painting to declare a historically established role for black Americans. Such a legacy demands an acknowledgement of moral responsibility at a moment when many would argue that blacks lacked the political power for such an admission to be possible. Ellison begs to differ. And in doing so, he advances his contention that African Americans have consistently contributed to the formation of U.S. character as well as to its most revered institutions. If Lee fills the role that comes closest to that of a son to Washington, the slave cannot escape all accountability for the early republic. Then again, acknowledging Lee's influence from the inception of the country makes it impossible to discount the impact of his vision. For Ellison, forthrightly accepting African American culpability for part of the country's failings guarantees black access to full, unfettered, citizenship and inclusion in the national family. Hickman's acceptance of Millsap's interpretation of the images – as well as his willingness to relate them to Bliss – displays the preacher's capacity for the kind of contemplative sight long associated with intellectual complexity. As Anne Dvinge argues, with Hickman Ellison portrays the "searching and experimenting element of 'Americanism'" that insists "on a more complex vision, one that can hold past, present and future in one gaze."[3]

Ellison's rendering of African American vision endows it with significance without proclaiming it inviolable. As a final example in my study that began with an examination of the moralizing vision of slaves and ended with the uncertain modernist vision of pre-Black Arts writers, Ellison signals the real goal of the trope of the Picture Book. Pondering the peculiarity of black vision constitutes reassessing the truth of American character. Whereas many black artists of the 1960s and 1970s would use their art to charge the nation with crimes of racial injustice, Ellison committed his second novel to initiating an extended rumination on shared guilt. For Ellison, accepting responsibility for American democracy depends on recognizing human fallibility. Ellison insists that African Americans have not only always been present, but part of the problem *and* solution of American democracy. And it is the profundity of this admission that represents the possibility of attaining the ideal pluralistic democracy the founding fathers envisioned.

Just as Hickman need not emerge in unblemished terms, his sophisticated vision need not represent the kind of improbable virtue too often assigned to respected national figures. After all, such claims initially led to the manipulation and negation of black sight in the rush to proclaim the righteousness of white American vision. Ellison refuses to repeat the errors of this history. He moves from a protagonist who advocates invisibility, the most extreme rejection of a legacy committed to befouling black appearance, to heralding the power of a "Hickman," an untutored man honest enough and courageous enough to accept himself and his country, faults and all. What he refuses to accept is an attitude of resignation that declines the challenge to change the legacy of denying, ignoring, and misrepresenting the vision of black Americans. Hickman's expansive vision embraces the totality of the U.S. in terms Ellison advocates more Americans should accept.

By tracing African American writers' portrayals of vision in literary texts from the late eighteenth into the late twentieth century, I appreciate Ellison's accomplishment as a fitting result of the unremitting investment in vision that pervades the tradition of black literature. African American writers and poets do not restrict their visualizing practices to one method or practice; rather, they revel in the multiplicity of literary acts that confirm the primary role vision plays in inaugurating, shaping, and developing black creative writing. *Visualizing Blackness* reminds us that although the rich vitality of black verbal arts have long enlivened and influenced African American literature, many of the works celebrated for their attention to the black voice show an equal, if not deeper, commitment to portraying black vision and contesting derogatory depictions of blackness. This signals the importance of both acknowledging and continuing to study the legacy of the trope of the Picture Book.

Notes

INTRODUCTION: THE TROPE OF THE PICTURE BOOK

1 Thomas Wooldridge to Earl of Dartmouth, November 24, 1772, in *Critical Essays on Phillis Wheatley*, ed. William Henry Robinson (Boston: G.K. Hall, 1982), 20–21.
2 Irving Howe, *Irving Howe: Selected Writings, 1950–1990* (New York: Harcourt Brace Jovanovich, 1990), 120, 129.
3 Nicholas Mirzoeff, *The Right to Look: A Counterhistory of Visuality* (Durham: Duke University Press, 2011), 1. The introduction fleshes out the consequences of looking whereas chapter 1, "Oversight: The Ordering of Slavery," details the history of the plantation complex of visuality. I stop short of subscribing to Mirzoeff's term, "countervisuality," to describe African American writers' methods of dramatizing their vision. Although they challenge the visual history that denies their humanity, the writers I study often appeal to similar methods employed by their white counterparts.
4 Jennifer L. Morgan, "'Some Could Suckle over Their Shoulder': Male Travelers, Female Bodies, and the Gendering of Racial Ideology, 1500–1770," *The William and Mary Quarterly* 54: 1 (January 1997), 170.
5 Robert B. Stepto incisively describes the goals of authenticating documents in the first chapter of his foundational work, *From Behind the Veil: A Study of Afro-American Narrative*, 2nd ed. (Urbana: University of Illinois Press, 1991), 3–31.
6 Ralph Ellison, *The Collected Essays of Ralph Ellison*, ed. John Callahan (New York: Modern Library, 1995), 159; hereafter cited in text as *CE*.
7 Ibid., 170.
8 Nicholas Mirzoeff, *An Introduction to Visual Culture* (New York: Routledge, 1999), 4, 5.
9 W. J. T. Mitchell, *Picture Theory: Essays on Verbal and Visual Representation* (Chicago, IL: University of Chicago Press, 1994), 162.
10 W. J. T. Mitchell, "Showing Seeing: A Critique of Visual Culture," *Journal of Visual Culture* 1:2 (2002), 166 and Martin Jay, *Downcast Eyes: The Denigration of Vision in Twentieth-Century French Thought* (Berkeley: University of California Press, 1993), 9.

11 Michele Wallace, *Dark Designs and Visual Culture* (Durham, NC: Duke University Press, 2004), 366.

12 Kenneth Warren claims that black literature itself only exists in a pre-Jim Crow state (although Warren also excludes slave-era writings from a proper definition of African American literature). See the first chapter of *What Was African American Literature* (Cambridge, MA: Harvard University Press, 2011), 1–43.

13 Mary Lou Emery, *Modernism, the Visual, and Caribbean Literature* (Cambridge: Cambridge University Press, 2007), 7.

14 Charles T. Davis and Gates helpfully present Hume's startling statement connecting black skin, character, and intellect in his famous essay "Of National Character" (1748). See *The Slave's Narrative* (Oxford: Oxford University Press, 1985), xxv–xxvi.

15 Ivy Wilson, *Specters of Democracy: Blackness and the Aesthetics of Politics in the Antebellum U.S.* (New York: Oxford University Press, 2011), 8.

16 Leigh Raiford makes a similar point regarding African American "looking" practices. She explains that black spectatorship is "'fluid,' 'negotiated,' 'heterogeneous,' and 'polyphonic'" because "the act of viewing elicits an array of responses from diverse individuals, in varying contexts, who differently interpret and incorporate visual messages into their lives." See *Imprisoned in a Luminous Glare: Photography and the African American Freedom Struggle* (Chapel Hill: University of North Carolina Press, 2011), 49.

17 For a complete overview of this history, see chapter 1 of Martin Jay's *Downcast Eyes*, 21–82.

18 Ibid., 236.

19 bell hooks, *Black Looks: Race and Representation* (Boston, MA: South End Press, 1999), 1–8.

20 William L. Andrews and Henry Louis Gates Jr. (eds.), *Slave Narratives* (New York: Library of America, 2000), 11–12.

21 Ibid., 85–86.

22 Ibid., 95.

23 For instance, the articles in *New Essays on Phillis Wheatley*, eds. John C. Shields and Eric D. Lamore (Knoxville: University Press, 2011) offer an array of readings that reassess Wheatley's appeal to classicism and provide a richer historical context for her work. These pieces invigorate Wheatley criticism from multiple angles ranging from using new archival resources to applying queer theoretics.

24 Karin Roffman, *From the Modernist Annex: American Women Writers in Museums and Libraries* (Tuscaloosa: University of Alabama Press, 2010), 24.

25 Les Harrison, *The Temple and the Forum: American Museum and Cultural Authority in Hawthorne, Melville, Stowe, and Whitman* (Tuscaloosa: University of Alabama Press, 2007), 45.

26 Carla Yanni, *Nature's Museums: Victorian Science and the Architecture of Display* (London: Athlone Press, 1999), 19.

27 Ibid., 31.

28 See Les Harrison's Introduction for a helpful review of studies that examine the appeal of the museum in literature. *The Temple and the Forum*, xx–xxi.

29 Elizabeth Loizeaux, *Twentieth-Century Poetry and the Visual Arts* (Cambridge: Cambridge University Press, 2008), 12, 13. For a superb overview of ekphrasis and the many theorists who have contributed useful definitions, see her introduction, 1–28.

30 Francoise Meltzer, *Salome and the Dance of Writing: Portraits of Mimesis in Literature* (Chicago, IL: University of Chicago Press, 1987), 1.

WITNESSING MORAL AUTHORITY IN PRE-ABOLITION LITERATURE

1 Winthrop Jordan, *White Over Black: American Attitudes Toward the Negro, 1550–1812* (Chapel Hill: University of North Carolina Press, 1968), 4–5.

2 David Walker, 1830, "Walker's Appeal, in Four Articles; Together with a Preamble, to the Coloured Citizens of the World, but in Particular, and Very Expressly, to Those of the United States of America, Written in Boston, State of Massachusetts, September 28, 1829," Documenting the American South, University Library, The University of North Carolina at Chapel Hill, 2001, http://docsouth.unc.edu/nc/walker/walker.html.

3 Milton Cantor, "The Image of the Negro in Colonial Literature," *The New England Quarterly* 36:4 (December 1963), 459. Cantor quotes John Woolman's 1762 text, *Considerations on Keeping Negroes*.

4 Phillip M. Richards, "Phillis Wheatley: The Consensual Blackness of Early African American Writing," in *New Essays on Phillis Wheatley*, eds. John C. Shields and Eric D. Lamore (Knoxville: The University of Tennessee Press, 2011), 252.

5 For excellent analyses of Wheatley's sense of her audience and their conception of her, see Mary Balkun, "Phillis Wheatley's Construction of Otherness and the Rhetoric of Performed Ideology," *African American Review* (Spring 2002), 121–135 and Kirstin Wilcox's superb "The Body into Print: Marketing Phillis Wheatley," *American Literature* 71:1 (March 1999), 1–29.

6 John Shields considers Wheatley's investment in neoclassicism at length in *Phillis Wheatley's Poetics of Liberation: Backgrounds and Contexts* (Knoxville: University of Tennessee Press, 2008). Eric Slauter provides one of the most compelling discussions of this issue in "Neoclassical Culture in a Society with Slaves: Race and Rights in the Age of Wheatley," *Early American Studies* (Spring 2004), 81–122.

7 Eric Slauter, "Neoclassical Culture in a Society with Slaves," 106.

8 John Shields, *Phillis Wheatley and the Romantics* (Knoxville: University of Tennessee Press, 2010), 4. Also see Shields, *Phillis Wheatley's Poetics of Liberation*, 150.

9 Winthrop Jordan, *White Over Black*, 284.

10 Gwendolyn Du Bois Shaw, "'On Deathless Glories Fix Thine Ardent View': Scipio Moorhead, Phillis Wheatley, and the Mythic Origins of Anglo-African

Portraiture in New England," in *Portraits of a People: Picturing African Americans in the Nineteenth Century* (Andover, MA: Addison Gallery of American Art, 2006), 27.

11 David Grimstead, "Anglo-American Racism and Phillis Wheatley's 'Sable Veil,' 'Length'ned Chain,' and 'Knitted heart,'" in *Women in the Age of the American Revolution*, eds. Peter J. Albert and Ronald Hoffman (Charlottesville: University Press of Virginia, 1989), 396–397.

12 Betsy Erkkilä, "Phillis Wheatley and the Black American Revolution," in *A Mixed Race: Ethnicity in Early America*, ed. Frank Shuffelton (New York: Oxford University Press, 1993), 229.

13 Walter Nott, "From 'Uncultivated Barbarian' to 'Poetical Genius': The Public Presence of Phillis Wheatley," MELUS, *Poetry and Poetics* 18:3 (Autumn 1993), 25.

14 Astrid Franke, "Phillis Wheatley, Melancholy Muse," *The New England Quarterly* 77:2 (June 2004), 225, 227.

15 Mary Balkun, "'To 'pursue th' unbodied mind': Phillis Wheatley and the Raced Body in Early America," in *New Essays on Phillis Wheatley*, 387–388.

16 Robert Kendrick, "Other Questions: Phillis Wheatley and the Ethics of Interpretation" *Cultural Critique* 38 (Winter 1997–1998), 47.

17 Studies that provide particularly helpful reviews of portrayals of African Americans in high art of the period include Guy McElroy, *Facing History: The Black Image in American Art 1710–1940* (San Francisco: Bedford Arts, 1990); Albert Boime, *The Art of Exclusion: Representing Blacks in the Nineteenth Century* (Washington, DC: Smithsonian Press, 1990); and, Elizabeth Johns, *American Genre Painting: the Politics of Everyday Life* (New Haven, CT: Yale University Press, 1991).

18 Gwendolyn Shaw provides one of the few extended close readings of Wheatley's portrait, and she places it within a legacy of visual portrayals of African women such as *The Voyage of the Sable Venus* (1794), *Joanna* (1796), and *Flagellation of a Female Slave* (1796). See "'On Deathless Glories Fix Thine Ardent View,'" 31–32.

19 For a comprehensive study of blacks in Western art, see the magisterial, three-volume set by David Bindman, Henry Louis Gates, Jr., and Karen C. C. Dalton (eds.), *The Image of the Black in Western Art* (Cambridge, MA: Belknap Press, 2010).

20 Boime argues that the black man is cast in a servant role as he holds the rope and waits for the other men to tell him what to do. He concludes that "at best," the black man "registers a sense of compassion for the hapless Watson." See *The Art of Exclusion*, 22.

21 Barbara Lacey, "Visual Images of Blacks in Early American Imprints," *The William and Mary Quarterly* 53:1 (January, 1996), 137.

22 Ibid., 144.

23 For a more expansive account of representations of slavery in the U.S., see Marcus Wood, *Blind Memory: Visual Representations of Slavery in England and America, 1780–1865* (New York: Routledge, 2000). Chapters 1 and 2 discuss

the iconography of the middle passage and the runaway, subjects especially relevant to my discussion.

24 See E. Jennifer Monaghan, "Literacy Instruction and Gender in Colonial New England," ed. Cathy Davidson, *Reading in America* (Baltimore: John Hopkins University Press, 1989), 53–80.

25 See Caroline Winterer, "The Female World of Classical Reading in Eighteenth-Century America" in *Reading Women: Literacy, Authorship, and Culture in the Atlantic World, 1500–1800* (Philadelphia: University of Pennsylvania Press, 2008), 109.

26 Vincent Carretta, *Phillis Wheatley: Biography of a Genius in Bondage* (Athens: University of Georgia Press, 2011), 38.

27 John Shields, "Phillis Wheatley's Subversive Pastoral," *American Society for Eighteenth-Century Studies* 27:4 (Summer 1994), 634.

28 Phillis Wheatley, *Complete Writings, Writings*, ed. Vincent Carretta (New York: Penguin Books, 2001), 9; hereafter cited parenthetically as *CW*.

29 Jennifer Billingsley, "Works of Wonder, Wondering Eyes, and the Wondrous Poet: The Use of Wonder in Phillis Wheatley's Marvelous Poetics," in *New Essays on Phillis Wheatley*, 170.

30 See Shields's discussion of Wheatley's use of "snatch." He explains that to "seize the laurel was, to ancient classical poets, to achieve success as a mature poet" and Wheatley "intends this ritual to be fully successful." *Phillis Wheatley's Poetics of Liberation*, 177.

31 Betsy Erkkilä similarly argues that Wheatley's use of Ethiop "suggests a figure of racial pride who speaks to the privileged white race from a position of moral authority," thereby undermining the common "social equation of black and African with sin and evil." See "Phillis Wheatley and the Black American Revolution," 232.

32 For a discussion of the first appearance of this poem, see Henry Foote, "Mr. Smibert Shows His Pictures, March, 1730" *New England Quarterly* 8:1/4 (1935), 14–28.

33 Ibid., 18.

34 Ibid., 20.

35 Ibid., 19.

36 Ibid., 20.

37 Mather Byles, *Works*, ed. Benjamin Franklin V (New York: Scholars' Facsimiles & Reprints, 1978), 90.

38 Ivy Wilson, "The Writing on the Wall: Revolutionary Aesthetics and Interior Spaces," in *American Literature's Aesthetic Dimensions*, eds. Cindy Weinstein and Christopher Looby (New York: Columbia University Press, 2012), 60.

39 Henry Foote, "Mr. Smibert Shows His Pictures, March 1730," 21.

40 Ivy Wilson, *Specters of Democracy,: Blackness and the Aesthetics of Politics in the Antebellum U.S.* (New York: Oxford University Press, 2011), 25.

41 Ibid., 108.

42 Karen Adams, "The Black Image in the Paintings of William Sidney Mount" *American Art Journal* 7:2 (November, 1975), 44. Adams examines

Mount's portrayal of African Americans as a means of discovering how antebellum Americans defined themselves as citizens in a rapidly changing nation.

43 As discussed in detail in Chapters 4 and 5, public galleries and museums did not proliferate in the U.S. until the late nineteenth century.

44 Marcus Wood, *Blind Memory*, 89.

45 For an expansive discussion of the impact of minstrelsy on ideas of blackness, see Eric Lott, *Love and Theft: Blackface Minstrelsy and the American Working Class* (New York: Oxford University Press, 1993), particularly chapter five, "'The Seeming Counterfeit': Early Blackface Acts, the Body, and Social Contradiction," 111–135.

46 Frances Smith Foster, *The Development of Ante-Bellum Slave Narratives*, 2nd ed. (Madison: University of Wisconsin Press, 1994), 41.

47 This description of the daguerreotype process is from Gordon Baldwin's *Looking at Photographs: A Guide to Technical Terms* (Malibu: J. Paul Getty Museum, 1991), 35.

48 Alan Tractenberg offers a compelling reading of Hawthorne's novel that makes rich use of the material composition of the daguerreotype. I am indebted to his reading for the similar approach I take in my assessment of the ex-slave's interest in these visual images. See "Seeing and Believing: Hawthorne's Reflections on the Daguerreotype in *The House of the Seven Gables*," *American Literary History* 9:3 (Autumn 1997), 475–479.

49 Alan Tractenberg, "Photography: The Emergence of a Keyword" in *Photography in Nineteenth Century America 1839–1900*, eds. Martha Sandweiss and Alan Tractenberg (Fort Worth: Amon Carter Museum, 1991), 26.

50 Frederick Douglass, "Pictures and Progress: An Address Delivered in Boston, Massachusetts, On 3 December 1861" in *The Frederick Douglass Papers 3:1865–63*, ed. John Blassingame (New Haven: Yale University Press, 1985), 454. Colin L. Westerbeck explains: "The daguerreotype was highly regarded in its own day as a kind of democratization of art, for it permitted those who had neither the time nor the money for painted portraits to obtain a likeness nonetheless." See "Frederick Douglass Chooses His Moment," *African Americans in Art: Selections from The Art Institute of Chicago* (Seattle: University of Washington Press, 1999), 18.

51 Alan Tractenberg, "Photography: The Emergence of a Keyword," 17.

52 Deborah Willis, *Reflections in Black: A History of Black Photographers, 1840 to the Present* (New York: Norton, 2000), 3.

53 Ball published a pamphlet that recorded every step of the slave experience and paired it with his 600-yard panorama of paintings and photographs illustrating the horrors of slavery described in the pamphlet. Washington operated a successful daguerrean portrait studio in Hartford and counted many white abolitionists as his patrons. See Willis, *Reflections in Black*, 7, 10.

54 Julia Sun-Joo Lee provides a compelling discussion of the frontispieces in *The American Slave Narrative and the Victorian Novel* (Oxford: Oxford University Press, 2010), 3–8.

55 John Stauffer, "Creating an Image in Black: The Power of Abolition Pictures" in Timothy McCarthy and John Stauffer (eds.), *Prophets of Protest: Reconsidering the History of American Abolitionism* (New York: New Press, 2006), 258, 260.

56 Ibid., 260, 262.

57 Frederick Douglass, *Narrative of the Life of Frederick Douglass, an American Slave Written by Himself*, 2nd ed., ed. David Blight (Boston: Bedford St. Martin's, 2003), 44–45.

58 Ibid., 46.

59 See Saidiya Hartman, *Scenes of Subjection: Terror, Slavery, and Scenes of Self-Making in Nineteenth Century America* (Oxford: Oxford University Press, 1997), 3 and Fred Moten, *In the Break: The Aesthetics of the Black Radical Tradition* (Minneapolis: University of Minnesota Press, 2003), 21, 1.

60 Lisa Yun Lee similarly interprets this scene as an example of Douglass proving that it "is by the acts of seeing that the truths of the slavery system are revealed." But Lee uses this claim to emphasize Douglass as a "powerless watcher" who only gains power through verbal acts. See "The Politics of Language in Frederick Douglass's Narrative of the Life of an American Slave," *MELUS* 17:2 (Summer 1991 – Summer 1992), 52, 53.

61 Dwight McBride analyzes Douglass's attention to the "discursive reader" of his text to consider the implications of witnessing in his *Narrative*. See chapter 6 in *Impossible Witness: Truth, Abolitionism, and Slave Testimony* (New York: New York University Press, 2001), 151–172.

62 Granville Ganter also focuses on the rhetoric of education. He suggests that Douglass hints at his white masters' lack of education by showing Auld and Captain Anthony substituting the word "learn" for "educate." See "'He Made Us Laugh Some': Frederick Douglass's Humor," *African American Review* 37:4 (Winter 2003), 544.

63 For incisive examples of such readings, see John Carlos Rowe, *At Emerson's Tomb: The Politics of Classic American Literature* (New York: Columbia University Press, 1997), 115; Paul Giles, "Narrative Reversals and Power Exchanges: Frederick Douglass and British Culture," *American Literature* 73:4 (December 2001), 785; and, David Van Leer, "Reading Slavery: The Anxiety of Ethnicity in Douglass's Narrative," in *Frederick Douglass: New Literary and Historical Essays*, ed. Eric Sundquist, 132. Deborah McDowell adds to this claim and emphasizes Douglass's broader depiction of the slave woman in "In the First Place: Frederick Douglass and the Afro-American Narrative Tradition," in *African American Autobiography: A Collection of Critical Essays*, ed. William L. Andrews (Englewood Cliffs: Prentice Hall, 1993), 50–51. Other critics extend this discussion by turning their attention to Douglass's return to this scene in *My Bondage and My Freedom*. For an example, see Carl Ostrowski's "Slavery, Labor Reform, and Intertextuality in Antebellum Print Culture: The Slave Narrative and the City-Mysteries Novel," *African American Review* 40:3 (Fall 2006), 502.

64 A good deal of criticism considers this, too. See Wilson J. Moses, "Dark Forests and Barbarian Vigo: Paradox, Conflict, and Africanity in Black Writing before 1914," *American Literary History* 1:3 (Autumn 1989), 639. For a more extensive consideration of this issue, see Hortense Spillers's "Mama's Baby, Papa's Maybe: An American Grammar Book," *Diacritics* 17:2 (Summer 1987), 75–76.

65 Ibid.

66 See Kathleen Collins, "The Scourged Back," *History of Photography* 9:1 (January– March 1985), 43–45.

67 Douglass, *Narrative*, 46.

68 Ibid., 103.

69 Ibid., 104. Also see Jeannine DeLombard's discussion of this scene. She impressively connects Douglass to Emerson arguing that his "burst eyeball ... represents the incompatibility of the ... universal subjectivity figured by Emerson's transparent eyeball." "'Eye-Witness to the Cruelty': Southern Violence and Northern Testimony in Frederick Douglass's 1845 Narrative," *American Literature* 73:2 (June 2001), 245.

70 Ibid, 117.

71 Sarah Blackwood and Michael Chaney capitalize on Jonathan Crary's work on the camera obscura to argue respectively that Jacobs appeals to this pre-photographic technology to redefine the agency of the gaze and readjust the reader's relation to the black body. See Blackwood's "Fugitive Obscura: Runaway Slave Portraiture and Early Photographic Technology," *American Literature* 81:1 (March 2009), 93–125 and Chaney's *Fugitive Vision: Slave Image and Black Identity in Antebellum Narrative* (Bloomington: Indiana University Press, 2008), 148–175. Ann Gelder claims that Jacobs reconfigures the pregnant slave body as an architectural space that allows her to broach subjects deemed unsuitable for polite conversation even as Brent challenges the very foundation of the cult of domesticity. See "Reforming the Body: 'Experience' and the Architecture of Imagination in Harriet Jacobs's *Incidents in the Life of a Slave Girl*," in *Inventing Maternity: Politics, Science, and Literature, 1660–1865*, eds. Susan Greenfield and Carol Barash (Lexington: University Press of Kentucky, 1999), 252–266. Similarly, Martha Cutter's reading reorients the focus on Jacobs's recreation of a language built on different principles. See "Dismantling 'The Master's House': Critical Literacy in Harriet Jacobs' *Incidents in the Life of a Slave Girl, Callaloo* 19:1 (Winter 1996), 209–225.

72 Harriet Jacobs, *Incidents in the Life of a Slave Girl* (USA: Seven Treasures Publications, 2009), 41.

73 Ibid., 40

74 Ibid., 30.

75 Ibid., 50.

76 Ibid., 75.

77 Ibid., 52.

78 Ibid., 115.

PICTURING EDUCATION AND LABOR IN WASHINGTON AND DU BOIS

1 W. E. B. Du Bois, "The Talented Tenth," in Booker T. Washington (ed.) *The Negro Problem: A Series of Articles by Representative Negroes of Today* (New York: James Pott & Company, 1903), 33.

2 Michael Bieze, *Booker T. Washington and the Art of Self-Representation* (New York: Peter Lang, 2008), 105.

3 For helpful discussions considering their oppositional philosophies, see chapter 6 in Kevern Verney, *The Art of the Possible: Booker T. Washington and black leadership in the United States, 1881–1925* (New York: Routledge, 2001), 79–93 and Jacqueline Moore, *Booker T. Washington, W. E. B. Du Bois, and the Struggle for Racial Uplift* (Lanham, MD: Scholarly Resources, 2003).

4 Leigh Raiford, *Imprisoned in a Luminous Glare: Photography and the African American Freedom Struggle* (Chapel Hill: University of North Carolina Press, 2011), 46. Raiford's larger argument on lynching photography pays special attention to the importance of "reframing" these horrific images for "black viewers" (34). Jacqueline Goldsby's meticulous consideration of lynching in both literature and photography further fleshes out the historical landscape that Washington and Du Bois inhabit. See *A Spectacular Secret: Lynching in American Life and Literature* (Chicago: University Press of Chicago, 2006).

5 See Deborah Willis's essay, "The Sociologist's Eye: W. E. B. Du Bois and the Paris Exposition," in *A Small Nation of People: W. E. B. Du Bois and African American Portraits of Progress*, The Library of Congress (New York: HarperCollins, 2003), 51–78 and Shawn Michelle Smith's *Photography on the Color Line: W. E. B. Du Bois, Race, and Visual Culture* (Durham: Duke University Press, 2004).

6 W. E. B. Du Bois, *The Souls of Black Folk*, eds. Henry Louis Gates and Terri Hume Oliver (New York: W. W. Norton, 1999), 5, 11; hereafter cited parenthetically as *SBF*.

7 Francille Rusan Wilson, *The Segregated Scholars: Black Social Scientist and the Creation of Black Labor Studies, 1890–1950* (Charlottesville: University of Virginia Press, 2006), 30.

8 For a rich discussion of Du Bois's relationship to the South, see chapter 3 in Harilaos Stecopoulos, *Reconstructing the World: Southern Fictions and U.S. Imperialisms, 1898–1976* (Ithaca, Cornell University Press, 2008), 77–100.

9 Francille Rusan Wilson, *The Segregated Scholars*, 31.

10 Kathleen Foster, *Thomas Eakins Rediscovered: Charles Bregler's Thomas Eakins Collection at the Pennsylvania Academy of the Fine Arts* (Philadelphia: Pennsylvania Academy of Fine Arts, 1997), 94.

11 Jan Nederveen Pieterse, *White on Black: Images of Africa and Blacks in Western Popular Culture* (New Haven: Yale University Press, 1992), 155.

12 Rob Boyte, "National Geographic: Primitivism in Body Acceptance" *Nude & Natural* 11.4 (1992), 23–24. Also see chapters 1 and 2 in Catherine Lutz and Jane Collins, *Reading National Geographic* (Chicago, IL: University

of Chicago Press, 1993), 1–46. Lutz and Collins explore how photography defines U.S. national identity by portraying a backward world.

13 Michael D. Harris, *Colored Pictures: Race and Visual Representation* (Chapel Hill: University of North Carolina Press, 2003), 68.

14 Ibid., 74–76. Also see Smith's discussion of the Dahomeyan village in *Photography on the Color Line*, 15–18.

15 Michael Harris, *Colored Pictures*, 75.

16 For expansive discussions of these photographers and their relationships to Du Bois and Washington respectively, see Deborah Willis, "The Sociologist's Eye," in *A Small Nation*, 58–64; Willis, *Reflections in Black: A History of Black Photographers, 1840 to the Present* (New York: Norton, 2000), 35–40; and chapter 3 in Bieze, *Booker T. Washington and the Art of Self-Representation*, 53–82.

17 Shawn Smith, *Photography on the Color Line*, 2.

18 See the Daniel Murray Collection, Library of Congress, Washington, DC. The collection can be viewed online at http://www.loc.gov/pictures/collection/anedub/.

19 Allan Sekula, "The Body and the Archive," *October* 39 (Winter 1986), 6.

20 Ibid., 10.

21 Sheila Lloyd argues that "Du Bois constructs a textual environment from the diverse tropes of the picturesque" in an effort to "supplement conventional formulations from sociology and political economy with aesthetics." See "Du Bois and the Production of the Racial Picturesque," *Public Culture* 17:2 (Duke University Press, 2005), 278.

22 Yogita Goyal, *Romance, Diaspora, and Black Atlantic Literature* (Cambridge: Cambridge University Press, 2010), 20–21.

23 George Fredrickson addresses the danger of Du Bois's "romantic racialist view of the Negro," noting that it was "a racial philosophy that could easily be transmuted into an overt doctrine of Negro inferiority, distinguished from harsher forms of racism only by a certain flavor of humanitarian paternalism." See *The Black Image in the White Mind: The Debate on Afro-American Character and Destiny, 1817–1914* (New York: Harper and Row, 1971), 125.

24 For an interesting discussion of Washington's work to populate the South with schools, see Stephanie Deutsch's *You Need a Schoolhouse: Booker T. Washington, Julius Rosenwald, and the Building of Schools for the Segregated South* (Evanston: Northwestern University Press, 2011).

25 Booker T. Washington, *Up from Slavery* (Oxford: Oxford University Press, 1995), 43; hereafter cited parenthetically as *US*.

26 Melissa Dabakis, *Visualizing Labor in American Sculpture: Monuments, Manliness, and the Work Ethic, 1880–1935* (Cambridge: Cambridge University Press, 1999), 22.

27 Wilson Moses notes that Du Bois was largely responsible for the now "common interpretation of Washington that isolates him from the realm of intellectualism" even though he likely recognized the sophistication of Washington's

ideas that anticipate "Max Weber's The Protestant Ethic and the Spirit of Capitalism." See *Creative Conflict in African American Thought: Frederick Douglass, Alexander Crummell, Booker T. Washington, W. E. B. Du Bois, and Marcus Garvey* (Cambridge: Cambridge University Press, 2004), 156.

28 See chapters 6, 7, and 8 in George Fredrickson's *The Black Image in the White Mind.*

29 Ibid, 276.

30 Eric Arnesen, "The Quicksands of Economic Insecurity: African Americans, Strikebreaking, and Labor Activism in the Industrial Era," in *The Black Worker: Race, Labor, and Civil Rights since Emancipation*, ed. Eric Arnesen (Urbana: University of Illinois, 2007), 43.

31 Ibid.

32 Frank Luther Mott, *American Journalism: A History: 1690–1960* (New York: Macmillan, 1962), 539. Mott also explains that pictures became more dominant through the advent of the color Sunday supplement with the first true comic strips and independent sports sections emerging at the turn of the century. See 585–588.

33 Frank Luther Mott, *A History of American Magazines, 1885–1905* (Cambridge, MA: Harvard University Press, 1957), 12.

34 Ibid, 13.

35 Michael Bieze, *Booker T. Washington and the Art of Self-Representation*, 55.

36 James Guimond, *American Photography and the American Dream* (Chapel Hill: University of North Carolina Press, 1991), 26.

37 Jan Nederveen Pieterse, *White on Black*, 154, 166, 168.

38 Barbara Bader, "Sambo, Babaji, and Sam," *The Horn Book Magazine* 72:5 (September–October 1996), 536.

39 Melissa Dabakis notes the absence of visual art depicting factories compared to the numerous images celebrating "industrial behemoths, like the steamboat and locomotive." She points to William Morris's 1884 essays as a corrective seeking to infuse an Arts and Crafts aesthetic into the architecture of factories. Washington sees the glory in Hampton without such influence. See *Visualizing Labor in American Sculpture*, 1, 15.

40 Michael Bieze, *Booker T. Washington and the Art of Self-Representation*, 41.

41 See chapter 3 in Michael Bieze, *Booker T. Washington and the Art of Self-Representation*, 53–82.

42 Michael Bieze, *Booker T. Washington and the Art of Self-Representation*, 68.

43 Ibid., 50.

44 Bettina Berch, *The Woman behind the Lens: The Life and Work of Frances Benjamin Johnston, 1864–1952* (Charlottesville: University Press of Virginia, 2000), 47.

45 Michael Bieze, *Booker T. Washington and the Art of Self-Representation*, 102.

46 Verney, *The Art of the Possible*, 81.

47 James Guimond, *American Photography and the American Dream*, 23, 29, 45.

48 Booker T. Washington, *Working with the Hands* (New York: Doubleday: Page & Company, 1904), 101.

49 Booker T. Washington, "Negro Homes," *Colored American Magazine* 5:5 (September 1902), 378.

50 W. W. Holland, "Photography for our Young People," *Colored American Magazine* 5:1 (May 1902), 6, 5.

51 In his appreciation of European art, Washington shares some similarities with Du Bois. Notwithstanding Du Bois's support for black artists, scholars like Arnold Rampersad and Bernard Bell maintain that he never became fully invested in African American art. See Arnold Rampersad, *The Art and Imagination of W. E. B Du Bois* (Cambridge, MA.: Harvard University Press, 1976), 74; and Bernard Bell, "W. E. B. Du Bois's Struggle to Reconcile Folk and High Art," in *Critical Essays on W. E. B. Du Bois*, ed. William Andrews (Boston: G. K. Hall, 1985), 106–122.

52 Du Bois's "The Art and Art Galleries of Modern Europe," a paper that he shared with his Wilberforce students, suggests that he most admired the masterpieces of Europe. David Levering Lewis, *W. E. B. Du Bois: Biography of a Race, 1868–1919* (New York: Henry Holt, 1993), 178. Even when he describes "Beauty" in his well-known essay "Criteria of Negro Art," he mentions only one traditional piece of art, and it is "the broken curves of the Venus de Milo." Interestingly, a miniature of the Venus de Milo is one of the pieces Johnston photographs in a Tuskegee office. See Du Bois, "Criteria of Negro Art" in *W. E. B. Du Bois: A Reader*, ed. David Levering Lewis (New York: Henry Holt, 1995), 510; and http://www.loc.gov/pictures/item/99471631/.

53 Michael Bieze, *Booker T. Washington and the Art of Self-Representation*, 100.

54 Katharine Martinez, "At Home with Mona Lisa: Consumers and Commercial Visual Culture, 1880–1920" in *Seeing High & Low: Representing Social Conflict in American Visual Culture*, ed. Patricia Johnston (Berkeley: University of California Press, 2006), 162–163.

55 Ibid., 166.

56 Kendrick Ian Grandison, "Landscapes of Terror: A Reading of Tuskegee's Historic Campus" in *The Geography of Identity*, ed. Patricia Yaeger (Ann Arbor: University of Michigan Press, 1996), 334–367.

57 Kendrick Ian Grandison, "Negotiated Space: The Black College Campus as a Cultural Record of Postbellum America," *American Quarterly* 51:3 (September 1999), 534, 535.

58 Ibid., 553.

GAZING UPON PLASTIC ART IN THE HARLEM RENAISSANCE

1 Quoted in Thadious Davis, *Nella Larsen: Novelist of the Harlem Renaissance* (Baton Rouge: Louisiana State University Press, 1994), 456.

2 W. E. B. Du Bois, "Criteria of Negro Art" in *W. E. B. Du Bois: A Reader*, ed. David Levering Lewis (New York: Holt Paperbacks, 1995), 509.

3 Alain Locke, "The Legacy of the Ancestral Arts," in *The New Negro*, ed. Alaine Locke (New York: Touchstone, 1997), 261.

4 For a helpful discussion of Locke's investment in modernism and poetry, see the conclusion of Sieglinde Lemke, *Primitivist Modernism: Black Culture and the Origins of Transatlantic Modernism* (Oxford: Oxford University Press, 1998), 147.

5 Jean Hagstrum, *The Sister Arts: The Tradition of Literary Pictorialism and English Poetry from Dryden to Gray* (Chicago: University of Chicago Press, 1958), 18.

6 Elizabeth Loizeaux, *Twentieth-Century Poetry and the Visual Arts*, 1.

7 Ibid, 5.

8 Murray Krieger, "The Ekphrastic Principle and the Still Movement of Poetry; or *Laokoön* Revisited" in Frank Lentricchia and Andrew Du Bois (eds.) *Close Reading: The Reader* (Durham: Duke University Press, 2003), 90.

9 Francoise Meltzer, *Salome and the Dance of Writing: Portraits of Mimesis in Literature* (Chicago, IL: University of Chicago Press, 1987), 11.

10 John Hollander, *The Gazer's Spirit: Poems Speaking to Silent Works of Art* (Chicago: University of Chicago Press, 1995), 4.

11 Bennett's time in Paris gave her new insight on the state of American artists. She became friendly with expatriate writers like Ernest Hemingway, whom she describes in a January 1926 letter as "a charming fellow – big and blustery with an out-doors quality about him coupled with a boyishness that makes him just right." Writing to Jackman in February, she reflects on the difference between U.S. and European visual artists and concludes: "Our American modernists are about a thousand years behind the Europeans." James Weldon Johnson Papers, Box A-Buc, Folder Bennett, Beinecke Library, Yale University.

12 Charita Ford, "Flowering a Feminist Garden: The Writings and Poetry of Anne Spencer," *SAGE* 5.1 (1988), 9.

13 J. Lee Greene records that the Spencer's hosted a variety of guests including "Paul Robeson, Roland Hayes, Walther White, Charles S. Johnson, George Washington Carver, Adam Clayton Powell, W. E. B. Du Bois, Langston Hughes, and Georgia Douglas Johnson." See *Time's Unfading Garden: Anne Spencer's Life and Poetry* (Baton Rouge: Louisiana State University Press, 1977), 68.

14 Anne Spencer to James Weldon Johnson, undated, Box 19, Folder 449. James Weldon Johnson Collection in the Yale Collection of American Literature, Beinecke Rare Book and Manuscript Library.

15 Ibid., November 17. Spencer refers to Carter Glass, a U.S. senator from Lynchburg who helped implement poll tests and other measures to disenfranchise African Americans; Theodore Lothrop Stoddard, a racial anthropologist, eugenicist, and political theorist; William Pickens, an outspoken linguist, writer, and official of the National Association for the Advancement of Colored People; and, Kelly Miller, the famous mathematician and dean at Howard University.

16 Evie Shockley expansively argues for addressing the radical race consciousness permeating Anne Spencer's poetry. See chapter 4, "Protest/Poetry: Anne Spencer's Garden of 'Raceless' Verse," in *Renegade Poetics: Black Aesthetics and*

Formal Innovation in African American Poetry (Iowa City: University of Iowa Press, 2011), 121–144.

17 Maureen Honey, *Shadowed Dreams: Women's Poetry of the Harlem Renaissance*, 2nd ed. (New Brunswick: Rutgers University Press, 2006), 261–262.

18 Greene, *Time's Unfading Garden*, 137.

19 See Adam Duvernay, "Statue of black man has history of controversy" in *The Daily Reveille*, October 6, 2009 and Ruth Laney, "The Journey of 'Uncle Jack,'" in *Country Roads: Adventures Close to Home*, November 2009.

20 Maya Angelou, *Even the Stars Look Lonesome* (New York: Random House, 1997), 92.

21 Ibid., 93.

22 Ibid., 94, 95.

23 See Greene's discussion in *Time's Unfading Garden*, 135. Spencer's granddaughter notes that Niagara, Concord, and Caco grapevines continue to grow in the garden Spencer planted. Spencer's historic home also continues to display "a large round tray in [her] dining room that is made of copper and fabric cut-outs of grapes." Shaun Spencer-Heston, e-mail message to author, February 19, 2013.

24 Maureen Honey, *Shadowed Dreams*, 265–266.

25 Anne Spencer to James Weldon Johnson, undated, Box 19, Folder 449.

26 Norman Bryson, *Looking at the Overlooked: Four Essays on Still Life Painting* (Cambridge: Harvard University Press, 1990), 177.

27 Kirsten Swinth, *Painting Professionals: Women Artists & the Development of Modern American Art, 1870–1930* (Chapel Hill: University of North Carolina Press, 2001), 73.

28 Maureen Honey, *Shadowed Dreams*, 130.

29 Du Bois, *W. E. B. Du Bois: A Reader*, 292–293.

30 Gloria Hull, *Color, Sex, & Poetry: Three Women Writers of the Harlem Renaissance* (Bloomington: Indiana University Press, 1987), 139.

31 Maureen Honey, *Shadowed Dreams*, 8.

32 Ibid. Honey explains this in her note to the poem.

33 The colors Bennett recalls echo the colors Larsen's protagonist, Helga Crane, wears that attract the suspicion of the proper matrons of Naxos. Helga loves dressing in the "dark purples, royal blues, rich greens, deep reds" that recall the "dim purples and fine reds / And blues" that inspire Bennett's verse (*Quicksand*, 21).

34 Maureen Honey, *Shadowed Dreams*, 10–11. In Bennett's original manuscript of the poem, the two stanzas are not presented as one poem. She seems to initially have planned a series of quatrains and cinquains. See Gwendolyn Bennett Papers, Box 2, Folder 5, Schomburg Center for Research in Black Culture, New York Public Library.

35 Anne Stavney, "'Mothers of Tomorrow': The New Negro Renaissance and the Politics of Maternal Representation," *African American Review* 32:4 (Winter 1998), 541.

36 Lisa Collins notes that scholars have discovered "only one full nude of an African American woman from the nineteenth century, and it was created by a visiting Swiss artist." See *The Art of History: African American Women Artists Engage the Past* (New Brunswick: Rutgers University Press, 2002), 38.

37 Ibid., 41, 42.

38 James Weldon Johnson Papers, Box A-Buc, Folder Bennett, Beinecke Library, Yale University.

39 Caroline Goeser reads Bennett's Adoration of the Kings as a radical racial statement of Mary's "bestowal of favor on [the] African youth, connecting the infant Christ in her arms symbolically with the African continent." See *Picturing the New Negro: Harlem Renaissance Print Culture and Modern Black Identity* (Lawrence: University Press of Kansas, 2007), 213.

40 James Weldon Johnson Papers, Box A-Buc, Folder Bennett, Beinecke Library, Yale University.

41 Elise McDougald, "The Task of Negro Womanhood," *The New Negro*, 379.

42 Ibid., 372.

43 See Thomas Otten's *A Superficial Reading of Henry James: Preoccupations with the Material World* (Columbus: The Ohio State University Press, 2006), 65.

44 Ibid, 63.

45 YCAL 76, Box 111, Folder 2278, Beinecke Library, Yale University. Thadious Davis refers to this letter in *Nella Larsen*, 251.

46 Pamela Barnett's comprehensive and compelling argument links Larsen's investment in Helga as an art object to a broader attempt to combat the Women's Club Movement. Barnett reads the opening pages as determining a "lack of agency" that "is essential for Larsen's depiction of visual and sexual objectification." See "'My Picture of You Is, after All, the True Helga Crane': Portraiture and Identity in Nella Larsen's *Quicksand*," *Signs* 20:3 (Spring 1995), 583. Cherene Sherrard-Johnson's chapter 1 thoughtfully connects Helga to Motley's paintings in *Portraits of the New Negro Woman: Visual and Literary Culture in the Harlem Renaissance* (New Brunswick: Rutgers University Press, 2007), 21–48. Ann Hostetler also provides a persuasive reading of the opening pages in "The Aesthetics of Race and Gender in Nella Larsen's *Quicksand*," *PMLA* 105:1 (January 1990), 35–46.

47 Nella Larsen, *Quicksand* (New York: Penguin, 2002), 7, 10, 9; hereafter cited parenthetically as *Q*.

48 Maude Owens, "Bathesda of Sinners Run," in *The Sleeper Wakes: Harlem Renaissance Stories by Women*, ed. Marcy Knopf (New Brunswick: Rutgers University Press, 1993), 148; hereafter cited parenthetically as *BSR*.

49 Jessie Fauset, *Plum Bun: A Novel without a Moral* (Boston, MA: Beacon Press, 1990), 66; hereafter cited parenthetically as *PB*.

50 Carolyn Sylvander, *Jessie Redmon Fauset, Black American Writer* (Albany: Whitston, 1981), 34.

51 Cherene Sherrard-Johnson makes a similar argument in her brilliant chapter on *Plum Bun*. See *Portraits of the New Negro Woman*, 49–76.

52 The painting is part of Angela's "14th Street Types" notebook which Deborah Barker claims represents Fauset's decision to connect Angela to the Fourteenth Street School of painting. See "Authenticating the African-American Female Artist: Frances Harper's *Iola Leroy* and Jessie Fauset's *Plum Bun*" in Barker's *Aesthetics and Gender in American Literature: Portraits of the Woman Artist* (London: Bucknell University Press, 2000), 162–197.

53 Kirsten Swinth, *Painting Professionals*, 73.

54 See Margaret Stetz's helpful discussion of *Plum Bun* in "Jessie Fauset's Fiction: Reconsidering Race and Revising Aestheticism," *Literature and Racial Ambiguity*, eds. Teresa Hubel, Neil Edward Brooks (Amsterdam: Rodopi, 2002), 260.

ZORA NEALE HURSTON: SEEING BY THE RULES OF THE NATURAL HISTORY MUSEUM

1 Zora Neale Hurston, *Zora Neale Hurston: Folklore, Memoirs, and Other Writings* (New York: Literary Classics, 1995), 826.

2 Ibid., 950, 951; hereafter cited parenthetically as *FM*.

3 Zora Neale Hurston, *Zora Neale Hurston: Novels & Stories* (New York: Literary Classics, 1995), 940; hereafter cited parenthetically as *NS*.

4 Sue Bridwell Beckham, "The American Front Porch: Women's Liminal Space," in *Making the American Home: Middle-Class Women & Domestic Material Culture, 1840–1940*, eds. Marilyn Ferris Motz and Pat Browne (Bowling Green: Bowling Green State University Popular Press, 1988), 76.

5 Ibid., 72.

6 Jocelyn Donlon, *Swinging in Place: Porch Life in Southern Culture* (Chapel Hill: University of North Carolina Press, 2001), 56.

7 Trudier Harris considers how Hurston, in the role of anthropologist in *Mules and Men*, identifies the porch as a site for collection that points toward other research opportunities beyond its limits. See chapter 1 of *The Power of the Porch: The Storyteller's Craft in Zora Neale Hurston, Gloria Naylor, and Randall Kenan* (Athens: University of Georgia Press, 1996), 1–50.

8 Elizabeth Loizeaux, *Twentieth-Century Poetry and the Visual Arts* (Cambridge: Cambridge University Press, 2008), 84.

9 Robert Hemenway, *Zora Neale Hurston: A Literary Biography* (Urbana-Champaign: University of Illinois Press, 1980), 63.

10 Vernon Williams, *Rethinking Race: Franz Boas and His Contemporaries* (Lexington: University Press of Kentucky, 1996), 22.

11 Carla Yanni, *Nature's Museums: Victorian Science and the Architecture of Display* (London: Athlone Press, 1999), 19.

12 Alice Conklin examines the "only major ethnographic museum in a world capitol" to open during the 1930s as a means of revealing the continued racist display practices that populated natural history museums even with liberal scientists at the helm. Paul Rivet, a proponent of Boas's techniques, nevertheless oversaw a large exhibition of skulls from different races in the Musée de l'Homme of Paris in 1938 even as he strove to make the Anthropology Gallery

a space for "diffusing as well as producing new knowledge" that parted ways with racist science of the past. See "Skulls on Display: The Science of Race in Paris's Musée de l'Homme, 1928–1950" in *Museums and Difference*, ed. Daniel J. Sherman (Bloomington: Indiana University Press, 2007), 251, 260.

13 Agassiz's instructional method is particularly ironic considering his own ridiculous response to seeing African Americans for the first time. In a letter to his mother, Agassiz concludes: "Nonetheless, it is impossible for me to repress the feeling that they are not of the same blood as us. In seeing their black faces with their thick lips and grimacing teeth, the wool on their head, their bent knees, their elongated hands, their curved nails, and especially the livid color of the palm of their hands, I could not take my eyes off their face." See Gould, *The Mismeasure of Man* (New York: W. W. Norton, 1981), 45.

14 Michael Elliott, *The Culture Concept: Writing and Difference in the Age of Realism* (Minneapolis: University of Minnesota Press, 2002), 6.

15 Ira Jacknis, "Franz Boas and Exhibits: On the Limitations of the Museum Method of Anthropology" in *Objects and Others: Essays on Museums and Material Culture*, ed. George W. Stocking, Jr. (Madison: University of Wisconsin Press, 1985), 82–83.

16 Michael Elliott makes a similar claim. He contends that Hurston's novels of the 1930s "extended her struggles to resolve the impasses of Boasian anthropology: ... to appreciate the complexity and power of culture while still accounting for the fate of the individual at odds with it." Elliot argues that "fiction became a medium in which she could sharpen her formulation of these problems by removing the literal social scientist and replacing her with characters who raised more difficult problems of cultural mobility and observation." See *The Culture Concept*, 177–178.

17 Franz Boas letter to Morris Jesup in George W. Stocking, Jr. (ed.), *The Shaping of American Anthropology, 1831–1911: A Franz Boas Reader* (New York: Basic Books, 1974), 299.

18 Douglas Cole, *Franz Boas: The Early Years, 1858–1906* (Seattle: University of Washington Press, 1999), 253.

19 Ibid. Jacknis quotes Boas's disappointment with his exhibits at length: "It is an avowed object of a large group to transport the visitor into foreign surroundings. He is to see the whole village and the way the people live. But all attempts at such an undertaking that I have seen have failed, because the surroundings of a Museum are not favorable to an impression of this sort. The cases, the walls, the contents of other cases, the columns, the stairways, all remind us that we are not viewing an actual village and the contrast between the attempted realism of the group and the inappropriate surroundings spoils the whole effect." See "Franz Boas and Exhibits," 101.

20 Michael Elliott, *The Culture Concept*, 11.

21 Daphne Lamothe, *Inventing the New Negro: Narrative, Culture, and Ethnography* (Philadelphia: University of Pennsylvania Press, 2008), 5.

22 Ibid., 6.

23 Karen Jacobs, *The Eye's Mind: Literary Modernism and Visual Culture* (Ithaca, NY: Cornell University Press, 2001), 126.

24 Hazel Carby, "The Politics of Fiction, Anthropology, and the Folk: Zora Neale Hurston," in *New Essays on Their Eyes Were Watching God*, ed. Michael Awkward (Cambridge: Cambridge University Press, 1990), 85, 78.

25 Ibid., 88.

26 Martyn Bone provides one of the most compelling challenges to Carby's assessment of Hurston's portrayal of the folk. Placing his work amid Southern literary criticism that takes up Hurston, he accuses Carby of over-looking Hurston's complex rendering of the Bahamian workers who compli-cate the image of the folk and highlight the textured nature of transnational migrant labor. See "The (Extended) South of Black Folk: Intraregional and Transnational Migrant Labor in *Jonah's Gourd Vine* and *Their Eyes Were Watching God*," *American Literature* 79.4 (December 2007), 753–779.

27 Elaine Charnov, "The Performative Visual Anthropology Films of Zora Neale Hurston," *Film Criticism* 23:1 (Fall 1998), 39.

28 Fatimah Rony, *The Third Eye: Race, Cinema, and the Ethnographic Spectacle* (Durham, NC: Duke University Press, 1996), 207.

29 Ann Du Cille provides a sustained critique of marriage in Hurston's fiction. She challenges critics who see Janie's marriage to Tea Cake as liberating and insists that *Their Eyes* fits a larger template of novels of the 1930s in which marriage "is no longer the relation of rescue and protection it was in the nineteenth century; holy wedlock is no longer a site of utopian partner-ship, but a seat of emotional confinement, and male domination, as well as infidelity, brutality, and betrayal." See *The Coupling Convention: Sex, Text and Tradition in Black Women's Fiction* (New York: Oxford University Press, 1993), 112.

30 Stephen Jay Gould, *The Mismeasure of Man*, 116–117.

31 Ibid., 117.

32 Ibid., 224–225.

33 Ibid., 231.

34 Douglas Cole, *Franz Boas*, 263.

35 Franz Boas, Commencement Address at Atlanta University, May 31, 1906, in *The Shaping of American Anthropology*, 315.

36 In his excellent reading of *Jonah's Gourd Vine*, John Lowe traces the repetition of what he describes as "the entry of the hero from a journey of rebirth into a strange culture." Lowe proceeds to aver that John, named after a preacher "Two-Eye John," should be read as a text himself." See *Jump at the Sun: Zora Neale Hurston's Cosmic Comedy* (Urbana: University of Illinois Press, 1997), 103–104, 195.

37 Benigno Sánchez-Eppler reminds readers that to "apply the term 'participant-observer' ... as early as the 1930s should be acknowledged as anachronistic" because it only became widely used in the mid-1960s. Nevertheless, he claims that the term is useful in relation to Hurston given "Boas's insistence on being over the field to observe became for Hurston ... de facto participation." See

"Telling Anthropology: Zora Neale Hurston and Gilberto Freyre Disciplined in Their Field-Home-Work," *American Literary History* 4:3 (Autumn 1992), 485–486.

38 Michael Elliott offers a similar argument in his reading of *Jonah's Gourd Vine* and *Their Eyes Were Watching God*. See *The Culture Concept*, 177–188.

39 Susan Meisenhelder goes further to argue persuasively that John's fascination with whiteness echoes his stepfather's outlook. See *Hitting a Straight Lick with a Crooked Stick: Race and Gender in the Work of Zora Neale Hurston* (Tuscaloosa: University of Alabama Press, 1999), 45.

40 I. C. Jarvie, "The Problem of Ethical Integrity in Participant Observation," in *Field Research: A Sourcebook and Field Manual*, ed. Robert Burgess (New York: Routledge, 1989), 105.

41 Ira Jacknis, "Franz Boas and Exhibits," 82.

42 Ibid., 95.

43 Deborah Clarke, "'The Porch Couldn't Talk for Looking': Voice and Vision in *Their Eyes Were Watching God*," *African American Review* 35:4 (Winter 2001), 603–604.

44 Karla Holloway, "The Emergent Voice: The Word within its Texts," in *Zora Neale Hurston: Critical Perspectives, Past and Present*, eds. Henry Louis Gates and Anthony Appiah (New York: Amistad Press, 1993), 70 and Dolan Hubbard, "'…Ah said Ah'd save de text for you': Recontextualizing the Sermon to Tell (Her) Story in Zora Neale Hurston's *Their Eyes Were Watching God*," 27:2 (June 1993), 168.

45 Stuart Burrows, "'You heard her, you ain't blind': Seeing What's Said in *Their Eyes Were Watching God*," *Novel* 34:3 (Summer 2001), 444.

46 In Hurston's play, *Spunk* (1935), Evaline tells her husband: "You always trying to put your mind in my head." See *Zora Neale Hurston: Collected Plays*, eds. Jean Lee Cole and Charles Mitchell (New Brunswick: Rutgers University Press, 2008), 237. Janie's contention also echoes Henry James's Isabel Archer. In assessing Osmond, she observes: "The real offense … was her having a mind of her own at all. Her mind was to be his. … It would be a pretty piece of property for a proprietor already far-reaching" (*The Portrait of a Lady* [Oxford: Oxford University Press, 1998], 463). Hurston imagines Janie as part of a long line of women whose thoughts are circumscribed by their husband.

47 For this reading, I am indebted to Michael Hill's lecture, "Adolescence in the African American Novel" (University of Iowa, Iowa City, IA, August 28, 2010).

48 Hurston, *Zora Neale Hurston: A Life in Letters*, ed. Carla Kaplan (New York: Doubleday, 2001), 234.

49 Ibid., 137, 114.

50 Alain Locke, review of *Their Eyes Were Watching God*, by Zora Neale Hurston, *Opportunity*, June 1, 1938, in *Zora Neale Hurston: Critical Perspectives Past and Present*, eds. Henry Louis Gates, Jr. and K. A. Appiah (New York: Amistad, 1993),18.

51 Richard Wright, "Between Laughter and Tears," *New Masses*, (October 5, 1937), 22.

52 Ibid., 23.

53 Valerie Boyd, *Wrapped in Rainbows: The Life of Zora Neale Hurston* (New York: Scribner, 2003), 308.

54 Deborah Plant claims that *Moses* "reveals more about Hurston's personal philosophy and worldview than any other work." See *Every Tub Must Sit on Its Own Bottom: The Philosophy and Politics of Zora Neale Hurston* (Urbana: University of Illinois Press, 1995), 125.

55 Mark Christian Thompson argues that Hurston uses Moses to critique Nazi Germany and its emphasis on racial purity, thereby deriding "National Socialism" while advocating for "black cultural nationalism." See "National Socialism and Blood-Sacrifice in Zora Neale Hurston's *Moses, Man of the Mountain*," *African American Review* 38:3 (Fall 2004), 395–414. Erica Edwards provocatively contends that Hurston emphasizes Moses's violence, particularly against Miriam, to underscore the gothic nature of the charismatic male leader. See her chapter, "Moses, Monster of the Mountain: Gendered Violence in Zora Neale Hurston's Gothic" in *Charisma and the Fictions of Black Leadership* (Minneapolis: University of Minnesota Press, 2012), 77–103. Judylyn Ryan also reads Moses's harsh treatment of Miriam as proof of "the limitation of his prophetic vision." See *Spirituality as Ideology in Black Women's Film and Literature* (Charlottesville: University of Virginia Press, 2005), 70.

56 In a well-known exchange with Nick Ford, Hurston responded to criticism of *Jonah's Gourd Vine* for dealing inadequately with racism: "I was writing a novel and not a treatise on sociology." See *The Contemporary Negro Novel: A Study in Race Relations,* 1936 (College Park: McGrath, 1968), 96.

57 Barbara Johnson, "Moses and Intertexuality: Sigmund Freud, Zora Neale Hurston, and the Bible" in *Poetics of the Americas: Race, Founding, and Textuality*, eds. Bainard Cowan and Jefferson Humphries (Baton Rouge: Louisiana State University Press, 1997)," 18, 19.

58 Werner Sollors, "Modernization as Adultery: Richard Wright, Zora Neale Hurston, and American Culture of the 1930's and 1940's," quoted in Carla Cappetti, *Writing Chicago: Modernism, Ethnography, and the Novel* (New York: Columbia University Press, 1993), 186.

59 Ralph Ellison, "Recent Negro Fiction," *New Masses*, August 5 (1941), 22, 24.

60 Barbara Johnson, "Moses and Intertexuality," 25. Meisenhelder claims under Mentu's teaching, Moses represents the "ideal male," but he later becomes a "dictator as ruthless as ... Pharaoh." See *Hitting a Straight Lick*, 117, 118.

61 Ira Jacknis, "Franz Boas and Exhibits," 86.

62 Ibid., 103.

63 Franz Boas, September 12, 1934, Franz Boas Papers, American Philosophical Society.

64 Valerie Boyd, *Wrapped in Rainbows*, 252.

MELVIN TOLSON: GAINING MODERNIST PERSPECTIVE IN THE ART GALLERY

1 Romare Bearden, "The Negro Artist and Modern Art," *Opportunity: Journal of Negro Life* 12 (December 1934), 371.

2 Robert Farnsworth describes Tolson's reputation on the campuses of both Wiley College and Langston University. See *Melvin B. Tolson 1898–1966: Plain Talk and Poetic Prophecy* (Columbia: University of Missouri Press, 1984), 101, 111.

3 Melvin Tolson, *The Harlem Group of Negro Writers*, ed. Edward Mullen (Westport: Greenwood Press, 2001), 136.

4 For a comprehensive discussion of Tolson's literary reputation, see Michael Bérubé's chapter 3: "Tolson's Neglect: African-American of Modernism and Its Representations" in *Marginal Forces/Cultural Centers: Tolson, Pynchon, and the Politics of the Canon* (Ithaca, NY: Cornell University Press, 1992), 133–206.

5 Tolson's heightened attention to the problem of white mentorship is part of a larger concern of black writers that escalates after the Vietnam War. Michael Hill examines this challenge at length in *The Ethics of Swagger: Prizewinning African American Literature* (Columbus: Ohio State University Press, 2013).

6 See Tolson's "The Odyssey of a Manuscript," *New Letters* (Fall 1981), 8, 9.

7 For helpful discussions of Tolson's admiration of Hughes's work as well as their personal relationship, see Craig Werner's "Blues for T. S. Eliot and Langston Hughes: The Afro-Modernist Aesthetic of Harlem Gallery," *Black American Literature Forum* 24:3 (Autumn 1990), 453–472; Robert Farnsworth's "What Can a Poet Do? Langston Hughes and M.B. Tolson," *New Letters* (Fall 1981), 19–29; and Mariann Russell's "Langston Hughes and Melvin Tolson: Blues People," in *The Furious Flowering of African American Poetry*, ed. Joanne Gabbin (Charlottesville: University Press of Virginia, 1999), 38–46.

8 Joy Flasch, *Melvin B. Tolson* (New York: Twayne Publishers, 1972), 81.

9 Robert Farnsworth, *Melvin B. Tolson*, 167.

10 David Gold, "'Nothing Educates Us like a Shock': The Integrated Rhetoric of Melvin B. Tolson," *College Composition and Communication* 55:2 (December 2003), 235.

11 Ibid., 227.

12 Ibid., 230, 231,229.

13 See Mariann Russell's *Melvin B. Tolson's Harlem Gallery: A Literary Analysis* (Columbia: University of Missouri Press, 1980), 2. Langston Hughes also commented on Tolson's reputation at Wiley: "Kids from the cottonfields like him. Cowpunchers understand him. He is a great teacher of the kind any college might be proud." See Robert Farnsworth, "What Can a Poet Do? Langston Hughes and M. B. Tolson," *New Letters* (Fall 1981), 26.

14 Gold makes a similar point. He notes that HBCUs "were frequently hierarchical and authoritarian. Yet they also were set up to serve explicitly civic purposes." See "'Nothing Educates Us like a Shock'," 227–228.

15 Les Harrison, *The Temple and the Forum: American Museum and Cultural Authority in Hawthorne, Melville, Stowe, and Whitman* (Tuscaloosa: University of Alabama Press, 2007), xiii.

16 Ibid., xiv.

17 Christy S. Coleman, "African American Museums in the Twenty-first Century," *Museum Philosophy for the Twenty-first Century*, ed. Hugh H. Genoways (Lanham, MD: Alta Mira Press, 2006), 151.

18 *To Conserve a Legacy: American Art from Historically Black Colleges and Universities*, eds. Richard Powell and Jock Reynolds (Cambridge, MA: MIT Press, 1999), 12.

19 Christy Coleman, "African American Museums in the Twenty-first Century," 152. Also see Spencer Crew, "African Americans, History and Museums: Preserving African American History in the Public Arena," *Making Histories in Museums*, ed. Gaynor Kavanagh (London: Leicester University Press, 1996), 82.

20 Christy Coleman, "African American Museums in the Twenty-first Century," 152, 154.

21 Robert Farnsworth, *Melvin B. Tolson*, 145.

22 Ibid., 145–146.

23 Mariann Russell, *Melvin B. Tolson's Harlem Gallery*, 62, 63.

24 Jean Toomer's *Cane* (1923) is the obvious and highly successful exception. His daring experiments with form, however, did not inspire a wide following among other Harlem Renaissance writers and poets.

25 For further discussion, see Caroline Goeser, *Picturing the New Negro*, 13 and Helen Langa, *Radical Art: Printmaking and the Left in 1930s New York* (Berkeley University of California Press, 2004).

26 Melvin Tolson, *A Gallery of Harlem Portraits*, ed. Robert Farnsworth (Columbia: University of Missouri Press, 1979), 4.

27 Keith Leonard, *Fettered Genius: The African American Bardic Poet from Slavery to Civil Rights* (Charlottesville: University of Virginia Press, 2005), 208. Werner, Craig, "Blues for T. S. Eliot and Langston Hughes: The Afro-Modernist Aesthetic of Harlem Gallery," *Black American Literature Forum* 24:3 (Autumn 1990), 457.

28 In my spring 2011 graduate course, Studies in African American Literature: Visualizing Blackness, Brent Krammes's essay, "Aesthetic Headings: Printmaking and Tolson's *Rendezvous with America* and *A Gallery of Harlem Portraits*," inspired my consideration of the relation between Tolson's musical and visual headings.

29 See Michael Bérubé's discussion of white critical response and Tolson's inclusion in anthologies in *Marginal Forces/Cultural Centers*, 154–188.

30 Aldon Nielsen helpfully considers the acerbic nature of black critical responses to Tolson's work as well as the destructive nature of white scholarly examinations. See "Melvin B. Tolson and the Deterritorialization of Modernism," *African American Review* 26:2 (Summer 1992), 241–255.

31 Robert Farnsworth, *Melvin B. Tolson*, 139.

32 Ibid, 145.

33 Ibid., 112.

34 Scott Deveaux, *The Birth of Bebop: A Social and Musical History* (Berkeley: University of California Press, 1999), 11, 12.

35 Brian McHale persuasively notes that Tolson's positioning of the Curator as his main speaker tellingly contrasts Ishmael Reed's "art nappers" in *Mumbo Jumbo* (1972): Tolson's Curator offers "a conservator where they are desecrators." See *The Obligation Toward the Difficult Whole: Postmodernist Long Poems* (Tuscaloosa: University of Alabama Press, 2004), 59.

36 Raymond Nelson, "*Harlem Gallery*: An Advertisement and User's Manual," *Virginia Quarterly Review* (1999), 532.

37 Michael Bérubé, *Marginal Forces/Cultural Centers*, 59, 86.

38 Melvin Tolson, "*Harlem Gallery*" *and Other Poems of Melvin B. Tolson*, ed. Raymond Nelson (Charlottesville: University Press of Virginia, 1999), 342; hereafter cited parenthetically as *HG*.

39 See Diana Cruz's "Refuting Exile: Rita Dove Reading Melvin B. Tolson," *Callaloo* 31:3 (Summer 2008).

40 Elizabeth Loizeaux, *Twentieth-Century Poetry and the Visual Arts*, 167.

41 Brian McHale considers the uncertain time period of the poem and highlights Tolson's refusal to show any "awareness of contemporary art ... of the sixties" or "any midcentury art movement." See *The Obligation toward the Difficult Whole*, 94. Bérubé makes a similar point wondering, "Where ... are Jackson Pollock, Robert Motherwell, William de Kooning?" See *Marginal Forces/Cultural Centers*, 105.

42 This trend toward more frequent appeals to visual art shows up throughout the drafts. In the 1956 draft, the section of "Beta" in which the Curator compares himself to "The Lost, The Bright, The Angry, The Beat" is missing the line, "Absent like shadow in Byzantine painting." See Box 7, Folder Harlem Gallery, c. 1956, Melvin Tolson Papers.

43 Tolson suggests that Hideho experiences the danger of the changing jazz scene. As bebop became more closely aligned with what had once been seen as its seedy underside, patrons came to expect eccentric personalities, like those of Charlie Parker and Thelonious Monk. David Rosenthal notes that although black bebop artists were by no means universally drug addicts, the "number of junkies among the hard boppers was alarming." See *Hard Bop: Jazz and Black Music, 1955–1965* (New York: Oxford University Press, 1992), 83.

44 For example, Michael Bérube and Keith Leonard offer compelling readings that interpret the Curator as closely aligned with Tolson and therefore highly critical of Hideho. See *Marginal Forces/Cultural Centers*, 118–132 and *Fettered Genius*, 240–251.

45 See Tolson, "The Odyssey of a Manuscript," 12.

46 See Library of Congress, Box 7, Harlem Gallery, c. 1956.

47 Quoted in Michael Bérubé, *Marginal Forces/Cultural Centers*, 144.

48 Early manuscript drafts stress the comparison between memories and pictures. A page from Tolson's 1956 draft begins with the line reading "Every

mind has a picture gallery, Curator. / In mine is an etching of a streetwalker giving birth" (see Box 7, Harlem Gallery, c. 1956).

49 Robert Farnsworth, *Melvin B. Tolson*, 297.

50 Ibid., 271.

51 Ibid., 300.

RALPH ELLISON: ENGAGING RACIAL PERCEPTION BEYOND MUSEUM WALLS

1 André Malraux, "Museum Without Walls," in Stuart Gilbert (trans) *The Voices of Silence* (Princeton, NJ: Princeton University Press, 1978), 13–14, 16. The 1949 edition that Ellison likely read reads very similarly except that it refers to an "Imaginary Art Museum" in place of the "Museum Without Walls." See Malraux, trans. Stuart Gilbert *The Psychology of Art: Museum Without Walls* (New York: Pantheon Books, 1949), 13, 17.

2 *Conversations with Ralph Ellison*, eds. Maryemma Graham and Amritjit Singh (Jackson: University Press of Mississippi, 1995), 364.

3 Barbara Foley also suggests that Ellison placed great emphasis on Malraux's leftist politics, and she argues that his sympathies profoundly shaped his creation of *Invisible Man*. Although I disagree with her conclusion, her careful consideration of Ellison's investment in Malraux is useful. See *Wrestling with the Left: The Making of Ralph Ellison's Invisible Man* (Durham, NC: Duke University Press, 2010), 87–88.

4 Ralph Ellison, April 14, 1940, Box 97, Folder 1314, Richard Wright Papers, Beinecke Library. All material from these papers comes from this box and folder, hereafter cited as RWP.

5 Tony Bennett, *The Birth of the Museum: History, Theory, Politics* (London: Routledge, 1995), 20.

6 Ibid., 24.

7 André Malraux, *The Psychology of Art*, 17.

8 Ibid., 16.

9 Barbara Foley argues that Ellison's subscription to communist ideas lasted much longer than he acknowledged. See *Wrestling with the Left*.

10 A letter to Richard Wright in 1945 reveals Ellison's view of Marxism as he delved into the craft of creative writing. He declares, "I was never dead, but I was amorphous as hell, literally; and after my discovery of Marx too, too many questions, nebulous emotions and moods were left waiting breathlessly behind the doors of dogma." August 18, 1945, RWP.

11 Arnold Rampersad, *Ralph Ellison: A Biography* (New York: Alfred A. Knopf, 2007), 83.

12 August 24, 1936, Box 54, Folder "Correspondence," 1936–1964, Langston Hughes Papers, Beinecke Library.

13 Margaret Vendryes explains that black critics accused Barthé of "perpetuating damaging stereotypes" and objectifying "black people." See "Casting Feral Benga: A Biography of Richmond Barthé's Signature Work," *Anyone Can Fly*

Foundation, www.anyonecanflyfoundation.org/library/Vendryes_on_Barthe_ Essay.html and *Barthé: A Life in Sculpture* (Jackson: University of Mississippi Press, 2008), 101.

14 Lawrence Jackson thoroughly examines Ellison's early musical training in *Ralph Ellison: Emergence of Genius* (New York: Wiley, 2002), 54–82.

15 Ibid., 140.

16 Vendryes recounts, "Ellison's apprenticeship under Barthé was tumultuous and short-lived"; see "The Lives of Richmond Barthé" in *The Greatest Taboo: Homosexuality in Black Communities*, ed. Delroy Constantine-Simms (Los Angeles: Alyson Books, 2001), 274–287.

17 Ellison remembers getting to know Tolson in New York, and he notes that they disagreed over the work of modernist writers like Pound and Eliot, poets Tolson later came to regard highly. See *Conversations with Ralph Ellison*, 370.

18 Horace A. Porter's *Jazz Country: Ralph Ellison in America* (Iowa City: University of Iowa Press, 2001) provocatively examines Ellison's friendship with Bearden. Kimberly Lamm also considers their connection in "Visuality and Black Masculinity in Ralph Ellison's *Invisible Man* and Romare Bearden's Photomontages," *Callaloo* 26 (July 2003), 813–835.

19 Horace Porter, *Jazz Country*, 57.

20 November 3,1941, RWP.

21 November 3, 1941, RWP.

22 August 5, 1945, RWP.

23 Lawrence Jackson, *Emergence*, 308.

24 August 8, 1945, RWP.

25 For an overview of the *Invisible Man* manuscript, see Michael and Lena Hill's *Ralph Ellison's Invisible Man: A Reference Guide* (Westport, CT: Greenwood Press, 2008), 39–53.

26 Ellison's attention to "packaging" extended beyond narrative to the material book itself. The cover of the first edition of *Invisible Man* recalls *Memento*, a piece Ellison discovered at an exhibition he visited in 1947. See Box 180, Folder 3, Ralph Ellison Papers, Library of Congress; further references to this collection will be cited as REP. In the introduction to *Invisible Man*, Ellison describes doing "free-lance photography (including book-jacket portraits of Fancis Steegmuller and Mary McCarthy)." See Ralph Ellison, *Invisible Man* (New York: Vintage, 1980), x; further references to *Invisible Man* are to this edition and will be cited parenthetically as *IM*.

27 Ross Posnock offers a compelling analysis of Ellison's investment in James, as well as his relationship to Locke and Hurston, as a means for understanding the complex nature of his literary cosmopolitanism. See *Color and Culture: Black Writers and the Making of the Modern Intellectual* (Cambridge, MA: Harvard University Press, 1998), 184–219.

28 Robert Stepto, *From Behind the Veil: A Study of Afro-American Narrative*, 2nd ed. (Urbana: University of Illinois Press, 1991), 177.

29 Box 144, Folder "Chapel," REP.

30 Francoise Meltzer, *Salome and the Dance of Writing: Portraits of Mimesis in Literature* (Chicago, IL: University of Chicago Press, 1987), 120.

31 Ibid., 121.

32 Ibid., 55.

33 The most substantial relationships documented in the drafts occur between Invisible Man and a black woman, Cleo, and a white woman, Louise. See Box 142, Folder "At Mary's" and Box 143, Folder "Brotherhood," REP.

34 Albert Murray and John F. Callahan, eds., *Trading Twelves: The Selected Letters of Ralph Ellison and Albert Murray* (New York: Vintage Books, 2000), 25.

35 See Shelly Eversley, "Female Iconography in *Invisible Man,*" *The Cambridge Companion to Ralph Ellison* (Cambridge: Cambridge University Press, 2005), 172–187.

36 This metaphorical framing evokes Hemingway's technique in *The Sun Also Rises* (1926). The arena, as well as a group of dancing boys, frame the bull, and later, also frame Brett. The framing symbolizes the shared status of the bull and Brett as spectacles. Ellison's blatant allusions to *The Sun Also Rises* suggest his familiarity with Hemingway's modernist technique of relating ideas through double metaphorical frames.

37 Maurice O. Wallace, *Constructing the Black Masculine: Identity and Ideality in African American Men's Literature and Culture, 1775–1995* (Durham, NC: Duke University Press, 2002), 30–31.

38 Invisible Man similarly stands on "soiled canvas" to deliver his maiden Brotherhood speech in the arena (340). Earlier drafts reveal Ellison selecting this language over his initial description of the flooring as a "flag-draped platform." Box 143, Folder "Brotherhood, Arena Speech," REP.

39 Susan Stewart made these points in her lecture "The Eidos in the Hand," Andrew Carnduff Ritchie Lecture Series (Yale Art Gallery, New Haven, December 15, 2000).

40 Robin Jaffee Frank, *Love and Loss: American Portrait and Mourning Miniatures* (New Haven, CT: Yale University Press, 2000), 10.

41 Stepto astutely comments on this picture but designates it a "cameo" (*From Behind the Veil*, 181). My designation of it as a miniature acknowledges Ellison's attention to distinct forms of portraiture and their sociohistorical significance.

42 Box 144, Folder (2) "Campus," REP.

43 For the ideas in this paragraph, I am indebted to Tamar Garb's discussion of Renoir in *Bodies of Modernity: Figure and Flesh in Fin-de-Siècle France* (London: Thames and Hudson, 1998), 147.

44 Box 146, Folder "Red Robe," REP.

45 Ibid.

46 Rampersad notes Ellison's expert work in photography with a specific "emphasis on portraiture" (241). For a comprehensive, richly nuanced discussion of Ellison and photography, see Sara Blair's superb chapter in *Harlem Crossroads: Black Writers and the Photograph in the Twentieth Century* (Princeton, NJ: Princeton University Press, 2007), 112–159.

47 Marc Conner's keen analysis draws a similar conclusion about the eviction scene and expounds on the significance of memory and history. See "The Litany of Things: Sacrament and History in *Invisible Man*" in *Ralph Ellison and the Raft of Hope: A Political Companion to Invisible Man* (Lexington: University Press of Kentucky, 2004), 171–192.

48 Box 143, Folder (3) "Brotherhood," REP.

49 Box 144, Folder "Hattie and Julius Franklin," REP.

50 In "Ambivalent Man: Ellison's Rejection of Communism," *African American Review* 34 (January 2000): 621–637, Jesse Wolfe examines Ellison's relationship to communism and its deployment in *Invisible Man*.

51 Kimberly Lamm, "Visuality and Black Masculinity," 818.

52 Ibid., 825.

53 Box 142, Folder "Brotherhood," REP.

54 The manuscript boasts a long scene crafted around these remembered words. Following his browbeating by Bledsoe, the protagonist visits Woodridge, a brilliant young professor rumored to be homosexual. He finds Woodridge drunk in his apartment decorated with "prints of modern paintings which [the protagonist] could not understand" (Ellison pencils above the typescript to describe the paintings as "a maze of wonderful colors and meaningless forms"). A different version notes: "Prints of abstract paintings puzzled me from the walls." Woodridge points to "a chest on one end of which there stood a nude male torso and on the other an ugly primitive African statue," and he tells the protagonist, "Relax like the white boy there. You live like the other all the time. ... Forced into extreme positions. Distorted in the interest of design." In keeping with the general philosophy of his revisions, Ellison excludes this museum episode which features a character verbally challenging Invisible Man to reassess his projected image. Box 144, Folder (4) "Chapel" and Box 146, Folder (16) "Woodridge," REP. In *Aberrations in Black: Toward a Queer of Color Critique* (Minneapolis: University of Minnesota Press, 2004), 54–81, Roderick Ferguson provocatively considers the unpublished Woodridge scenes at length.

55 Box 143, Folder (3) "Brotherhood," REP.

56 Box 143, Folder (5) "Brotherhood," REP.

57 Box 142, Folder "At Mary's," REP.

58 Elizabeth Yukins studies the relationship between Ellison's interest in cubism and his writing in "An 'Artful Juxtaposition on the Page': Memory, Perception, and Cubist Technique in Ralph Ellison's *Juneteenth*," *PMLA* 119 (October 2004), 1247–1263.

59 See William Rubin, ed., *Picasso and Portraiture: Representation and Transformation* (New York: Museum of Modern Art, 1996), 23.

60 This major revision was also encouraged by a reader whose initials are "HF," likely Harry Ford of Knopf Publishing: "Careful reading leads me to feel quite strongly that Leroy's diary should be dropped entirely. Prolix, didactic and inimical to the narrative – a crutch for the narrator which never entirely works. ... It seems to me that either Leroy has to be introduced as a *character*

(if it is really necessary to project his highly sophisticated viewpoint) or eliminated entirely. I would prefer the latter." See Box 151, Folder 6, REP.

61 January 21, 1953, RWP.

62 See letter from Fanny Ellison, October 23, 1979 Box 154, Folder 4, REP.

63 Box 153, Folder 4, REP.

64 Box 154, Folder 7, REP.

65 Adam Bradley persuasively makes this argument in *Ralph Ellison in Progress* (New Haven, CT: Yale University Press, 2010).

66 Editors John Callahan and Adam Bradley surmise that "Ellison uses Hickman as the mouthpiece for all of what [Ellison] came to know and think and feel about being African American in America." See *Three Days Before the Shooting...* (New York: Modern Library, 2010), xxiii; hereafter cited as TD.

67 Conflicting details in *Three Days* make it somewhat unclear as to whether Ellison intended Hickman to visit the Christ painting before he studies the tapestry or afterward, but considering the numerous drafts, it seems more likely that he favored the sequence I note.

CODA: REDEFINING THE LOOK OF AMERICAN CHARACTER

1 Albert Murray and John F. Callahan, eds, *Trading Twelves: The Selected Letters of Ralph Ellison and Albert Murray* (New York: Vintage Books, 2000), 25.

2 Box 127, Folder 4, REP.

3 Anne Dvinge, "Complex Fate – Complex Vision: The Vernacular and Identity in Ralph Ellison's *Juneteenth*," *Amerikastudien/American Studies* 51:2 (2006), 203.

Bibliography

ARCHIVAL SOURCES

Bennett, Gwendolyn. *James Weldon Johnson Collection.* Beinecke Library, Yale University, New Haven, CT.

Bennett, Gwendolyn. *Gwendolyn Bennett Papers.* Schomburg Center for Research in Black Culture, New York City, NY.

Boas, Franz. *Franz Boas Papers,* American Philosophical Society. Philadelphia, PA.

Ellison, Ralph. *Ralph Ellison Papers.* Manuscript Collection. Library of Congress, Washington, DC.

Ellison, Ralph. *Langston Hughes Papers.* Beinecke Library, Yale University, New Haven, CT.

Ellison, Ralph. *Richard Wright Papers.* Beinecke Library, Yale University, New Haven, CT.

Johnston, Frances Benjamin. *Frances Benjamin Johnston Collection.* Prints & Photographs Division, Library of Congress, Washington, DC.

Spencer, Anne. *James Weldon Johnson Collection.* Beinecke Library, Yale University, New Haven, CT.

Tolson, Melvin. *Melvin Tolson Papers.* Manuscript Collection. Library of Congress, Washington, DC.

PUBLISHED WORKS

Adams, Karen. "The Black Image in the Paintings of William Sidney Mount." *American Art Journal* 7, no. 2 (1975): 42–59.

Angelou, Maya. *Even the Stars Look Lonesome.* New York: Random House, 1997.

Arnesen, Eric. "The Quicksands of Economic Insecurity: African Americans, Strikebreaking, and Labor Activism in the Industrial Era." In *The Black Worker: Race, Labor, and Civil Rights since Emancipation,* edited by Eric Arnesen, 41–71. Urbana: University of Illinois, 2007.

Baldwin, Gordon. *Looking at Photographs: A Guide to Technical Terms.* New York: Oxford University Press, 1991.

Balkun, Mary. "Phillis Wheatley's Construction of Otherness and the Rhetoric of Performed Ideology." *African American Review* 36, no. 1 (2002) 121–135.

Barker, Deborah. "Authenticating the African-American Female Artist: Frances Harper's *Iola Leroy* and Jessie Fauset's *Plum Bun*." In *Aesthetics and Gender in American Literature: Portraits of the Woman Artist*, 162–197. London: Bucknell University Press, 2000.

Barnett, Pamela. "'My Picture of You Is, After All, the True Helga Crane': Portraiture and Identity in Nella Larsen's *Quicksand*." *Signs* 20, no. 3 (Spring 1995): 575–600.

Bearden, Romare. "The Negro Artist and Modern Art." *Opportunity: Journal of Negro Life* 12 (December 1934): 371–372.

Beckham, Sue Bridwell. "The American Front Porch: Women's Liminal Space." In *Making the American Home: Middle-Class Women & Domestic Material Culture, 1840–1940*, edited by Marilyn Ferris Motz and Pat Browne, 69–89. Bowling Green, OH: Bowling Green State University Popular Press, 1988.

Bell, Bernard. "W. E. B. Du Bois's Struggle to Reconcile Folk and High Art." In *Critical Essays on W. E. B. Du Bois*, edited by William L. Andrews, 106–122. Boston: G. K. Hall, 1985.

Bell, Kevin. "The Embrace of Entropy: Ralph Ellison and the Freedom Principle of Jazz Invisible." *Boundary* 2 30 (July 2003): 21–45.

Bennett, Tony. *The Birth of the Museum: History, Theory, Politics*. London: Routledge, 1995.

Berch, Bettina. *The Woman behind the Lens: The Life and Work of Frances Benjamin Johnston, 1864–1952*. Charlottesville: University Press of Virginia, 2000.

Bérubé, Michael. "Tolson's Neglect: African-American Modernism and Its Representations." In *Marginal Forces/Cultural Centers: Tolson, Pynchon, and the Politics of the Canon*, 133–206. Ithaca: Cornell University Press, 1992.

Bieze, Michael. *Booker T. Washington and the Art of Self-Representation*. New York: Peter Lang, 2008.

Bindman, David, Henry Louis Gates, Jr., and Karen C. C. Dalton. *The Image of the Black in Western Art*. Cambridge, MA: Belknap Press, 2010.

Blackwood, Sarah. "Fugitive Obscura: Runaway Slave Portraiture and Early Photographic Technology." *American Literature* 81, no. 1 (March 2009): 93–125.

Blair, Sara. *Harlem Crossroads: Black Writers and the Photograph in the Twentieth Century*. Princeton, NJ: Princeton University Press, 2007.

Boas, Franz. *The Shaping of American Anthropology, 1831–1911: A Franz Boaz Reader*, edited by George W. Stocking, Jr. New York: Basic Books, 1974.

Boime, Albert. *The Art of Exclusion: Representing Blacks in the Nineteenth Century*. Washington, DC: Smithsonian Press, 1990.

Bone, Martyn. "The (Extended) South of Black Folk: Intraregional and Transnational Migrant Labor in *Jonah's Gourd Vine* and *Their Eyes Were Watching God*." *American Literature* 79, no. 4 (December 2007): 753–779.

Boyd, Valerie. *Wrapped in Rainbows: The Life of Zora Neale Hurston*. New York: Scribner, 2003.

Boyte, Rob. "National Geographic: Primitivism in Body Acceptance." *Nude & Natural* 11, no. 4 (1992): 23–24.

Bradley, Adam. *Ralph Ellison in Progress: From Invisible Man to Three Days Before the Shooting ....* New Haven: Yale University Press, 2010.

Bryson, Norman. *Looking at the Overlooked: Four Essays on Still Life Painting.* Cambridge, MA: Harvard University Press, 1990.

Burrows, Stuart. "'You Heard Her, You Ain't Blind': Seeing What's Said in *Their Eyes Were Watching God.*" *Novel* 34, no. 3 (Summer 2001): 434–452.

Byles, Mather. *Works,* edited by Benjamin Franklin V. New York: Scholars' Facsimiles & Reprints, 1978.

Cantor, Milton. "The Image of the Negro in Colonial Literature." *The New England Quarterly* 36, no. 4 (1963): 452–477.

Cappetti, Carla. *Writing Chicago: Modernism, Ethnography, and the Novel.* New York: Columbia University Press, 1993.

Carby, Hazel. "The Politics of Fiction, Anthropology, and the Folk: Zora Neale Hurston." In *New Essays on Their Eyes Were Watching God,* edited by Michael Awkward, 72–90. Cambridge: Cambridge University Press, 1990.

Carretta, Vincent. *Phillis Wheatley: Biography of a Genius in Bondage.* Athens: University of Georgia Press, 2011.

Chaney, Michael A. *Fugitive Vision: Slave Image and Black Identity in Antebellum Narrative.* Bloomington, IN: Indiana University Press, 2008.

Charnov, Elaine. "The Performative Visual Anthropology Films of Zora Neale Hurston." *Film Criticism* 23, no. 1 (Fall 1998): 38–47.

Clarke, Deborah. "'The Porch Couldn't Talk for Looking': Voice and Vision in *Their Eyes Were Watching God.*" *African American Review* 35, no. 4 (Winter 2001): 599–613.

Cole, Douglas. *Franz Boas: The Early Years, 1858–1906.* Seattle: University of Washington Press, 1999.

Coleman, Christy S. "African American Museums in the Twenty-First Century." In *Museum Philosophy for the Twenty-First Century,* edited by Hugh H. Genoways, 151–160. Lanham: Alta Mira Press, 2006.

Collins, Kathleen. "The Scourged Back." *History of Photography* 9, no. 1 (January–March 1985): 43–45.

Collins, Lisa. *The Art of History: African American Women Artists Engage the Past.* New Brunswick, NJ: Rutgers University Press, 2002.

Conklin, Alice. "Skulls on Display: The Science of Race in Paris's Musée de l'Homme, 1928–1950." In *Museums and Difference,* edited by Daniel J. Sherman, 250–288. Bloomington: Indiana University Press, 2007.

Connor, Marc. "The Litany of Things: Sacrament and History in *Invisible Man.*" In *Ralph Ellison and the Raft of Hope: A Political Companion to Invisible Man,* edited by Lucas E. Morel, 171–192. Lexington: University Press of Kentucky, 2004.

Conwill, Kinshasha Holman. "Introduction." In *To Conserve a Legacy: American Art from Historically Black Colleges and Universities,* edited by Richard Powell and Jock Reynolds, 11–17. Cambridge, MA: MIT Press, 1999.

Crew, Spencer. "African Americans, History and Museums: Preserving African American History in the Public Arena." In *Making Histories in Museums,* edited by Gaynor Kavanagh, 80–91. London: Leicester University Press, 1996.

Cruz, Diana. "Refuting Exile: Rita Dove Reading Melvin B. Tolson." *Callaloo* 31, no. 3 (Summer 2008): 789–802.

Cutter, Martha. "Dismantling 'The Master's House': Critical Literacy in Harriet Jacobs' Incidents in the Life of a Slave Girl." *Callaloo* 19, no. 1 (Winter 1996): 209–225.

Dabakis, Melissa. *Visualizing Labor in American Sculpture: Monuments, Manliness, and the Work Ethic, 1880–1935.* New York: Cambridge University Press, 1999.

Davis, Charles T. and Henry Louis Gates, Jr. *The Slave Narrative.* Oxford: Oxford University Press, 1985.

DeLombard, Jeannine. "'Eye-Witness to the Cruelty': Southern Violence and Northern Testimony in Frederick Douglass's 1845 Narrative." *American Literature* 73, no. 2 (June 2001): 245–275.

Deveaux, Scott. *The Birth of Bebop: A Social and Musical History.* Berkeley: University of California Press, 1999.

Donlon, Jocelyn. *Swinging in Place: Porch Life in Southern Culture.* Chapel Hill: University of North Carolina Press, 2001.

Douglass, Frederick. *Narrative of the Life of Frederick Douglass, an American Slave Written by Himself,* 2nd ed., edited by David Blight. Boston: Bedford St. Martin's, 2003.

Douglass, Frederick. "Pictures and Progress: An Address Delivered in Boston, Massachusetts, on 3 December 1861." In *The Frederick Douglass Papers: Series One: Speeches, Debates, and Interviews Volume 3:1855–63,* 452–473, edited by John Blassingame. New Haven, CT: Yale University Press, 1985.

Du Bois, W. E. B. *The Souls of Black Folk,* edited by Henry Louis Gates, Jr. and Terri Hume Oliver. New York: W. W. Norton, 1999.

Du Bois, W. E. B. *W. E. B. Du Bois: A Reader,* edited by David Levering Lewis. New York: Henry Holt, 1995.

Du Cille, Ann. *The Coupling Convention: Sex, Text and Tradition in Black Women's Fiction.* New York: Oxford University Press, 1993.

Duvernay, Adam. "Statue of Black Man Has History of Controversy." *The Daily Reveille* (Baton Rouge, LA), October 6, 2009.

Dvinge, Anne. "Complex Fate – Complex Vision: The Vernacular and Identity in Ralph Ellison's *Juneteenth.*" *Amerikastudien/American Studies* 51, no. 2 (2006): 193–206.

Edwards, Erica. *Charisma and the Fictions of Black Leadership.* Minneapolis: University of Minnesota Press, 2012.

Elliot, Michael. *The Culture Concept: Writing and Difference in the Age of Realism.* Minneapolis: University of Minnesota Press, 2002.

Ellison, Ralph. *The Collected Essays of Ralph Ellison,* edited by John Callahan. New York: Modern Library, 1995.

Ellison, Ralph. *Invisible Man.* New York: Vintage, 1980.

Ellison, Ralph. *Three Days Before the Shooting ...,* edited by John Callahan and Adam Bradley. New York: Modern Library, 2010.

Emery, Mary Lou. *Modernism, the Visual, and Caribbean Literature.* Cambridge: Cambridge University Press, 2007.

Erkkilä, Betsy. "Phillis Wheatley and the Black American Revolution." In *A Mixed Race: Ethnicity in Early America*, edited by Frank Shuffleton, 225–240. New York: Oxford University Press, 1993.

Eversley, Shelly. "The Female Iconography in *Invisible Man*." In *The Cambridge Companion to Ralph Ellison*, edited by Ross Posnock, 172–187. Cambridge: Cambridge University Press, 2005.

Farnsworth, Robert. *Melvin B. Tolson 1898–1966: Plain Talk and Poetic Prophecy*. Columbia: University of Missouri Press, 1984.

Farnsworth, Robert. "What Can a Poet Do? Langston Hughes and M. B. Tolson." *New Letters* 48 (Fall 1981): 19–29.

Fauset, Jessie. *Plum Bun: A Novel without a Moral*. Boston, MA: Beacon Press, 1990.

Ferguson, Roderick. *Aberrations in Black: Toward a Queer of Color Critique*. Minneapolis: University of Minnesota Press, 2004.

Flasch, Joy. *Melvin B. Tolson*. New York: Twayne Publishers, 1972.

Foley, Barbara. "From Communism to Brotherhood: The Drafts of *Invisible Man*." In *Left of the Color Line: Race, Radicalism, and Twentieth-Century Literature of the United States*, edited by Bill V. Mullen and James Smethurst, 163–182. Chapel Hill: University of North Carolina Press, 2003.

Foley, Barbara. *Wrestling with the Left: The Making of Ralph Ellison's Invisible Man*. Durham, NC: Duke University Press, 2010.

Foote, Henry. "Mr. Smibert Shows His Pictures, March, 1730." *New England Quarterly* 8, no. ¼ (1935): 14–28.

Ford, Charita. "Flowering a Feminist Garden: The Writings and Poetry of Anne Spencer." *SAGE* 5, no. 1 (1988): 7–14.

Foster, Frances Smith. *The Development of Ante-Bellum Slave Narratives*, 2nd ed. Madison: University of Wisconsin Press, 1994.

Foster, Kathleen. *Thomas Eakins Rediscovered: Charles Bregler's Thomas Eakins Collection at the Pennsylvania Academy of the Fine Arts*. Philadelphia: Pennsylvania Academy of Fine Arts, 1997.

Frank, Robin Jaffee. *Love and Loss: American Portrait and Mourning Miniatures*. New Haven, CT: Yale University Press, 2000.

Franke, Astrid. "Phillis Wheatley, Melancholy Muse." *The New England Quarterly* 77, no. 2 (2004): 224–251.

Frederickson, George M. *The Black Image in the White Mind: The Debate on Afro-American Character and Destiny, 1817–1914*. New York: Harper and Row, 1971.

Ganter, Granville. "'He Made Us Laugh Some': Frederick Douglass's Humor." *African American Review* 37, no. 4 (Winter 2003): 535–552.

Garb, Tamar. *Bodies of Modernity: Figure and Flesh in Fin-de-Siècle France*. London: Thames and Hudson, 1998.

Gates, Henry Louis, Jr. *The Signifying Monkey: A Theory of African-American Literary Criticism*. New York: Oxford University Press, 1988.

Gates, Henry Louis, "*Their Eyes Were Watching God*: Hurston and the Speakerly Text." In *Zora Neale Hurston: Critical Perspectives Past and Present*, edited by Henry Louis Gates, Jr. and K. A. Appiah. New York: Amistad, 1993.

Gelder, Ann. "Reforming the Body: 'Experience' and the Architecture of Imagination in Harriet Jacobs's Incidents in the Life of a Slave Girl." In *Inventing Maternity: Politics, Science, and Literature, 1660–1865*, edited by Susan Greenfield and Carol Barash, 252–266. Lexington: University Press of Kentucky, 1999.

Giles, Paul. "Narrative Reversals and Power Exchanges: Frederick Douglass and British Culture." *American Literature* 73, no. 4 (December 2001): 779–810.

Goeser, Caroline. *Picturing the New Negro: Harlem Renaissance Print Culture and Modern Black Identity*. Lawrence: University Press of Kansas, 2007.

Gold, David. "'Nothing Educates Us Like a Shock': The Integrated Rhetoric of Melvin B. Tolson." *College Composition and Communication* 55, no.2 (December 2003): 226–253.

Goldsby, Jacqueline. *A Spectacular Secret: Lynching in American Life and Literature*. Chicago: University of Chicago Press, 2006.

Gould, Steven J. *The Mismeasure of Man*. New York: W. W. Norton, 1981.

Goyal, Yogita. *Romance, Diaspora, and Black Atlantic Literature*. Cambridge: Cambridge University Press, 2010.

Grandison, Kendrick Ian. "Landscapes of Terror: A Reading of Tuskegee's Historic Campus." In *The Geography of Identity*, edited by Patricia Yaeger, 334–367. Ann Arbor: University of Michigan Press, 1996.

Grandison, Kendrick Ian. "Negotiated Space: The Black College Campus as a Cultural Record of Postbellum America." *American Quarterly* 51, no. 3 (September 1999): 529–579.

Greene, J. Lee. *Time's Unfading Garden: Anne Spencer's Life and Poetry*. Baton Rouge: Louisiana State University Press, 1977.

Grimstead, David. "Anglo-American Racism and Phillis Wheatley's 'Sable Veil,' 'Length'ned Chain,' and 'Knitted Heart.'" In *Women in the Age of the American Revolution*, edited by Peter J. Albert and Ronald Hoffman, 338–444. Charlottesville: University Press of Virginia, 1989.

Guimond, James. *American Photography and the American Dream*. Chapel Hill: University of North Carolina Press, 1991.

Hagstrum, Jean. *The Sister Arts: The Tradition of Literary Pictorialism and English Poetry from Dryden to Gray*. Chicago: University of Chicago Press, 1958.

Harris, Michael D. *Colored Pictures: Race and Visual Representation*. Chapel Hill: University of North Carolina Press, 2003.

Harris, Trudier. *The Power of the Porch: The Storyteller's Craft in Zora Neale Hurston, Gloria Naylor, and Randall Kenan*. Athens: University of Georgia Press, 1996.

Harrison, Les. *The Temple and the Forum: American Museum and Cultural Authority in Hawthorne, Melville, Stowe, and Whitman*. Tuscaloosa: University of Alabama Press, 2007.

Hartman, Saidiya. *Scenes of Subjection: Terror, Slavery, and Scenes of Self-Making in Nineteenth Century America*. Oxford: Oxford University Press, 1997.

Hemenway, Robert. *Zora Neale Hurston: A Literary Biography.* Urbana-Champaign: University of Illinois Press, 1980.

Hill, Michael and Lena Hill. *Ralph Ellison's Invisible Man: A Reference Guide.* Westport: Greenwood Press, 2008.

Holland, W. W. "Photography for our Young People." *Colored American Magazine* 5, no.1 (May 1902): 5–6.

Hollander, John. *The Gazer's Spirit: Poems Speaking to Silent Works of Art.* Chicago: University of Chicago Press, 1995.

Holloway, Karla. "The Emergent Voice: The Word within Its Texts." In *Zora Neale Hurston: Critical Perspectives, Past and Present,* edited by Henry Louis Gates, Jr. and K. A. Appiah, 67–75. New York: Amistad Press, 1993.

Honey, Maureen. *Shadowed Dreams: Women's Poetry of the Harlem Renaissance,* 2nd ed. New Brunswick, NJ: Rutgers University Press, 2006.

hooks, bell. *Black Looks: Race and Representation.* Boson, MA: South End Press, 1999.

Hostetler, Anne. "The Aesthetics of Race and Gender in Nella Larsen's *Quicksand.*" *PMLA* 105, no. 1 (January 1990): 35–46.

Howe, Irving. *Irving Howe: Selected Writings, 1950–1990.* New York: Harcourt Brace Jovanovich, 1990.

Hull, Gloria. *Color, Sex, & Poetry: Three Women Writers of the Harlem Renaissance.* Bloomington: Indiana University Press, 1987.

Hurston, Zora Neale. *Zora Neale Hurston: Folklore, Memoirs, and Other Writings,* edited by Cheryl A. Wall. New York: Literary Classics, 1995.

Hurston, Zora Neale. *Zora Neale Hurston: A Life in Letters,* edited by Carla Kaplan. New York: Doubleday, 2001.

Hurston, Zora Neale. *Zora Neale Hurston: Novels and Stories: Jonah's Gourd Vine / Their Eyes Were Watching God / Moses, Man of the Mountain / Seraph on the Suwanee / Selected Stories,* edited by Cheryl A. Wall. New York: Literary Classics, 1995.

Jacknis, Ira. "Franz Boas and Exhibits: On the Limitations of the Museum Method of Anthropology." In *Objects and Others: Essays on Museums and Material Culture,* edited by George W. Stocking, Jr., 75–111. Madison: University of Wisconsin Press, 1985.

Jackson, Lawrence. *Ralph Ellison: Emergence of Genius.* New York: Wiley, 2002.

Jacobs, Harriet. *Incidents in the Life of a Slave Girl.* USA: Seven Treasures Publications, 2009.

Jacobs, Karen. *The Eye's Mind: Literary Modernism and Visual Culture.* Ithaca, NY: Cornell University Press, 2001.

Jarvie, I. C. "The Problem of Ethical Integrity in Participant Observation." In *Field Research: A Sourcebook and Field Manual,* edited by Robert Burgess, 104–113. New York: Routledge, 1989.

Jay, Martin. *Downcast Eyes: The Denigration of Vision in Twentieth-Century French Thought.* Berkeley: University of California Press, 1994.

Jefferson, Thomas. *Notes on the State of Virginia,* edited by David Waldstreicher. New York: Palgrave, 2002.

Johns, Elizabeth. *American Genre Painting: the Politics of Everyday Life.* New Haven, CT: Yale University Press, 1991.

Johnson, Barbara. "Moses and Intertextuality: Sigmund Freud, Zora Neale Hurston, and the Bible." In *Poetics of the Americas: Race, Founding, and Textuality,* edited by Bainard Cowan and Jefferson Humphries, 15–29. Baton Rouge: Louisiana State University Press, 1997.

Jordan, Winthrop D. *White Over Black: American Attitudes toward the Negro 1550–1812.* Chapel Hill, NC: University of North Carolina Press, 1968.

Kendrick, Robert. "Other Questions: Phillis Wheatley and the Ethics of Interpretation." *Cultural Critique* 38 (Winter 1997–1998): 39–64.

Krieger, Murray. "The Ekphrastic Principle and the Still Movement of Poetry; or *Laokoön* Revisited." In *Close Reading: The Reader,* edited by Frank Lentricchia and Andrew Du Bois, 88–110. Durham, NC: Duke University Press, 2003.

Lacey, Barbara. "Visual Images of Blacks in Early American Imprints." *The William and Mary Quarterly* 53, no.1 (1996): 137–180.

Lamm, Kimberly. "Visuality and Black Masculinity in Ralph Ellison's *Invisible Man* and Romare Bearden's Photomontages." *Callaloo* 26 (July 2003): 813–835.

Lamothe, Daphne. *Inventing the New Negro: Narrative, Culture, and Ethnography.* Philadelphia: University of Pennsylvania Press, 2008.

Laney, Ruth. "The Journey of 'Uncle Jack.'" *Country Roads: Adventures Close to Home* November 2009.

Langa, Helen. *Radical Art: Printmaking and the Left in 1930s New York.* Berkeley: University of California Press, 2004.

Larsen, Nella. *Quicksand.* New York: Penguin, 2002.

Lee, Julia Sun-Joo. *The American Slave Narrative and the Victorian Novel.* Oxford: Oxford University Press, 2010.

Lee, Lisa Yun. "The Politics of Language in Frederick Douglass's Narrative of the Life of an American Slave." *MELUS* 17, no. 2 (Summer 1991–Summer 1992): 51–59.

Lemka, Sieglinde. *Primitive Modernism: Black Culture and the Origins of Transatlantic Modernism.* Oxford: Oxford University Press, 1998.

Leonard, Keith. *Fettered Genius: The African American Bardic Poet from Slavery to Civil Rights.* Charlottesville: University of Virginia Press, 2005.

Lewis, David Levering. *W. E. B. Du Bois: Biography of a Race, 1868–1919.* New York: Henry Holt, 1993.

Lloyd, Sheila. "Du Bois and the Production of the Racial Picturesque." *Public Culture* 17, no. 2 (2005): 277–298.

Locke, Alain. *Opportunity,* June 1, 1938. In *Zora Neale Hurston: Critical Perspectives Past and Present,* edited by Henry Louis Gates, Jr. and K. A. Appiah, 18. New York: Amistad, 1993.

Locke, Alain. "The Legacy of the Ancestral Arts." In *The New Negro: Voices of the Harlem Renaissance,* edited by Alain Locke, 254–270. New York: Touchstone, 1997.

Loizeaux, Elizabeth Bergmann. *Twentieth-Century Poetry and the Visual Arts.* Cambridge: Cambridge University Press, 2008.

Lott, Eric. *Love and Theft: Blackface Minstrelsy and the American Working Class.* New York: Oxford University Press, 1993.

Lowe, John. *Jump at the Sun: Zora Neale Hurston's Cosmic Comedy.* Urbana: University of Illinois Press, 1997.

Lutz, Catherine and Jane Collins. *Reading National Geographic.* Chicago: University of Chicago Press, 1993.

Malraux, André. *The Psychology of Art: Museum Without Walls,* translated by Stuart Gilbert. New York: Pantheon Books, 1949.

Martinez, Katherine. "At Home with Mona Lisa: Consumers and Commercial Visual Culture, 1880–1920." In *Seeing High and Low: Representing Social Conflict in American Visual Culture,* edited by Patricia Johnston, 160–176. Berkeley: University of California Press, 2006.

McBride, Dwight. *Impossible Witness: Truth, Abolitionism, and Slave Testimony.* New York: New York University Press, 2002.

McDougald, Elise. "The Task of Negro Womanhood." In *The New Negro: Voices of the Harlem Renaissance,* edited by Alain Locke, 369–384. New York: Touchstone, 1997.

McDowell, Deborah. "In the First Place: Frederick Douglass and the Afro-American Narrative Tradition." In *African American Autobiography: A Collection of Critical Essays,* edited by William L. Andrews, 35–58. Englewood Cliffs, NJ: Prentice Hall, 1993.

McElroy, Guy. *Facing History: The Black Image in American Art 1710–1940.* San Francisco, CA: Bedford Arts, 1990.

McHale, Brian. *The Obligation Toward the Difficult Whole: Postmodernist Long Poems.* Tuscaloosa: University of Alabama Press, 2004.

Meisenhelder, Susan. *Hitting a Straight Lick with a Crooked Stick: Race and Gender in the Work of Zora Neale Hurston.* Tuscaloosa: University of Alabama Press, 1999.

Meltzer, Francoise. *Salome and the Dance of Writing: Portraits of Mimesis in Literature.* Chicago, IL: University of Chicago Press, 1987.

Mitchell, W. T. J. *Picture Theory: Essays on Verbal and Visual Representation.* Chicago, IL: University of Chicago Press, 1994.

Mitchell, W. T. J. "Showing Seeing: A Critique of Visual Culture." *Journal of Visual Culture* 1, no. 2 (2002): 165–181.

Mirzoeff, Nicholas. *An Introduction to Visual Culture.* New York: Routledge, 1999.

Mirzoeff, Nicholas. *The Right to Look: A Counterhistory of Visuality.* Durham, NC: Duke University Press, 2011.

Monaghan, E. Jennifer. "Literacy Instruction and Gender in Colonial New England." In *Reading in America,* edited by Cathy Davidson, 53–80. Baltimore, MD: John Hopkins University Press, 1989.

Moore, Jacqueline. *Booker T. Washington, W. E. B. Du Bois, and the Struggle for Racial Uplift.* Lanham, MD: Scholarly Resources, 2003.

Morgan, Jennifer L. "'Some Could Suckle over Their Shoulder': Male Travelers, Female Bodies, and the Gendering of Racial Ideology, 1500–1770." *William and Mary Quarterly* 54, no. 1 (January 1997): 167–192.

Moses, Wilson J. *Creative Conflict in African American Thought: Frederick Douglass, Alexander Crummell, Booker T. Washington, W. E. B. Du Bois, and Marcus Garvey*. Cambridge: Cambridge University Press, 2004.

Moses, Wilson J. "Dark Forests and Barbarian Vigor: Paradox, Conflict, and Africanity in Black Writing before 1914." *American Literary History* 1, no. 3 (Autumn 1989): 637–55.

Moten, Fred. *In the Break: The Aesthetics of the Black Radical Tradition*. Minneapolis: University of Minnesota Press, 2003.

Mott, Frank Luther. *American Journalism: A History: 1690–1960*. New York: Macmillan, 1962.

Mott, Frank Luther. *A History of American Magazines, 1885–1905*. Cambridge, MA: Harvard University Press, 1957.

Murray, Albert and John F. Callahan. *Trading Twelves: The Selected Letters of Ralph Ellison and Albert Murray*. New York: Vintage Books, 2000.

Nelson, Raymond. "*Harlem Gallery*: An Advertisement and User's Manual." *Virginia Quarterly Review* 75, no. 3 (1999): 528–543.

Nielsen, Aldon. "Melvin B. Tolson and the Deterritorialization of Modernism." *African American Review* 26, no. 2 (Summer 1992): 241–255.

Nott, Walter. "From 'Uncultivated Barbarian' to 'Poetical Genius': The Public Presence of Phillis Wheatley." *MELUS* 18, no. 3 (Autumn 1993): 21–32.

Ostrowski, Carl. "Slavery, Labor Reform, and Intertextuality in Antebellum Print Culture: The Slave Narrative and the City-Mysteries Novel." *African American Review* 40, no. 3 (Fall 2006): 493–506.

Otten, Thomas. *A Superficial Reading of Henry James: Preoccupations with the Material World*. Columbus: Ohio State University Press, 2006.

Owens, Maude. "Bathesda of Sinners Run." In *The Sleeper Wakes: Harlem Renaissance Stories by Women*, edited by Marcy Knopf, 146–158. New Brunswick, NJ: Rutgers University Press, 1993.

Pieterse, Jan Nederveen. *White on Black: Images of Africa and Blacks in Western Popular Culture*. New Haven: Yale University Press, 1992.

Plant, Deborah. *Every Tub Must Sit on Its Own Bottom: The Philosophy and Politics of Zora Neale Hurston*. Urbana: University of Illinois Press, 1995.

Posnock, Ross. *Color and Culture: Black Writers and the Making of the Modern Intellectual*. Cambridge, MA: Harvard University Press, 1998.

Porter, Horace A. *Jazz Country: Ralph Ellison in America*. Iowa City: University of Iowa Press, 2001.

Raiford, Leigh. *Imprisoned in a Luminous Glare: Photography and the African American Freedom Struggle*. Chapel Hill: University of North Carolina Press, 2011.

Rampersad, Arnold. *The Art and Imagination of W. E. B. Du Bois*. Cambridge, MA: Harvard University Press, 1976.

Rampersad, Arnold. *Ralph Ellison: A Biography*. New York: Alfred A. Knopf, 2007.

Richards, Phillip. "Phillis Wheatley: The Consensual Blackness of Early African American Writing." In *New Essays on Phillis Wheatley*, edited by John C. Shields and Eric D. Lamore, 247–270. Knoxville: The University of Tennessee Press, 2011.

Roffman, Karin. *From the Modernist Annex: American Women Writers in Museums and Libraries*. Tuscaloosa: University of Alabama Press, 2010.

Rony, Fatimah. *The Third Eye: Race, Cinema, and the Ethnographic Spectacle*. Durham, NC: Duke University Press, 1996.

Rosenthal, David. *Hard Bop: Jazz and Black Music, 1955–1965*. New York: Oxford University Press, 1992.

Rowe, John Carlos. *At Emerson's Tomb: The Politics of Classic American Literature*. New York: Columbia University Press, 1997.

Rubin, William. *Picasso and Portraiture: Representation and Transformation*. New York: Museum of Modern Art, 1996.

Russell, Mariann. "Langston Hughes and Melvin Tolson: Blues People." In *The Furious Flowering of African American Poetry*, edited by Joanne Gabbin, 38–46. Charlottesville: University Press of Virginia, 1999.

Russell, Mariann. *Melvin B. Tolson's Harlem Gallery: A Literary Analysis*. Columbia: University of Missouri Press, 1980.

Sánchez-Eppler, Benigno. "Telling Anthropology: Zora Neale Hurston and Gilberto Freyre Disciplined in Their Field-Home-Work." *American Literary History* 4, no. 3 (Autumn 1992): 464–488.

Sekula, Allan. "The Body and the Archive." *October* 39 (Winter 1986): 3–64.

Sherrard-Johnson, Cherene. *Portraits of the New Negro Woman: Visual and Literary Culture in the Harlem Renaissance*. New Brunswick, NJ: Rutgers University Press, 2007.

Shields, John. *Phillis Wheatley's Poetics of Liberation: Backgrounds and Contexts*. Knoxville, TN: University of Tennessee Press, 2008.

Shields, John. "Wheatley's Subversive Pastoral." *American Society for Eighteenth-Century Studies* 27, no. 4 (Summer 1994): 631–647.

Slauter, Eric. "Neoclassical Culture in a Society with Slaves: Race and Rights in the Age of Wheatley." *Early American Studies* 2, no. 1 (Spring 2004): 81–122.

Smith, Shawn Michelle. *Photography on the Color Line: W. E. B. du Bois, Race, and Visual Culture*. Durham, NC: Duke University Press, 2004.

Sollors, Werner. "Modernization as Adultery: Richard Wright, Zora Neale Hurston, and American Culture of the 1930's and 1940's." *Hebrew University Studies in Literature and the Arts* 18 (1990): 1–37.

Spillers, Hortense. "Mama's Baby, Papa's Maybe: An American Grammar Book." *Diacritics* 17, no. 2 (Summer 1987): 65–81.

Stauffer, John. "Creating an Image in Black: The Power of Abolition Pictures." In *Prophets of Protest: Reconsidering the History of American Abolitionism*, edited by Timothy McCarthy and John Stauffer, 256–267. New York: New Press, 2006.

Stavney, Anne. "'Mothers of Tomorrow': The New Negro Renaissance and the Politics of Maternal Representation." *African American Review* 32, no.4 (Winter 1998): 533–561.

Stecopoulos, Harilaos. *Reconstructing the World: Southern Fictions and U.S. Imperialisms, 1898–1976*. Ithaca: Cornell University Press, 2008.

Stepto, Robert. *From Behind the Veil: A Study of Afro-American Narrative*, 2nd ed. Urbana: University of Illinois Press, 1991.

Stetz, Margaret. "Jessie Fauset's Fiction: Reconsidering Race and Revising Aestheticism." In *Literature and Racial Ambiguity*, edited by Teresa Hubel and Neil Edward Brooks, 253–270. Amsterdam: Rodopi, 2002.

Stewart, Susan. "The Eidos in the Hand." *Presentation in the Andrew Carnduff Ritchie Lecture Series*, Yale Art Gallery, New Haven, CT, December 15, 2000.

Swinth, Kirsten. *Painting Professionals: Women Artists & the Development of Modern American Art, 1870–1930*. Chapel Hill: University of North Carolina Press, 2001.

Sylvander, Carolyn. *Jessie Redman Fauset, Black American Writer*. Albany, NY: Whitston, 1981.

Thompson, Mark Christian. "National Socialism and Blood-Sacrifice in Zora Neale Hurston's *Moses, Man of the Mountain*." *African American Review* 38, no. 3 (Fall 2004): 395–414.

Tolson, Melvin B. *A Gallery of Harlem Portraits*, edited by Robert Farnsworth. Columbia: University of Missouri Press, 1979.

Tolson, Melvin B. *"Harlem Gallery" and Other Poems of Melvin B. Tolson*, edited by Raymond Nelson. Charlottesville: University of Press of Virginia, 1999.

Tolson, Melvin B. *The Harlem Group of Negro Writers*, edited by Edward Mullen. Westport, CT: Greenwood Press, 2001.

Tolson, Melvin B. "The Odyssey of a Manuscript." *New Letters* 48 (Fall 1981): 5–18.

Trachtenberg, Alan. "Photography: The Emergence of a Keyword." *Photography in Nineteenth-Century America 1839–1900*, edited by Martha A. Sandweiss and Alan Trachtenberg, 17–18. Fort Worth, TX: Amon Carter Museum, 1991.

Van Leer, David. "Reading Slavery: The Anxiety of Ethnicity in Douglass's Narrative." In *Frederick Douglass: New Literary and Historical Essays*, edited by Eric Sundquist, 118–140. Cambridge: Cambridge University Press, 1990.

Vendryes, Margaret. *Barthé: A Life in Sculpture*. Jackson: University of Mississippi Press, 2008.

Vendryes, Margaret. "Casting Feral Benga: A Biography of Richmond Barthé's Signature Work." *Anyone Can Fly Foundation*, www.anyonecanflyfoundation.org/library/Vendryes_on_Barthe_Essay.html.

Vendryes, Margaret. "The Lives of Richmond Barthé." In *The Greatest Taboo: Homosexuality in Black Communities*, edited by Delroy Constantine-Simms, 274–287. Los Angeles: Alyson Books, 2001.

Verney, Kevern. *The Art of the Possible: Booker T. Washington and Black Leadership in the United States, 1881–1925*. New York: Routledge, 2001.

Walker, David. 1830. "Walker's Appeal, in Four Articles; Together with a Preamble, to the Coloured Citizens of the World, but in Particular, and Very Expressly, to Those of the United States of America, Written in Boston, State of Massachusetts, September 28, 1829." Documenting the American South. University Library, The University of North Carolina at Chapel Hill, 2001. http://docsouth.unc.edu/nc/walker/walker.html.

Wallace, Maurice O. *Constructing the Black Masculine: Identity and Ideality in African American Men's Literature and Culture, 1775–1995.* Durham, NC: Duke University Press, 2002.

Wallace, Michele. *Dark Designs & Visual Culture.* Durham, NC: Duke University Press, 2004.

Warren, Kenneth. *What Was African American Literature?* Cambridge, MA: Harvard University Press, 2011.

Washington, Booker T. "Negro Homes." *Colored American Magazine* 5, no. 5 (September 1902): 378–379.

Washington, Booker T. *Up from Slavery.* Oxford: Oxford University Press, 1995.

Washington, Booker T. *Working With the Hands: Being a Sequel to 'Up from Slavery' Covering the Author's Experiences in Industrial Training at Tuskegee.* New York: Doubleday, Page & Company, 1904.

Werner, Craig. "Blues for T.S. Eliot and Langston Hughes: The Afro-Modernist Aesthetic of Harlem Gallery." *Black American Literature Forum* 24, no. 3 (Autumn 1990): 453–472.

Westerbeck, Colin L. "Frederick Douglass Chooses His Moment." In *African Americans in Art: Selections from The Art Institute of Chicago*, 145–161. Seattle: University of Washington Press, 1999.

Wheatley, Phillis. *Complete Writings*, edited by Vincent Carretta. New York: Penguin Books, 2001.

Wilcox, Kirstin. "The Body into Print: Marketing Phillis Wheatley." *American Literature* 71, no. 1 (March 1999): 1–29.

Williams, Vernon. *Rethinking Race: Franz Boas and His Contemporaries.* Lexington: University Press of Kentucky, 1996.

Willis, Deborah. *Reflections in Black: A History of Black Photographers, 1840 to the Present.* New York: Norton, 2000.

Willis, Deborah. "The Sociologist's Eye: W. E. B. Du Bois and the Paris Exposition." In *A Small Nation of People: W. E. B. Du Bois and African American Portraits of Progress*, edited by David L. Lewis, Deborah Willis, and The Library of Congress, 51–78. New York: HarperCollins, 2003.

Wilson, Francille Rusan. *The Segregated Scholars: Black Social Scientists and the Creation of Black Labor Studies, 1890–1950.* Charlottesville: University of Virginia Press, 2006.

Wilson, Ivy. *Specters of Democracy: Blackness and the Aesthetics of Politics in the Antebellum U.S.* New York: Oxford University Press, 2011.

Wilson, Ivy. "The Writing on the Wall: Revolutionary Aesthetics and Interior Spaces." In *American Literature's Aesthetic Dimensions*, edited by Cindy

Weinstein and Christopher Looby, 56–72. New York: Columbia University Press, 2012.

Winterer, Caroline. "The Female World of Classical Reading in Eighteenth-Century America." In *Reading Women: Literacy, Authorship, and Culture in the Atlantic World, 1500–1800*, edited by Heidi Brayman Hackel and Catherine E. Kelly, 105–123. Philadelphia: University of Pennsylvania Press, 2007.

Winthrop, Jordan. *White Over Black: American Attitudes toward the Negro, 1550–1812*. Chapel Hill: University of North Carolina Press, 1968.

Wolfe, Jesse. "Ambivalent Man: Ellison's Rejection of Communism." *African American Review* 34 (January 2000): 621–637.

Wood, Marcus. *Blind Memory: Visual Representations of Slavery in England and America, 1780–1865*. New York: Routledge, 2000.

Wooldridge, Thomas. "... a very Extraordinary female Slave .... " In *Critical Essays on Phillis Wheatley*, edited by William Robinson, 20–21. Boston: G.K. Hall, 1982.

Wright, Richard. "Between Laughter and Tears." *New Masses*. October 5, 1937.

Yanni, Carla. *Nature's Museums: Victorian Science and the Architecture of Display*. London: Athlone Press, 1999.

Yukins, Elizabeth. "An 'Artful Juxtaposition on the Page': Memory, Perception, and Cubist Technique in Ralph Ellison's *Juneteenth*." *PMLA* 119 (October 2004): 1247–1263.

Index

265